# Create Web Charts
# With jqPlot

Fabio Nelli

Apress®

## Create Web Charts with jqPlot

ISBN-13 (pbk): 978-1-4842-0863-2

ISBN-13 (electronic): 978-1-4842-0862-5

Managing Director: Welmoed Spahr
Lead Editor: Ben Renow-Clarke
Technical Reviewer: Matthew Canning
Editorial Board: Steve Anglin, Mark Beckner, Ewan Buckingham, Gary Cornell, Louise Corrigan, Jim DeWolf, Jonathan Gennick, Jonathan Hassell, Robert Hutchinson, Michelle Lowman, James Markham, Matthew Moodie, Jeff Olson, Jeffrey Pepper, Douglas Pundick, Ben Renow-Clarke, Dominic Shakeshaft, Gwenan Spearing, Matt Wade, Steve Weiss
Coordinating Editor: Jill Balzano
Copy Editors: Lisa Vecchione, Kezia Endsley, and Brendan Frost
Compositor: SPi Global
Indexer: SPi Global
Artist: SPi Global
Cover Designer: Anna Ishchenko

*This book is dedicated to my grandfather Polo and my grandmother Franca,*
*for all the support they have given me in life*

# Contents at a Glance

# Contents

# About the Author

**Fabio Nelli** is an information technology scientific application specialist at IRBM Science Park, a private research center in Pomezia, Italy. He was a computer consultant for many years at IBM, EDS, and Merck Sharp and Dohme, along with several banks and insurance companies. He worked as well as a specialist in information technology and automation systems at Beckman Coulter.

He holds a Master's degree in Organic Chemistry from La Sapienza University of Rome. He recently earned a Bachelor's degree in Automation and Computer Engineering from eCampus University of Novedrate.

Nelli is currently developing Java applications that interface Oracle databases, using scientific instrumentation to generate data, and web server applications that provide analysis to researchers in real time.

Web site: www.meccanismocomplesso.org

# About the Technical Reviewer

**Matthew Canning** is an author, speaker and experienced technical leader who has served in engineering and management roles at some of the world's largest companies. Aside from technology, he writes and presents on subjects such as memory, mental calculation and productivity. He currently lives outside Philadelphia with his wife and daughter.

    Twitter: @MatthewCanning

    Website: matthewcanning.com

# Acknowledgments

I would like to express my gratitude to all the people who played a part in developing this book. First, a special thanks to Ben Renow-Clarke for giving me the opportunity to write the book. Thanks to Jill Balzano and Mark Powers for their guidance and direction. Thanks also to everyone who took part in the review and editing of the book for their professionalism and enthusiasm: Chris Nelson, Matthew Canning, James Markham, Lisa Vecchione, Kezia Endsley, Brendan Frost, and Dhaneesh Kumar.

# Introduction

Welcome to the world of charts. If you are holding this book in your hands, you are undoubtedly interested in data visualization, perhaps with the hope of developing web pages filled with interactive charts. Or, maybe your purpose is to improve your knowledge of the jqPlot library. Whatever your objective, I hope this book enables you to achieve it.

In addition to the various types of charts implemented using the jqPlot library, this book covers a range of topics: the jQuery library and selections, HTML5 and the canvas, widgets and controls and mathematical concepts (scales and domains, curve fitting and trend lines, and much more).

I have enriched this wide range of topics with many examples, each tightly focused on a particular one and presented to you in an ordered sequence, with step-by-step instructions.

Chart development can be easy once you know the process and have the right tools at the ready. Therefore, in presenting this material, I have included helpful, reusable code snippets as well as explanations of underlying concepts. After reading this book, you will be equipped to create any type of data visualization, either traditional or newer, with confidence.

■ ■ ■

# CHAPTER 1

# Charting Technology Overview

When we need to represent data or qualitative structures graphically in order to show a relationship—to make a comparison or highlight a trend—we make use of charts. A chart is a graphic structure consisting of symbols, such as lines, in a line chart; bars, in a bar chart; or slices, in a pie chart. Charts serve as valid tools that can help us discern and understand the relationships underlying large quantities of data. It is easier for humans to read graphic representations, such as a chart, than raw numeric data. Nowadays, use of charts has become common practice in a wide variety of professional fields as well as in many other aspects of daily life. For this reason, charts have come to take on many forms, depending on the stucture of the data and the phenomenon that is being highlighted. For example, if you have data separated into different groups and want to represent the percentage of each, with respect to the total, you usually display these groups of data in a pie chart or a bar chart. In contrast, if you want to show the trend of a variable over time, a line chart is typically the best choice.

In this book, you will learn how to create, draw, and adapt charts to your needs, using various technologies based on JavaScript. Before you start using JavaScript to develop charts, however, it is important that you understand the basic concepts that will be covered in the chapters of this book. In this chapter, I will provide a brief overview of these concepts.

First, I will show you how to recognize the most common elements that make up a chart. Knowledge of these elements will prove helpful, because you will find them in the form of components, variables, and objects defined within the specialized JavaScript libraries created for the realization of charts.

Next, I will present a list of the most common types of charts. The greater your knowledge of charts and their features, the easier it will be to choose the right representation for your data. Making the right choice is essential if you are to underline the relationships you want to represent, and just reading the data will not be sufficent. Only when you have become familiar with the most common types of charts will you be able to choose which is the most suitable for your purposes.

Once you have become familiar with these concepts, you will need to learn how it is possible to realize them via the Web and what the current technologies are that can help you achieve this aim. Thus, in the second part of the chapter, I will discuss these technical aspects, presenting one by one the technologies involved in the development of the examples provided in this book.

Finally, given that all our work will focus on the development of code in JavaScript, I thought it would be helpful to provide a brief description of certain types of data. Those who are not familiar with JavaScript can benefit from this quick reference source on the forms that the data will take within the code. However, I strongly recommend that the reader research in greater depth the concepts and technologies discussed in this chapter.

## Elements in a Chart

As you will soon see, charts can assume a variety of forms. In a chart the data take on graphic structure through the use of symbols specific to the type of chart; there are, however, some features that are common to all charts.

Generally, every chart has a title, appearing at the top, that provides a short description of the data. Less frequently, subtitles or footnotes are used to supply additional descriptions (mostly data-related information, such as references, places, dates, and notes).

Charts often have axes—two perpendicular lines that allow the user to refer to the values of the coordinates (x, y) for each data point P(x, y), as shown in Figure 1-1. The horizontal line usually represents the x axis, and the vertical line, the y axis.

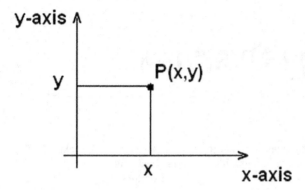

**Figure 1-1.** *A two-dimensional chart*

A scale is defined on each axis. The scale can be either numerical or categorical. Each axis is divided into segments corresponding to the particular range of values represented by the scale. The boundaries between one segment and the next are called ticks. Each tick reports the value of the scale associated with that axis. Generally, call these tick labels.

Figure 1-2 shows four axes with different scales. Axes a and b have numerical scales, with a being a linear scale, and b, a logarithmic scale. Axes c and d have categorical scales, with c being ordinal and therefore following an ascending order, whereas d is only a sequence of categories without any particular order.

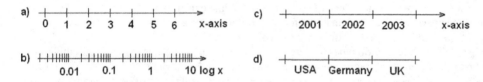

**Figure 1-2.** *Four axes with different scales*

Along with each axis, it is good practice to display a label briefly describing the dimension represented; these are called axis labels. If the scale is numerical, the label should show the units of measure in brackets. For instance, if you had an x axis reporting the timing for a set of data, you might write "time" as an axis label, with the second unit (in this case, seconds) in square brackets as [s] (see Figure 1-3).

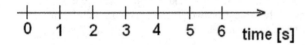

**Figure 1-3.** *An axis label*

In the drawing area displaying the chart, a line grid may be included to aid in the visual alignment of data. Figure 1-4 shows a grid for a chart with a linear time scale on the x axis and a logarithmic scale on the y axis.

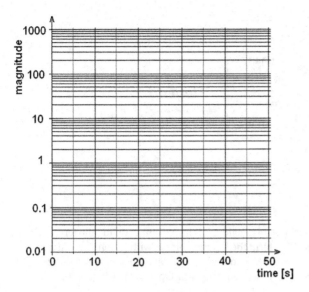

**Figure 1-4.** *A chart with two different scales*

You have seen how data can be represented symbolically. However, text labels can also be used to highlight specific data points. Point labels provide values in a chart right at the corresponding points in a chart, whereas tool tips are small frames that appear dynamically, when you pass the mouse over a given point. These two types of labels are shown in Figure 1-5.

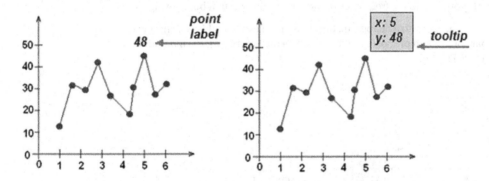

**Figure 1-5.** *The point label and the tooltip of a data point*

Data are often grouped in several series, and in order to represent these in the same chart, they must be distinguishable. The most common approach is to assign a different color to each series. In other cases, for example, with line charts, the line stroke (dashed, dotted, and so on) can also be used to distinguish different series. Once you have established a sequence of colors (or strokes), it is necessary to add a table demonstrating the correspondence between colors and groups. This table is called the legend and is shown in Figure 1-6.

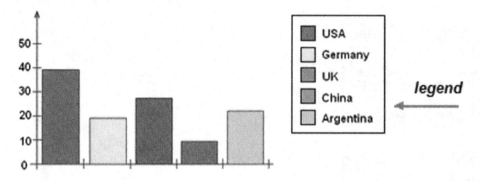

*Figure 1-6.* *A legend*

Although it may seem trivial to discuss the concepts covered in this section, it is important to define the terminology of the elements that I will be referring to throughout the book. They form the building blocks with which you will be building your charts. You will also see how JavaScript libraries specializing in the representation of charts use these terms, associating them with editing and setting components (see the section "Inserting Options" in Chapter 8).

# Most Common Charts

This section contains a brief overview of the most common types of charts. These charts will each be described more thoroughly in the following chapters of the book.

**Histogram:** Adjacent rectangles erected on the x axis, split into discrete intervals (bins) and with an area proportional to the frequency of the observation for that bin (see Figure 1-7).

**Bar chart:** Similar in shape to a histogram, but different in essence, this is a chart with rectangular bars of a length proportional to the values they represent. Each bar identifies a group of data (see Figure 1-7).

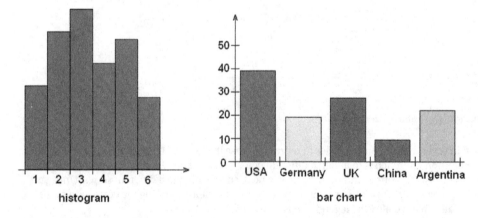

*Figure 1-7.* *A histogram and a bar chart*

**Line chart:** A sequence of ordered data points connected by a line. Data points P (x, y) are reported in the chart, representing the scales of two axes, x and y (see Figure 1-8).

**Pie chart:** A circle (pie) divided into segments (slices). Each slice represents a group of data, and its size is proportional to the percentage value (see Figure 1-8).

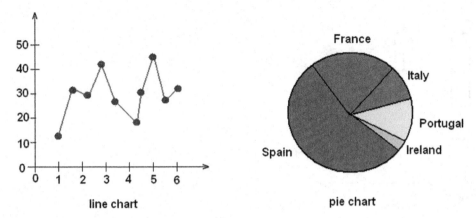

**Figure 1-8.** *A line chart and a pie chart*

**Bubble chart:** A two-dimensional scatterplot in which a third variable is represented by the size of the data points (see Figure 1-9).

**Radar chart:** A chart in which a series of data is represented on many axes, starting radially from a point of origin at the center of the chart. This chart often takes on the appearance of a spiderweb (see Figure 1-9).

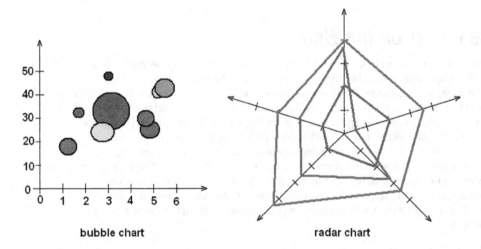

**Figure 1-9.** *A bubble chart and a radar chart*

**Candlestick chart:** A type of chart specifically used to describe price trends over time. Each data point consists of four values, generally known as open-high-low-close (OHLC) values, and assumes a shape resembling a candlestick (see Figure 1-10).

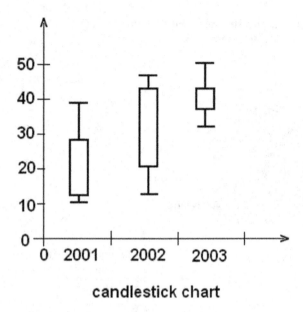

**Figure 1-10.** *A candlestick chart*

---

■ **Note** Open-high-low-close (OHLC) are four numeric values typically used to illustrate movement in the price of a financial instrument over time.

---

# How to Realize Charts on the Web

Now that I have described the most common types of charts and the elements that compose them, the next step is to take a quick look at the technologies available today that will allow you to realize your chart.

Nowadays, web technologies are in constant flux: each day, new solutions are proposed, solving problems that only a short time ago would have proven to be quite complex. These innovations will afford you the possibility to realize highly interactive charts, with eye-catching graphics, all by writing only a few lines of JavaScript code. The whole thing can be done fast and easily, as most of the work is done for you, by the JavaScript libraries, which are highly specialized in chart representation. These libraries are now to be found all over the network.

In this book, you will work with jqPlot which is currently one of the most widely used libraries and which can provide general solutions to practically any problem that may arise in the process of chart realization.

But, before stepping through these libraries one by one (which you will do in later chapters), you must first survey all the technologies that constitute the basis for chart development in JavaScript, as these will accompany you throughout the rest of the book.

# HTML5

Recently, there has been a lot of talk about HTML5, which is practically revolutionizing the way in which web applications are developed. Before its advent, if you wanted to introduce interactive graphical content, the use of applications such as Adobe Flash was pretty much the obligatory path. But, dealing with Flash or similar applications for developing charts or other graphic representations on the Web involves an obvious limitation: dependency on a plug-in, to be installed on the end user's machine. In addition, these kinds of applications are not supported on smartphones. Thanks to HTML5, developers can now create advanced graphics and animation without relying on Flash.

As you read through this book, you will see how HTML5 has also led to the birth of many other technologies, some new, others old but renewed, such as JavaScript. In fact, as a language, JavaScript is experiencing a rebirth, as a result of the new libraries developed precicely to take advantage of the innovations introduced by HTML5. HTML5 has many new syntactical features, including the <canvas> elements and the integration of scalar vector graphics (SVG) content. Owing to these elements, it will be very easy to integrate multimedia and graphical content on the Web without using Flash.

In Flash's place, you will be using JavaScript libraries, such as jQuery and jqPlot. Currently, these are a good example of complete libraries available for the realization tasks such as the graphic visualization of data. The world of web technologies is constantly evolving, however; on the Internet, you can always find new libraries, with characteristics similar to those contained in this book.

# Charting with SVG and CANVAS

Among all the possible graphic applications that can be implemented with the new technologies introduced by HTML5, I will focus on the representation and visualization of data through charts. Using JavaScript as a programming language, we can now take advantage of the powerful rendering engines embedded in new browsers. As the basis of the new capabilities of this language, I will refer to the HTML5 canvas and SVG. Instead of drawing static images on the server and then downloading them into the browser, SVG and canvas allow you to develop fully interactive charts and thus to enrich your graphic representations with built-in animation, transitions, and tool tips. This is because SVG and canvas content is drawn in the browser, and so the graphic elements that make up the chart can be transformed without refreshing the page. This feature is essential for visualizing real-time data, which require that the chart be continually updated, as the data change. Operating in this way will ensure a true client-side charting. In fact, by making use of these technologies, charts are actually drawn on the client and only require that the data be passed from the server. This aspect affords a considerable number of advantages, the foremost being elimination of the need for large graphics files to be downloaded from the server.

## Canvas vs SVG

Both HTML5 canvas and SVG are web technologies that allow you to create rich graphics in the browser, but they are fundamentally different. Throughout this text, you will see mainly a JavaScript frameworks: **jqPlot**. jqPlot, based on the jQuery framework, makes use of the HTML5 <canvas> element to draw its charts. Other libraries (such as the D3 library) instead make use of SVG

The HTML5 canvas specification is a versatile JavaScript API, allowing you to code programmatic drawing operations. Canvas, by itself, lets you define a canvas context object, shown as a <canvas> element on your HTML page. This element can then be drawn inside, using either a two-dimensional or three-dimensional drawing context, with Web Graphics Library (WebGL). I will cover only the first option; jqPlot uses a two-dimensional drawing context. The two-dimensional context provides you with a powerful API that performs quick drawing operations on a bitmap surface—the canvas. Unlike SVG, there are no DOM nodes for the shapes, only pixels.

SVG is an XML-based vector graphic format. SVG content can be static, dynamic, interactive, or animated, which makes it very flexible. You can also style the SVG elements with Cascading Style Sheets (CSS) and add dynamic behavior to them, using the application programming interface (API) methods provided by the SVG document object model (DOM).

The advantages of canvas, compared with SVG, are high drawing performance and faster graphics and image editing. Whenever it is necessary to work at the pixel level, canvas is preferable. However, with canvas, not having DOM nodes on which to work can be a disadvantage, especially if you do not use a JavaScript framework, such as jqPlot. Another disadvantage is poor text-rendering capabilities.

The advantages of SVG, compared with canvas, are resolution independence, good support for animation, and the ability to animate elements, using a declarative syntax. Most important, though, is having full control over each element, using the SVG DOM API in JavaScript. Yet, when complexity increases, slow rendering can be a problem, but browser providers are working hard to make browsers faster (see Tables 1-1 and 1-2).

***Table 1-1.*** *Web Browsers and Engines*

| Browser | Current | Engine | Developer | License |
|---|---|---|---|---|
| Google Chrome | 29 | Blink | Google, Opera, Samsung, Intel, others | GNU Lesser General Public License (LGPL), Berkeley Software Distribution (BSD) style |
| Mozilla Firefox | 23 | Gecko | Netscape/Mozilla Foundation | Mozilla Public License (MPL) |
| Internet Explorer | 10 | Trident | Microsoft | Proprietary |
| Apple Safari | 6 | WebKit | Apple, KDE, Nokia, Blackberry, Palm, others | GNU LGPL, BSD style |

***Table 1-2.*** *Web Technology Support: Comparison of Web Browsers*

| | Browser | | | |
|---|---|---|---|---|
| Technology | Internet Explorer 10 | Chrome 29 | Firefox 23 | Safari 6 |
| SVG (v.1.1) | | | | |
| Filters | Yes (from 10) | Yes | Yes | Yes (from 6) |
| Synchronized Multimedia Integration Language (SMIL) animation | No | Yes | Yes | Partial |
| Fonts | No | Yes | No | Yes |
| Fragment identifiers | Yes | No | Yes | No |
| HTML effects | Partial | Partial | Yes | Partial |
| CSS backgrounds | Yes | Yes | Partial | Yes |
| CSS | Yes | Yes | Yes | Yes |
| HTML5 | | | | |
| Canvas | Yes (from 9) | Yes | Yes | Yes |
| New elements | Yes | Yes | Yes | Yes |
| Video elements | Yes (from 9) | Yes | Yes | Yes |
| JavaScript API | | | | |
| JavaScript Object Notation (JSON) parsing | Yes | Yes | Yes | Yes |
| WebGL | No | Yes | Partial | Partial |

# The DOM

Working with libraries that act at the level of the structural elements of an HTML page, we cannot avoid talking about the DOM. I will be referring to this concept often, as it is the basic structure underlying every web page. The World Wide Web Consortium (W3C) felt the need, and rightly so, to create an official standard for the representation of structured documents, so as to develop guidelines for all programming languages and platforms.The tree structure of HTML documents, as well as those of XML, follows the guidelines developed by this standard perfectly. Following is an example of an HTML document:

```
<HTML>
    <HEAD>
      <TITLE>A title</TITLE>
    </HEAD>
    <BODY>
      Hello
      <BR>
    </BODY>
</HTML>
```

The DOM tree of this document can be represented as shown in Figure 1-11.

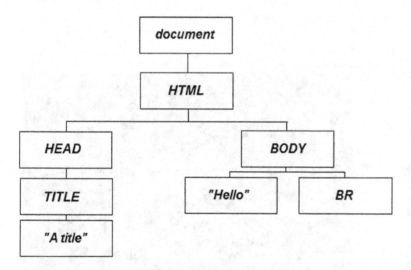

**Figure 1-11.** *An example of tree structure of the DOM*

But, the DOM standard is not limited to developing guidelines on how the DOM should be structured in a document; the standard also defines a number of features designed to act on the elements that compose a document. Thus, any action pertaining to a document (creating, inserting, deleting) should follow the DOM standard. As a result, regardless of the programming language that you are using or the platform on which you are working, you will always find the same functionality expressed by this standard. Often, the term *DOM* also applies to the API, which manages all the elements of a web page.

All this is important, because anyone choosing to read this book is interested in developing charts that not only use the DOM, but that are also part of it and whose every aspect can be inspected and manipulated in JavaScript. Throughout the book, you will learn how to make the best use of jQuery and jqPlot. With these JavaScript libraries, you can access every chart element, such as changing the color and position of objects.

# Developing in JavaScript

Although it is likely that most people who have chosen to read this book already have a good knowledge of JavaScript, this may not in fact be the case. For this reason, I have structured the book in a practical way, giving step-by-step examples and providing all the code that must be written in the examples. As such, this book offers newcomers an opportunity to study the language and those who have not used it for some time a chance to refresh their memories.

To start working with the JavaScript libraries that you will be using to develop your charts, it is necessary to prepare a development environment. It is true that to develop JavaScript code, you could simply use a text editor, such as Notepad (or, even better, Notepad++), but developers generally prefer to use specialized applications, usually called integrated development enviroments (IDEs), to develop code. As well as providing a text editor with differentiated colors corresponding to the keywords used in the code, such applications also contain a set of tools designed to facilitate the work. These applications can check if there are any errors in the code, supply debugging tools, make it easy to manage files, and assist in deployment on the server, among many other operations.

Nowadays, there are many JavaScript IDEs on the network, but some of the most prominent are **Aptana Studio** (see Figure 1-12); **Eclipse Web Developer**, with the JavaScript test driver (JSTD) plug-in installed; and **NetBeans**. These editors also allow you to develop Hypertext Preprocessor (PHP), CSS, and HTML (for information on how to use the Aptana Studio IDE to set up a workspace in which to implement the code for this book, see Appendix A, or use the source code accompanying the book directly; you can find the code samples in the Source Code/Download area of the Apress web site [www.apress.com]).

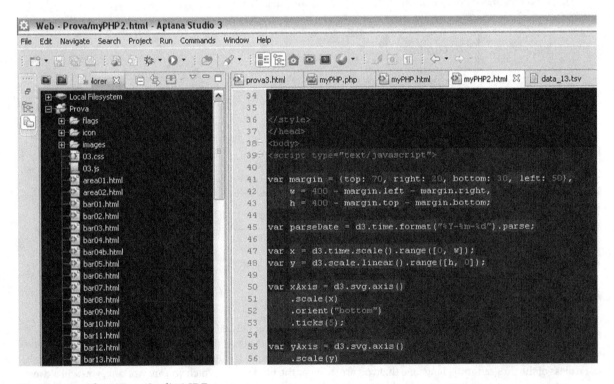

***Figure 1-12.*** *The Aptana Studio 3 IDE*

For those who prefer not to install too many applications on their computer, there are online JavaScript IDEs. These allow users to edit JavaScript code in a web page working as an IDE and to check their result directly from the same web page. Unfortunately, many of these IDEs charge a fee. However, **jsFiddle** (http://jsfiddle.net) is an online IDE that requires no payment and that, in addition to editing, provides code sharing and the option of adding libraries, such as jQuery and D3.(see Figure 1-13).

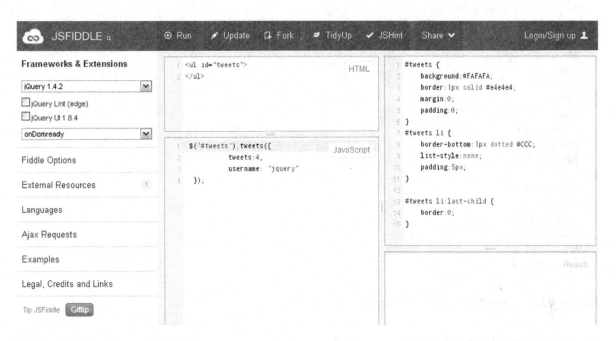

***Figure 1-13.*** *The online IDE jsFiddle*

jsFiddle can prove very useful. As well as letting the user include many JavaScript libraries (see Figure 1-14), it offers the respective different versions released, thus allowing him or her to test any incompatibilities in real time.

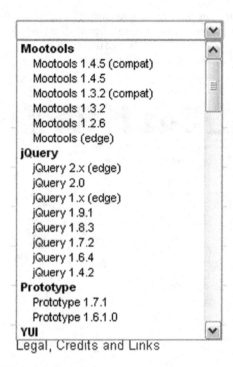

*Figure 1-14. jsFiddle offers a set of the most popular JavaScript libraries*

# Running and Debugging JavaScript

JavaScript, if we want to define it in a client–server framework, is a completely client-side programming language. It is not subject to compilation, and parts of the code, apart from HTML documents, can be found in many other types of files that are specific to other languages, such as .JSP or .PHP.

These code fragments pass unaffected through the application servers without ever being processed. Only the browser is responsible for running the JavaScript code. Therefore, JavaScript code is run only when a web page is downloaded or afterward, in response to an event. If the JavaScript code is of a considerable size or might be useful subsequently, it can be defined externally in a .JS file; here, you will find all the JavaScript libraries and frameworks that will be mentioned throughout this text. Regardless of its form, however, JavaScript runs directly from the browser.

So, even if you do not use a real IDE for the development and debugging of JavaScript code, you can simply insert the code in an empty HTML file and then load this file directly in a browser (Chrome, Internet Explorer, and Firefox are the most common). To distinguish it from the rest of the text on the page, you must separate the code by putting it inside the <script></scripts> tags:

```
<script type="text/javascript">
// JavaScript code
</script>
```

If the JavaScript code resides in an external file, then it will be necessary to include it in the HTML page, writing

```
<script type="text/javascript" src="library.js"></script>
```

Therefore, as long as the execution of JavaScript is not required for the purpose of installing something, you have everything you need. Who does not have a web browser on his or her operating system?

# Data Types in JavaScript

As mentioned earlier, this book will neither explain the rules and syntax for the programming of good JavaScript code nor will it linger too long on programming details. Nevertheless, the code that we are going to develop is centered on charts, or rather the processing of data and how to display them. Let us start with the simplest case. The smallest building block of all data structures is the variable (when it contains a single value). In handling the types of data, JavaScript is very different from other programming languages. , You do not have to specify the type of value (int, string, float, boolean, and so on) when you want to store JavaScript in a variable; you need only define it with the var keyword.

In Java or C a variable containing an integer value is declared differently from one containing a text:

```
int value = 3;
String text = "This is a string value";
```

In JavaScript the type of stored value does not matter. Everything is declared with var, so the same declarations are

```
var value = 3;
var text = "This is a string value";
```

Thus, in JavaScript we can think of variables as containers for storing any type of value.

For the sake of simplicity, here the variables are seen as containers of a single value, thus representing the simplest data structure. Actually, however, variables may also contain types of data that are more complex: arrays and objects.

---

■ **Note**   The use of variables in JavaScript is actually a bit more complicated. You can also use a variable without ever declaring it with the var keyword. The var keyword will declare the variable within the current scope. If var is missing, JavaScript will search for a variable with the same name declared at an upper level of scope. If JavaScript does not find this variable, a new one is declared; otherwise, JavaScript will use the values in the variable found. As a result, an incorrect use of variables can sometimes lead to errors that are difficult to detect.

---

## Arrays

An array is a sequence of values separated by a comma and enclosed in square brackets [ ]:

```
var array = [ 1, 6, 3, 8, 2, 4 ];
```

Arrays are the simplest and most widely used data structure in JavaScript, so you should become very familiar with them. It is possible to access any value in an array by specifying its index (position in the array) in the brackets, immediately following the name of the array. In JavaScript the indexes start from 0:

```
array[3]   //returns 8
```

Arrays can contain any type of data, not just integers:

```
var fruits = [ "banana", "apple", "peach" ];
```

There are a many functions that can help us handle this kind of object. Because of its usefulness, I will be using this object frequently throughout the book, and it therefore seems proper to give it a quick look.

It is possible to know the number of the values in an array by writing

```
fruits.length  //returns 3
```

Or, if you know the values, you can get the corresponding index with

```
fruits.indexOf("apple") //returns 1
```

Moreover, there is a set of functions that allow us to add and remove items in an array. **push()** and **pop()** functions add and remove the last element in an array, whereas **shift()** and **unshift()** functions add and remove the first element in an array:

```
fruits.push("strawberry");
// Now the array is ["banana", "apple", "peach", "strawberry"];
fruits.pop();     //returns "strawberry"
// Now the array is ["banana", "apple", "peach"];
fruits.unshift("orange", "pear");
// Now the array is ["orange", "pear", "banana", "apple", "peach"];
fruits.shift();   //returns "orange"
// Now the array is ["pear", "banana", "apple", "peach"];
```

Sometimes, it is necessary to make a loop through every value in an array in order to perform some action with it. An approach that is widely used in other programming languages is the use of the function for(). For example, to calculate the sum of the values in an array, you would write

```
var sum = 0;
for (var i = 0; i < array.length; i++) {
    sum += array[i];
}
```

But, in JavaScript it is more common to use the forEach() function, where d assumes the values in the array, one by one, following the sequence:

```
var sum = 0;
array.forEach(function(d) {
    sum += d;
});
```

# Objects

Arrays are useful for simple lists of values, but if you want structured data, you need to define an object. An object is a custom data structure whose properties and values you define. You can define an object by enclosing its properties between two curly brackets { }; every property is defined by a name followed by a colon (:) and the assigned value, and commas separate each property/value pair:

```
var animal = {
    species: "lion",
    class: "mammalia",
    order: "carnivora",
    extinct: false,
    number: 123456
};
```

In JavaScript code, dot notation refers to each value, specifying the name of the property:

```
animal.species        //Returns "lion"
```

Now that you have learned about both objects and arrays, you can see how it is possible to combine them in order to get more complex data structures in JavaScript. You can create arrays of objects or objects of arrays, or even objects of objects. Square brackets are used to indicate an array, curly brackets, an object. For example, let us define an array of objects in this way:

```
var animals = [
    {
        species: "lion",
        class: "mammalia",
        order: "carnivora",
        extinct: false,
        number: 123456
    },
    {
        species: "gorilla",
        class: "mammalia",
        order: "primates",
        extinct: false,
        number: 555234
    },
    {
        species: "octopus",
        class: "cephalopoda",
        order: "octopoda",
        extinct: false,
        number: 333421
    }
];
```

To get the values of these data structures, you need to use both the square brackets with the index and the name of the property:

```
animals[0].extinct  //return false
animals[2].species  //return "octopus"
```

# Firebug and DevTools

To debug, if you are using an IDE, you can easily make use of the various debugging tools that are included with it. If you do not have access to an IDE, however, you can still avail yourself of external tools. Think of the browser as a development environment, where debugging tools can be integrated through plug-ins that are downloadable from Internet. There are many tools currently available on the Internet, but the one I want to propose is Firebug, a web development tool for those who prefer to use the browser Mozilla Firefox. Firebug is an add-in that integrates seamlessly into the Firefox browser, as demonstrated in Figure 1-15.

**Figure 1-15.** *Firebug is an extention of Mozilla Firefox and is fully integrated into the browser*

Firebug will prove a very useful tool throughout, especially when using use the jQuery and D3 libraries, which require that the structure of the DOM always be kept under control. This tool will allow you to monitor the structure of the DOM directly.

For those who prefer to use Google Chrome, however, there is DevTools, which is already integrated into the browser (see Figure 1-16). To access this tool, simply click the button at the top-right corner of the browser.

**Figure 1-16.** *With DevTools it is possible to monitor a lot of information about your web page*

Next, select Tools ➤ Developer Tools, or simply right-click any page element, and then select Inspect element in the context menu.

With these two tools, you can easily inspect not only each element of the DOM—its attributes and their values—but also the CSS styles applied to them. You can also input changes to these values to observe the effects in real time without having to modify the code on file and save it every time. Firebug and DevTools also include various tools for monitoring the performance of the page, for both rendering and networking.

With DevTools, particular attention should be paid to the use of the console as well. Through it, you can access diagnostic information, using methods such as console.log(). This method is frequently used to display the values of many variables through the console, passing the name of the variable as an argument, with the addition of text as an indication:

```
var x = 3;
console.log("The value of x is " + x); // The value of x is 3
```

It is also possible to enter commands and perform interactions with the document, using methods such as $() or profile().For further information on these methods, see the documentation regarding the Console API (https://developers.google.com/chrome-developer-tools/docs/console-api) and the Command Line API (https://developers.google.com/chrome-developer-tools/docs/commandline-api).

# JSON

JSON is a specific syntax for organizing data as JavaScript objects. This format is generally used in browser-based code, especially in JavaScript. JSON represents a valid alternative to XML for organizing data. Both are independent from the programming language, but JSON is faster and easier to parse with JavaScript than XML, which is a full-markup language. Moreover, jqPlot and D3 work well with JSON. Its structure follows perfectly the rules that we have seen for objects and arrays defined in JavaScript:

```
var company = {
    "name": "Elusive Dinamics",
    "location": "France",
    "sites": 2,
    "employees": 234,
    "updated": true
};
```

# Summary

This first chapter has introduced you to many of the fundamental concepts that will accompany you throughout the book. First, you examined the most common types of charts and the elements that compose them. You also took a quick look at many of the technical aspects you need to know when setting about developing a chart on the Web. Finally, you briefly explored the types of data used in the JavaScript examples in this book.

I mentioned that the majority of your work will be done by specialized JavaScript libraries. In the next chapter, you will learn about the **jQuery** library. This library will provide you with a whole range of tools that act directly, at the level of the DOM. Later in the book, you will find that knowledge of this library is vital: many of the graphics libraries (including jqPlot) are built on it.

# CHAPTER 2

∎ ∎ ∎

# jQuery Basics

In the previous chapter, you learned about the DOM tree and saw how HTML documents are composed of many elements that can be created, modified, and deleted from the initial context. These operations are performed by the browser via JavaScript commands that, as discussed previously, can be executed either at the time of page loading or as a result of events that follow. A JavaScript library that manages all these operations in a simple and well-established manner has been developed for this purpose. This library is jQuery, and it is completely open source. It was created in 2006 by Jon Resig and continues to be improved on by a team of developers. Because of its usefulness, compared with classic JavaScript, and its ability to manipulate DOM elements, jQuery is currently the most widely used JavaScript library and constitutes a point of reference for all web developers.

Any developer who plans to include the jQuery library in a web page will soon discover the truth of the now well-known motto that accompanies thisUI libraries: "Write less, do more." In the spirit of this slogan, jQuery has introduced three new concepts in the development of JavaScript code—concepts you need to keep in mind when using the methods provided by thisUI libraries:

- Choosing elements of the HTML page (selections) on which to apply jQuery methods through Cascading Style Sheets (CSS) selectors

- Building chains of jQuery methods, applicable in sequence on a same selection

- Making implicit iterations, using jQuery wrappers

In this chapter, after seeing how to include the jQuery library in the Web pages that you will develop, the concept of the "selection" will be introduced. Selections are the base of the jQuery library and it will be important to understand them and how to implement them, as they will be discussed throughout the book. Through a series of small examples and using the technique of chaining methods, you will browse a range of functions provided by the jQuery library that will allow you to manipulate the selections in order to create, hide, and change the various DOM elements and their content.In the last part of this chapter, I will introduce the **jQuery user interface library** (**jQuery UI**), illustrating some of its most common widgets. You will learn their basic features and discover how to incorporate them within a web page.

The aim of this chapter is to provide a quick view of jQuery—its functionality and basic concepts. A detailed description of each of its methods is beyond the scope of this book. In all the examples in this text, these methods will be explained contextually. However, you may also want to consult the documentation on the official jQuery web site (`http://jquery.com/`).

# Including the jQuery Library

Now, there are two ways to include the jQuery library in your web page.

- **Local method**: Download the necessary libraries locally, and then add` them to the web page.

- **CDN method**: Set the link directly to the sites that provide these JavaScript libraries.

The sites offering these libraries are known as content delivery networks (CDNs). A CDN is a large system of servers that provide content with high availability and high performance to end users. When a user attempts to access a file, the CDN picks the server nearest to the user. One of the most used CDNs is Google Hosted Libraries. This service supplies web applications with reliable access to many of the most popular open source JavaScript libraries, such as jQuery.

To load the libraries from this service, you need to copy the following HTML snippet and paste it directly into your web page:

```
<script src="http://ajax.googleapis.com/ajax/libs/jquery/1.9.1/jquery.min.js">
</script>
```

Another CDN site from which to obtain any version of the jQuery library is the official CDN site of jQuery itself: **code.jquery.com**. If you prefer to use this site's URL, you need to copy and paste this HTML snippet:

```
<script src="http://code.jquery.com/jquery-1.9.1.min.js"></script>
```

---

■ **Note**    All the examples in this chapter use version 1.9.1 of the jQuery library.

---

If you choose to follow the local option instead, you need to copy and paste the relative path of the jQuery library. This path will vary, depending on where the library is situated on the web server or on your PC. It is good practice to create an appropriate local directory for loading all the libraries you will need to include.

For example, you may decide to put your jQuery library in an src directory and the web pages that you are developing in a charts directory, as shown in Figure 2-1. In this case, you have to use this relative path:

```
<script src="../src/js/jquery-1.9.1.js"></script>
```

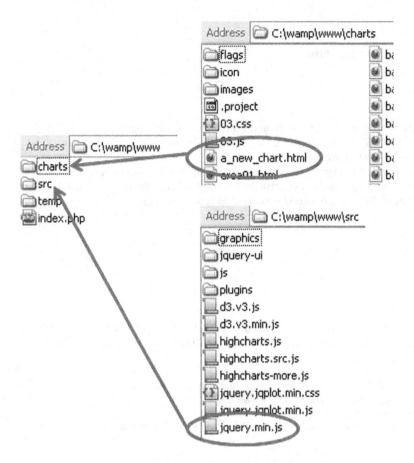

**Figure 2-1.** *An example of how a directory might be organized on a web server*

---

■ **Note**    For details on how to set up on a web server or PC a workspace in which to develop the examples in this book, see Appendix A. You will also find information on the different versions of the libraries, how to download them, and how to include them in the workspace.

---

## Selections

A selection is a group of HTML elements that have been chosen in order to be manipulated in some way. In effect, this is the main concept behind jQuery. Let us take as an example the simple HTML page in Listing 2-1:

**Listing 2-1.**  ch2_01a.html

```
<HTML>
<HEAD>
<script src="http://ajax.googleapis.com/ajax/libs/jquery/1.9.1/jquery.min.js"></script>
</HEAD>
```

```
<BODY>
<div> This is the first text</div>
<div class="selected"> This is the second text</div>
<div> This is the last text</div>
</BODY>
</HTML>
```

In this page there are three <div> elements containing three different texts. The second element in the list has been marked with the class name 'selected'. To select all three <div> elements, you can use the selector 'div', which identifies them among all the elements on the page.

Next, you write the jQuery() function, with the selector passed as an argument. In this way, you will have selected the three elements and their contents. To get the text, you use the function text(), placing it in chain to the jQuery() function call and adding this line at the end of the <body> section, as shown in Listing 2-2.

*Listing 2-2.* ch2_01a.html

```
<script>
var text = jQuery('div').text();
console.log(text);
</script>
```

All text contained in the three <div> elements has been assigned to the variable text. To view its contents (very useful in debugging), you can use the function console.log() and then, on Google Chrome, select Inspect element by right-clicking the page directly (see Figure 2-2).

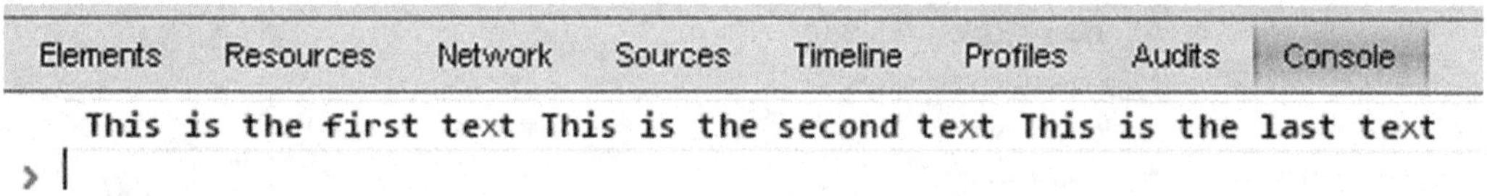

| Elements | Resources | Network | Sources | Timeline | Profiles | Audits | Console |
|----------|-----------|---------|---------|----------|----------|--------|---------|

This is the first text This is the second text This is the last text

›

*Figure 2-2. The variable text contains the text within the three <div> elements*

Depending on the frequency with which you make your selections, you can also call this function with $(), as shown in Listing 2-3. We will be using this option in the examples provided in this book.

*Listing 2-3.* ch2_01b.html

```
<script>
var text = $('div').text();
console.log(text);
</script>
```

In contrast, if you want to select only one of the three <div> elements, you can distinguish them by assigning a class name to each element and then apply the selector to the name of the element chosen, instead of the tag element (Listing 2-4).

*Listing 2-4.* ch2_01c.html

```
<script>
var text = $('.selected').text();
console.log(text);
</script>
```

In this case, the variable text contains only the text of the second <div> element, as demonstrated in Figure 2-3.

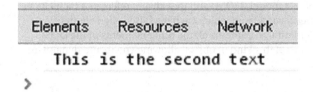

**Figure 2-3.** *The content of the text variable displayed by Inspect element in the Google Chrome browser*

Once you understand how to make a selection, you will discover how to manipulate any element by changing its content or attributes. You can even add other elements or remove an element from the page. In this regard, jQuery provides us with the necessary tools, thanks to the large number of methods it affords.

## Chaining Methods

jQuery is designed to allow jQuery methods to be chained. Once the selection of an element or a set of elements is made, the next step is to apply a sequence of methods to it. This sequence can be written using chaining.

Using the previous example (see Listing 2-1), let us say you want to replace the text in the second <div> element with another phrase and hide the other two elements so that they no longer appear in the web page. To do this, you are going to replace the line "This is the second text" with a new line, "This is a new text," hiding the other text at the same time. Figure 2-4 shows what appears before any change is applied.

This is the first text
This is the second text
This is the last text

**Figure 2-4.** *The text displayed by the web page without using the jQuery methods chain*

Now, you apply the following chain of methods:

```
$('div').hide().filter('.selected').text('This is a new text').show();
```

All three <div> elements are included in the selection and then hidden. In the selection you chose, only the elements with the class name `'selected'` and their content are replaced with a new text. Only these last elements must be shown. So, at the end of this chain of command, the result will be

This is a new text

## The Wrapper Set

When jQuery is involved, we deal with wrapper sets. In the previous example, there are three <div> elements. You will often make selections containing several elements, but you will never need to specify a programmatic loop. Here, when you applied the `hide()` method in order to hide all three elements, you did not use a `for` or `while` construct (i.e., `$('div').each(function() {})`). Therefore, a **wrapper set** may be defined as a group of elements (selection) amenable to any manipulation, as if it were a single item.

# jQuery and the DOM

jQuery is a library that principally works on the document object model (DOM) and that always refers to it for all its features. jQuery, like the DOM, treats each web page like a tree structure, in which each tag (also called element) is a node. The root of this tree is the document, which is the element that contains all the other elements of the DOM. jQuery provides a set of methods that simplify the manipulation of this kind of object, allowing you to add dynamism to your page.

## The ready() Method

If you want to write a JavaScript code that manipulates DOM elements, the DOM needs to be loaded before you can operate on it. But, you need to operate before the browser has loaded all assets completely. To this end, jQuery provides you with the ready() method. This is a custom event handler that is bound to the DOM of the document object. The ready() method takes only one parameter: a function containing the code, which should be executed just after the DOM is loaded, but before the user can see all the assets in the browser.

```
$(document).ready( function() {
    // we write the JavaScript code here.
});
```

## Traversing the DOM with Selections

You have seen how to select a group of DOM elements, using a specific CSS selector passed as an argument that identifies them. However, the potential of jQuery does not end there; starting from the position of the selection within the DOM, it is possible to traverse the DOM to get a new set of selected elements to operate on. jQuery provides us with a set of methods to apply to a selection.

Let us take as an example the simple HTML code in Listing 2-5:

***Listing 2-5.*** ch2_03a.html

```
<HTML>
<HEAD>
<script src="http://ajax.googleapis.com/ajax/libs/jquery/1.9.1/jquery.min.js"></script>
</HEAD>
<BODY>
<div class="fruits">
    <div>Apple</div>
    <div>Orange</div>
    <div>Banana</div>
    <div>Strawberry</div>
</div>
</BODY>
</HTML>
```

This page will show a list of four fruits. As you have already seen, if you make a selection with 'div' as selector, you will get a sequence of the five elements:

```
<div class="fruits">
    <div>Apple</div>
    <div>Orange</div>
    <div>Banana</div>
    <div>Strawberry</div>
</div>
<div>Apple</div>
<div>Orange</div>
<div>Banana</div>
<div>Strawberry</div>
```

You need to pay special attention to the first <div> element. You will find the other four <div> fruits in the selection, although these will then be repeated in successive elements. This is because the selector 'div' selects every <div> element, along with its contents, regardless of whether an element therein will in turn be selected. It is important to take this into account whenever you want to subject this type of selection to further manipulations.

Now, if you write the snippet in Listing 2-6, you get the text in an alert dialog box, as shown in Figure 2-5. You can see that the text in the last row includes all fruits.

*Listing 2-6.* ch2_03a.html

```
<script>
    var text = $('div').text();
    alert(text);
</script>
```

```
Apple
Orange
Banana
Strawberry
AppleOrangeBananaStrawberry
```

*Figure 2-5.* *The alert dialog box shows the text contained within the elements of the selection*

Often, however, you need to access a specific value of the selection directly. For example, to access the second element of the current selection directly, you can write

```
var text = $('div:eq(1)').text();
```

You have used the function eq() with the index of the element in the selection you wish to choose. Now, you have only this text:

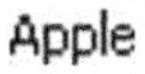

```
Apple
```

Similarly, if you want to select the third element of the sequence, you can directly write

```
var text = $('div:eq(2)').text();
```

Or, if you prefer, you can make a traversing, using the next() method to move the selection from one element to the next:

```
var text = $('div:eq(1)').next().text();
```

You then get this alert message:

Orange

Now, let us look at an example that demonstrates the difference between the selection and the DOM structure. This sometimes causes confusion. You must remember that the eq() method makes a sort of subselection; next(), prev(), parent(), children(), nextAll(), and prevAll() shift the selection onto the DOM.

In fact, if you write the chain

```
var text = $('div:eq(1)').prev().text();
```

you do not get anything, because the element selected by 'div:eq(1) ' is the first on the list (but second in the selection). Therefore, if you try to shift the selection to a previous element in the DOM, you do not get anything. If you want to shift the selection to the parent <div> element, called 'fruits', you need to use the parent() method:

```
var text = $('div:eq(1)').parent().text();
```

Now, you get the parent element, which is the same as the first element of the selection. Figure 2-6 presents the result.

Apple
Orange
Banana
Strawberry

***Figure 2-6.*** *The alert dialog box shows the four fruits within the first element*

Had you written the command

```
var text = $('div:eq(0)').text();
```

you would have obtained the same result.

## Create and Insert New Elements

So far, you have seen that by passing an argument in the function jQuery() or in its alias $(), you obtained a selection of all the items that have that tag in the DOM or the same class name. Now, suppose you pass as an argument a tag that is not present in the HTML page. Here, you have just created a new item to add to the DOM. Moreover, this element is, for all intents and purposes, a selection and may therefore be subjected to any kind of manipulation, even if it has not yet been physically added to the web page. By adding some specific jQuery methods at the end of the method chain, you will decide where to insert the newly created element.

For instance, as shown in the previous example, by writing the snippet

```
$('<div>Lemon</div>').appendTo('div:eq(2)');
```

you create a new element in the list of fruits. Then, you append it after the third element of the selection (the second element of the list). Figure 2-7 shows how the list in the web page appears after the change is applied.

Apple
Orange
Lemon
Banana
Strawberry

**Figure 2-7.** *The list can be increased dynamically, adding new elements*

There are many methods that specify where and how to insert the elements just created: prepend(), after(), before(), append(), appendTo(), prependTo(), insertAfter(), insertBefore(), wrap(), wrapAll(), wrapInner(), and so on.

For more details on the use of these functions, the reader is advised to consult the documentation on the official jQuery web site (http://jquery.com/).

## Remove, Hide, and Replace Elements

Another set of very useful jQuery methods includes those methods that allow us to eliminate static elements from the page (from the DOM) or at least to hide them. Sometimes, these methods can be useful even for replacing one element with another.

To remove the "Orange" fruit from the list, simply write

```
$('div:eq(2)').remove();
```

Apple
Banana
Strawberry

If you want to hide it, you write

```
$('div:eq(2)').hide();
  ...
$('div:eq(2)').show();
```

In this case, however, further on in the code, it will be possible to show "Orange" again.

If you use remove() instead (see Listing 2-7), the element corresponding to the selector 'div:eq(2)' changes, and it would not be possible to recover the removed element.

**Listing 2-7.** ch2_04c.html

```
$('div:eq(2)').remove();
var text = $('div:eq(2)').text();
alert(text); //returns 'Banana'
```

Finally, if you want to replace "Orange" with "Pineapple," you can do so with the replaceWith() method, as follows:

```
$('div:eq(2)').replaceWith('<div>Pineapple<div>');
```

Now, you have a new list of fruits, as demonstrated in Figure 2-8.

Apple
Pineapple
Banana
Strawberry

***Figure 2-8.*** *The list can be dynamically reduced by removing some of its elements*

# jQuery UI: Widgets

Along with the jQuery library, there is another library that can help you integrate your web page with interactive and graphic objects: the jQuery UI. This library provides a whole range of tools, such as widgets, themes, effects, and interactions, that enrich web pages, turning them into highly interactive web applications. For our purposes, widgets are of particular interest. These small graphic applications can prove a valuable tool that, when added to your web pages, makes your charts even more interactive. Widgets facilitate interaction the program beneath the web page and very often are real mini-applications. In their simplest forms, widgets appear as tables, accordions, combo boxes, or even buttons.

As with the jQuery library, you will need to include the plug-in file in the web page if you want to integrate its widgets. You must also include the CSS file representing the theme. This can be done through the Google Hosted Libraries service:

```
<link rel="stylesheet" href="http://ajax.googleapis.com/ajax/libs/jqueryui/1.10.3/themes/smoothness/
jquery-ui.css" />
<script src="http://ajax.googleapis.com/ajax/libs/jquery/1.9.1/jquery.min.js">
</script>
<script src="http://ajax.googleapis.com/ajax/libs/jqueryui/1.10.3/jquery-ui.min.js">
</script>
```

You can also download from the official CDN jQuery site:

```
<link rel="stylesheet" href="http://code.jquery.com/ui/1.10.3/themes/smoothness/jquery-ui.css" />
<script src="http://code.jquery.com/jquery-1.9.1.min.js"></script>
<script src="http://code.jquery.com/ui/1.10.3/jquery-ui.min.js"></script>
```

If you prefer to download the libraries locally or to use the workspace in the source code accompanying this book (see Appendix A), you can refer to the libraries as follows:

```
<link rel="stylesheet" href="../src/css/smoothness/jquery-ui-1.10.3.custom.min.css" />
<script src="../src/js/jquery-1.9.1.js"></script>
<script src="../src/js/jquery-ui-1.10.3.custom.min.js"></script>
```

---

■ **Note** The theme for the jQuery UI widgets used in this book is **smoothness**. The list of available themes is vast and covers many combinations of colors and shapes. This well-stocked list is available on ThemeRoller (http://jqueryui.com/themeroller). ThemeRoller is a page on the official jQuery web site that allows you to preview widgets and to then download your favorite theme from those available.

---

On visiting the official jQuery UI web site (http://jqueryui.com/), you will notice that the widgets provided by this library are numerous. Here, I will discuss only the most common examples, especially those that are most likely to be integrated into a page containing charts.

As you will see throughout this book, some of these widgets will be used as containers, exploiting their particular capabilities, such as resizing and encapsulation, including these:

- Accordions
- Tabs

Other widgets will be used to replace the simple controls that HTML offers, as the former are much more advanced and rich in functionality, including the following:

- Buttons
- Combo boxes
- Menu
- Sliders

Still other widgets will also perform the function of indicators. With these, you will see how to integrate a particular widget class:

- Progress bars

# Accordion

An accordion widget is a set of collapsible panels that enable the web page to show a large amount of information in a compact space. Each panel can hold a thematic area or, as you will see in later chapters, different types of charts. The content is revealed by clicking the tab for each panel, allowing the user to move from one panel to another without changing the page. The panels of the accordion expand and contract, according to the choice of the user, such that only one panel shows its content at any given time.

The HTML structure you need to write in order to obtain an accordion widget in the page is composed of an outer <div> tag containing all the panels. Each panel in turn is specified by a heading placed between two <h3> tags and a <div></div> pair, with the content in between. Listing 2-8 represents a simple accordion with four panels.

***Listing 2-8.*** ch2_05.html

```
<div id="accordion">
    <h3>First header</h3>
    <div>First content panel</div>
    <h3>Second header</h3>
    <div>Second content panel</div>
    <h3>Third header</h3>
    <div>Third content panel</div>
    <h3>Fourth header</h3>
    <div>Fourth content panel</div>
</div>
```

In JavaScript code, you need to add the snippet in Listing 2-9 in order to obtain an accordion widget.

**Listing 2-9.** ch2_05.html

```
$(function() {
    $( "#accordion" ).accordion();
});
```

Figure 2-9 illustrates our accordion.

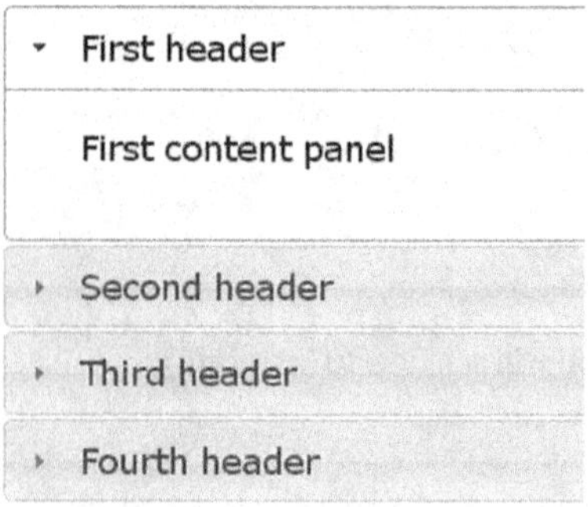

**Figure 2-9.** *An accordion consists of collapsible panels suitable for containing information in a limited amount of space*

But, that is not enough. It would be better if you could control the style of the accordion. This can be accomplished by adding the code given in Listing 2-10.

**Listing 2-10.** ch2_05.html

```
<style type="text/css">
    .ui-accordion {
        width: 690px;
        margin: 2em auto;
    }
    .ui-accordion-header {
        font-size: 15px;
        font-weight: bold;
    }
    .ui-accordion-content {
        font-size: 12px;
    }
</style>
```

The result is shown in Figure 2-10.

▾ First header

First content panel

▸ Second header

▸ Third header

▸ Fourth header

**Figure 2-10.** *By modifying the CSS style properties, you can change the accordion's appearance as you like*

## Tab

A widget that is very similar to the accordion in its functionality is the panel with tabs. Here, each panel is unique, but there are several tabs at the top, identified by different headings. Nonetheless, this widget affords the possibility to show a large amount of information in a limited space, and the user can choose to view the content of only one tab at a time. More significant is the loss of the vertical expansion of panels.

The HTML structure you need to write in order to obtain a tab widget in the web page is slightly more complex than the previous one. The headings are given in an unordered list <ul>, in which each item <li> must be referenced to an anchor tag <a>. The contents of every tab are enclosed in a <div></div> pair, with an id attribute corresponding to the references in the anchor tags (see Listing 2-11).

**Listing 2-11.** ch2_06.html

```
<div id="tabs">
  <ul>
    <li><a href="#tabs-1">First header</a></li>
    <li><a href="#tabs-2">Second header</a></li>
    <li><a href="#tabs-3">Third header</a></li>
    <li><a href="#tabs-4">Fourth header</a></li>
  </ul>
  <div id="tabs-1">
    <p>First tab panel</p>
  </div>
  <div id="tabs-2">
    <p>Second tab panel</p>
  </div>
   <div id="tabs-3">
    <p>Third tab panel</p>
  </div>
  <div id="tabs-4">
    <p>Fourth tab panel</p>
  </div>
</div>
```

In JavaScript code, you need to specify the tab widget, as shown in Listing 2-12.

**Listing 2-12.** ch2_06.html

```
$(function() {
    $( "#tabs" ).tabs();
});
```

The CSS style classes must also be defined, as shown in Listing 2-13.

**Listing 2-13.** ch2_06.html

```
<style type="text/css">
    .ui-tabs {
      width: 690px;
      margin: 2em auto;
    }
    .ui-tabs-header {
      font-size: 15px;
      font-weight: bold;
    }
    .ui-tabs-panel {
      font-size: 12px;
    }
</style>
```

When the procedure is complete, you will get the widgets illustrated in Figure 2-11.

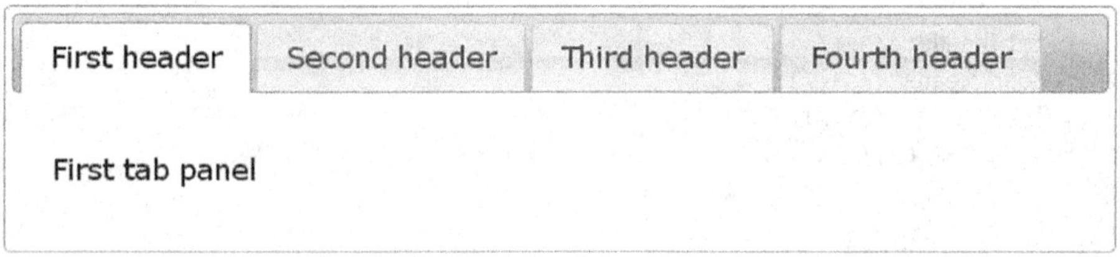

**Figure 2-11.** *The tab widget consists of multiple panels that occupy the same area*

## Button

Among all the widgets available, the button remains the most commonly used. Previously, there were two ways to insert a button in a web page. The first was the classic method, with the tag `<input type="button"/>`. A more modern approach was the <button> tag. But, thanks to jQuery, there is another kind of button that we have not yet considered. We can create an anchor tag <a> as a button, calling it "anchor button." When the user clicks it on the page, the browser loads the corresponding link. How to insert in a blank web page all three of the examples described is shown in Listing 2-14.

***Listing 2-14.*** ch2_07.html

```
<button>A button element</button>
<input type="submit" value="A submit button" />
<a href="#">An anchor</a>
```

Without further specification or JavaScript code, when you load the page, you see the buttons presented in Figure 2-12.

A button element    A submit button   An anchor

***Figure 2-12.*** *The web page shows three types of buttons: a simple button element, a submit button, and an anchor button*

To refer to them by using a JavaScript function, write the snippet provided in Listing 2-15.

***Listing 2-15.*** ch2_07.html

```
$(function() {
    $( "input[type=submit], a, button" )
      .button()
      .click(function( event ) {
         event.preventDefault();
      });
});
```

In this way, you will get a more presentable set of buttons, as demonstrated in Figure 2-13.

A button element     A submit button     An anchor

***Figure 2-13.*** *The three types of buttons are now represented by the jQuery UI button widgets*

You can enrich your buttons by adding icons. jQuery UI offers a huge set of icons, but you may also use larger, personal icons. Listing 2-16 shows how to write the four buttons into your web page:

***Listing 2-16.*** ch2_08.html

```
<button>Button with icon only</button>
<button>Button with custom icon on the left</button>
<button>Button with two icons</button>
<button>Button with two icons and no text</button>
```

You have added four buttons to highlight four possible cases: a button with only an icon; a button with text and an icon on the left side; a button with text and an icon on each side; and a button with two icons and no text (see Figure 2-14). Looking at the HTML code, you can see that actually all four buttons have text inside, but this feature can be disabled in order to get a button without text. Listing 2-17 illustrates the assignment of icons to the various buttons, with the icon name being assigned to the primary and secondary (optional) attributes. Furthermore, by setting the text attribute to 'false', you can obtain a button without text.

**Listing 2-17.** ch2_08.html

```
$(function() {
    $( "button:first" ).button({
        icons: {
            primary: "ui-icon-locked"
        },
        text: false
    }).next().button({
        icons: {
            primary: "ui-icon-italy"
        }
    }).next().button({
        icons: {
            primary: "ui-icon-gear",
            secondary: "ui-icon-triangle-1-s"
        }
    }).next().button({
        icons: {
            primary: "ui-icon-gear",
            secondary: "ui-icon-triangle-1-s"
        },
        text: false
    });
});
```

To insert customized icons, you need to define their address as a CSS file, using the function url(), as demonstrated in Listing 2-18.

**Listing 2-18.** ch2_08.html

```
<style>
.ui-button .ui-icon-italy {
    background-image: url("icon/exit24x24.png");
    width: 24px;
    height: 24px;
}
</style>
```

Figure 2-14 shows the set of buttons you have just created.

**Figure 2-14.** *Each button can be easily enriched with icons*

# Combo Box

The combo box is another widely used control in web pages and in many applications. A combo box is an editable drop down menu, from which the user can select an entry. To insert a combo box in your page, you need to define a specific structure of elements, as shown in Listing 2-19.

***Listing 2-19.*** ch2_09.html

```html
<div class="ui-widget">
    <label>Select your destination:</label>
    <select id="combobox">
        <option value="">Select one...</option>
        <option value="Amsterdam">Amsterdam</option>
        <option value="London">London</option>
        <option value="Rome">Rome</option>
    </select>
</div>
```

Next, you need to refer this structure using the JavaScript code, first choosing the elements with $() and then activating the structure as a jQuery combo box widget:

```javascript
$(function() {
    $( "#combobox" ).combobox();
});
```

Let us add a pinch of CSS style:

```css
<style>
    .ui-widget {
        font-size: 18px;
    }
</style>
```

Figure 2-15 illustrates the combo box widget, which represents the starting point for a whole series of functionalities for enabling the capture of events.

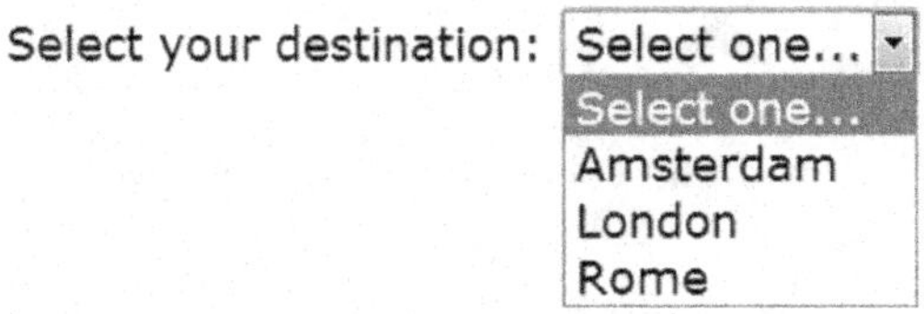

***Figure 2-15.*** *A combo box is a drop-down menu allowing the user to make a choise among various options*

# Menu

Having just considered the combo box, you cannot overlook the possibility of including an interactive menu on your home page. With such a menu, the user can make a series of choices, such as selecting options on how to represent a chart.

In HTML an unordered list is defined as <ul>, and a list of items, as <li>. If you want to add a submenu as an item, you only need to insert an embedded unordered list <ul>. To illustrate how to build a menu, let us take a look at Listing 2-20.

***Listing 2-20.*** ch2_10.html

```
<ul id="menu">
    <li class="ui-state-disabled"><a href="#">Advanced</a></li>
    <li><a href="#">Filter</a></li>
    <li>
        <a href="#">Zoom</a>
        <ul>
            <li><a href="#">10%</a></li>
            <li><a href="#">25%</a></li>
            <li><a href="#">50%</a></li>
            <li><a href="#">100%</a></li>
        </ul>
    </li>
</ul>
```

As with the preceding widgets, you must activate the menu by adding the following function:

```
$(function() {
    $( "#menu" ).menu();
});
```

You also need to include the CSS style settings:

```
<style>
    .ui-menu {
        width: 150px;
    }
</style>
```

Now, you have a menu on the page, as shown in Figure 2-16.

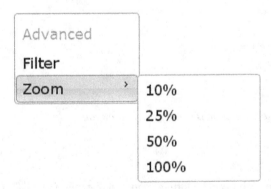

***Figure 2-16.*** *A drop-down menu lets you categorize different options*

# Slider

When you begin to develop various types of charts, you will find that several parameters have to be set each time. These parameters may be modified in real time by the user by means of sliders. These sliders enable the user to change parameters within a certain range.

As with many of the other widgets, first you add the <div> element to represent the slider in the web page.

```
<div id="slider"></div>
```

Then, as always, you activate the widget with a JavaScript function, specifying the widget's attributes within. For example, to specify the default position of the slider handle, you set the value attribute to a percentage value ranging from 0 to 100. Similarly, the orientation can be set by assigning the string 'horizontal' or 'vertical' to the orientation attribute. For the range attribute, you can indicate if the range (the shaded area of the slider track) covered by the slider should start from the 'min' value or the 'max' value (see Figure 2-19). Thus, if you were to set the range attribute to 'min', the range would extend from the minimum value to the slider handle. The animation attribute is another setting to consider. The slider widget has animation built in: when the user clicks the slider track, the handle moves from its current position to reach the clicked point; this can be done slowly or quickly. You can choose how fast the handle moves by setting the animation attribute to 'fast' or 'slow'. The attributes 'true' and 'false' indicate if the animation is enabled or disabled (see Listing 2-21).

*Listing 2-21.* ch2_12.html

```
$(function() {
    $( "#slider" ).slider({
        value: 60,
        orientation: 'horizontal',
        range: 'min',
        animate: 'slow'
    });
});
```

Once you have defined the fundamental attributes of the slider, you have to decide its size (and that of the handle) and add CSS style settings. When you define the length and width of the slider, you need to take into account the orientation you have chosen, setting the height and width attributes accordingly. In this case, we want to represent a slider horizontally; thus, the width attribute will be far greater than the height attribute (see Listing 2-22).

*Listing 2-22.* ch2_12.html

```
<style>
    .ui-slider {
        width: 400px;
        height: 10px;
    }
    .ui-slider .ui-slider-handle {
        width: 12px;
        height: 20px;
    }
</style>
```

If you load the web page in a browser, you can see the slider (see Figure 2-17).

*Figure 2-17. A slider is a widget that allows you to select a numeric value in a range*

Sometimes, you will need to use multiple sliders; you will need to organize these horizontally (you can find a similar structure, e.g., in the equalizer of a stereo). When specifying several sliders, it is not necessary to define multiple <div> elements: all that is required is a single <div> element, with "eq" as its id, to mark it. Then, within this <div> element, you define each slider as a <span></span> pair containing its default value (i.e., where the respective handles appear on the slider tracks), as demonstrated in Listing 2-23.

*Listing 2-23.* ch2_13.html

```
<div id="eq">
    <span>88</span>
    <span>77</span>
    <span>55</span>
    <span>33</span>
    <span>40</span>
    <span>45</span>
    <span>70</span>
</div>
```

Now, you must implement a JavaScript function, this time one that is slightly more complex. First, using the $("#eq > span") selector, you make a selection on the seven <span> elements. Then, with the parseInt() function, you assign all the values contained in <span></span> pairs to the corresponding value attributes in order that the handles be in the positions shown in Figure 2-18 (see Listing 2-24).

*Listing 2-24.* ch2_13.html

```
$(function() {
    $( '#eq > span' ).each(function() {
        // read initial values from markup and remove that
        var value = parseInt( $( this ).text(), 10 );
        $( this ).empty().slider({
            value: value,
            range: 'min',
            animate: 'slow',
            orientation: 'vertical'
        });
    });
});
```

Even for this equalizer-like structure, it is necessary to add some CSS style settings, such as the margins between the different sliders (see Listing 2-25).

**Listing 2-25.** ch2_13.html

```
<style>
    #eq span {
        height:180px;
        float:left;
        margin:15px;
        width:10px;
    }
</style>
```

In the end, you get the bars illustrated in Figure 2-18.

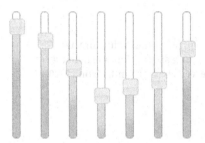

**Figure 2-18.** *The sliders can also be grouped in series to achieve more complex controls (e.g., an equalizer)*

## Progress Bar

When you are developing complex operations, the system may require a long time to finish its tasks. While the user is on hold, to prevent the system from appearing to be locked, it is usual to represent the percentage of the process completed with a progress bar. Defining a progress bar is very simple:

```
<div id="progressbar"></div>
```

You must also write the corresponding function in JavaScript in order to activate the progress bar, as shown in Listing 2-26.

**Listing 2-26.** ch2_11a.html

```
$(function() {
    $( "#progressbar" ).progressbar({
        value: 37
    });
});
```

Next, you add the CSS style settings, as illustrated in Listing 2-27.

**Listing 2-27.** ch2_11a.html

```
<style>
    .ui-progressbar {
        height: 20px;
        width: 600px;
    }
</style>
```

But, what you get is not the desired result; you get a static progress bar, fixed at the 37 percent mark (see Figure 2-19).

**Figure 2-19.** *With a progress bar, you can display the status of a process*

To obtain a fully functional progress bar, you need to set its attribute value with a counter value directly connected to the underlying iteration of the process. Furthermore, if you want to increase the dynamism of the progress bar, you can use an animated graphics interchange format (GIF) image as its background. Listing 2-28 displays the addition of CSS style properties to the progress bar.

**Listing 2-28.** ch2_11b.html

```
<style>
    .ui-progressbar {
        height: 20px;
        width: 600px;
    }
    .ui-progressbar .ui-progressbar-value {
        background-image: url(images/pbar-ani.gif);
    }
</style>
```

The GIF image in Figure 2-20 gives a greater sense of the progress of the operation.

**Figure 2-20.** *A progress bar with an animated GIF gives a highly dynamic appearance to the web page*

■ **Note**    Animated GIFs suitable for any kind of progress bar can be easily and safely obtained from the web site ajaxload (www.ajaxload.info). Simply choose the type of progress bar that you want to use, then the foreground and background colors, and the site automatically generates a preview of the animated GIF. If the image is to your liking, you can proceed with downloading it.

Otherwise, you can use the animated GIF (pbar-ani.gif) included in the code that accompanies this book, in the charts/images directory (you can find the code samples in the Source Code/Download area of the Apress web site [www.apress.com]).

# Concluding Thoughts on the jQuery Library

By now, you are probably wondering why we started with a library (jQuery) that, apparently, does not have anything to do with the development of charts or with data visualization in general. You have seen that the jQuery UI library provides us with graphic elements, but its use is far from what you would expect when thinking about charts.

Actually, we had to start here. You have decided to work with the JavaScript language, with the aim of implementing graphic elements (which are nothing more than DOM elements) in web pages. At the heart of all this are the concepts introduced through this library. The selections, the chains of methods, the structure, the practice of using CSS styles—these are the basis of web programming and, even more so, of chart development. And, what better way to obtain these fundamentals than with the jQuery library?

As you progress through the book, you will find that the jqPlot library must necessarily include the jQuery library. That is why it is important to know jQuery.

# Summary

Before starting to develop charts directly with JavaScript, it was necessary to introduce some fundamental tools that form the basis of the development of this type of code. In this second chapter, then, you were introduced to the **jQuery** and **jQuery UI** libraries. With jQuery, you learned how to manipulate DOM elements dynamically, through selections and chains of methods. With **jQuery UI**, you discovered how to enrich your pages with interactive graphic elements: the **jQuery UI widgets**.

In the next chapter, you will take your first steps with the jqPlot library. In particular, you will look at how the library is designed and at key concepts, such as plug-ins and options.

# CHAPTER 3

■ ■ ■

# Introducing jqPlot

In the course of this chapter, you will be introduced to the basic concepts that underlie this library. After seeing how the library is structured and the files that compose it, you will begin to understand how easy it is to make a chart using only a few lines of code.

With a series of examples, and through the use of plug-ins, you will gradually learn how to represent any type of chart. Everything will be done using the `$.jqPlot()` function, whose three arguments characterize all the features of the jqPlot library: the target canvas, the input data array, and the options object.

Finally, after a brief illustration of how to customize a chart through the use of Cascading Style Sheets (CSS) styles, you will take a quick look at how thinking in modules can make your implementations ordered, maintainable, and reusable. Let us, therefore, begin our introduction to this wonderful library.

## The jqPlot library

jqPlot is a JavaScript library specialized for the generation of charts in web pages. Written completely in pure JavaScript, jqPlot is an open source project, fully developed and maintained by Chris Leonello since 2009. When extended, the jQuery library reaches its full potential functionality. It is for this reason, in addition to its simplicity, that jqPlot is one of the most popular libraries for the representation of charts today.

jqPlot has been very successful and has virtually supplanted other, previous libraries, such as Flot, many aspects of which, including look and feel, jqPlot retains. In fact, the author of jqPlot often admits that he was a dedicated user of Flot but that, over time, he came to realize its limitations. The old library lacked many capabilities; moreover, its architecture was structured in such a way as to make it difficult to expand. So, Leonello felt the need to create a new library that preserved all that was good in Flot but that allowed it to grow. As such, he rewrote its architecture completely. jqPlot has a highly modular structure and, as you will see, is based on a large number of plug-ins, each of which plays a certain role. Hence, its strongest feature is its pluggability. Every object the user draws, be it a line, an axis, a shadow, or the grid itself, is handled by a plug-in. Every plot element has customizable setting options, and every added plug-in can expand the functionality of the plot.

The plug-ins gradually increased in number, widening the library's targets further. jqPlot is now a versatile and expandable library, suitable for those who want to develop professional charts in a just a few steps.

In most cases, jqPlot allows you to draw beautiful charts without adding too many lines of code. Indeed, you will see that jqPlot (perhaps even more than jQuery) has embraced the philosophy "Write less, do more." I think that this is the libary's most appreciated aspect. Every day, more and more developers are added to the list of jqPlot users.

# Including Basic Files

When you decide to take advantage of jqPlot to draw a chart on your web site, there is, as a starting point, a set of critical files that needs to be included.

As mentioned earlier, jqPlot is essentially an extention of jQuery, and so operating with it requires the inclusion of the jQuery plug-in (see Table 3-1). You can download this plug-in from the official jqPlot web site (www.jqplot.com), along with all the other plug-ins that make up the jqPlot library, including the CSS file. These files are grouped in different distributions, depending on the release version.

*Table 3-1.* *The distributions of jqPlot and versions of jQuery on which they are based*

| jqPlot Version | jQuery Version |
| --- | --- |
| 1.0.6–1.0.8 | 1.9.1 |
| 1.0.2–1.0.5 | 1.6.4 |

■ **Note**   All the examples in this book use version 1.0.8 of the jqPlot library.

However, there is a small set of files that represents the core of the library and that is indispensable if you want to include every function made possible by jqPlot. This set of basic files consists of the jQuery plug-in, the jqPlot plug-in, and a jqPlot CSS file. There is another file that needs to be imported, but only if you want to load the page in an Internet Explorer browser that is below version 9: an ExplorerCanvas (excanvas) script. This optional file compensates for the lack of canvas functionality introduced by HTML5.

Thus, within the <head></head> tags of your web page, you are going to include these files (for further information on how to set up a workspace, see Appendix A):

```
<!--[if lt IE 9]><script type="text/javascript" src="../src/excanvas.js"></script><![endif]-->
<script type="text/javascript" src="../src/jquery.min.js"></script>
<script type="text/javascript" src="../src/jquery.jqplot.min.js"></script>
<link rel="stylesheet" type="text/css" href="../src/jquery.jqplot.min.css"/>
```

Instead of working with the jqPlot library locally, by downloading it from the web site, you can also use a content delivery network (CDN) service, just as you have done with jQuery. jsDelivr (www.jsdelivr.com/#!jqplot) is a CDN web site that offers all the most recent distributions of jqPlot.If you want to use this service, you can modify the URL as follows:

```
<!--[if lt IE 9]><script type="text/javascript" src="http://cdn.jsdelivr.net/excanvas/r3/excanvas.js">
</script><![endif]-->
<script src="http://code.jquery.com/jquery-1.9.1.min.js"></script>
<script type="text/javascript" src="http://cdn.jsdelivr.net/jqplot/1.0.8/jquery.jqplot.min.js">
</script>
<link rel="stylesheet" type="text/css" href="http://cdn.jsdelivr.net/jqplot/1.0.8/jquery.jqplot.min.css"/>
```

As you will soon discover, in the network, you will come across similar files, some with and others without the abbreviation "min" (for "minified"). You should always try to use the min versions, the compressed versions of these files. They are faster to load. You should use their normal versions (without "min") only when your intent is to modify these libraries internally.

# Plot Basics

Now that you have seen how the jqPlot library is structured and have looked at the set of files you require to operate with it, you can begin to learn how to use these files within your web page. In chart development, there are two basic steps: the creation of an area in which to represent the chart and the insertion of a section for the JavaScript code needed to call all the functions, variables, and series of objects that the jqPlot library makes available.

## Adding a Plot Container

The jqPlot library requires the definition of a container (a <div> element) within the <body> section of the HTML page. This container will function as a canvas for the library.

Throughout this chapter, this container is referred to as the **target**. Within a web page, each target (in this case, the plot container) is identified by a specific id. In this book, you will always find myChart as an identifier of the target, but it can take any name, and you must always bear in mind that more than one target may be assigned to the same web page. Furthermore, it is also important to specify a width and a height for the target. These will define the size of the drawing area within the web page (see Listing 3-1).

***Listing 3-1.*** Ch3_01.html

```
<BODY>
    ...
    <div id="myChart" style="height:400px; width:500px;"></div>
    ...
</BODY>
```

## Creating the Plot

To be entered, jqPlot commands and almost all JavaScript code must be enclosed within a <scripts> tag. But, a web page is divided into two sections: head and body. So, which is the best place to insert JavaScript code? Although it is possible to place code in both sections of a library, it is preferable to place it in only one, depending on the library. Considering how jqPlot works, you will be putting the code between the <head></head> tags.

Furthermore, jqPlot is an extension of jQuery, so you need to call all its methods inside the $(document).ready() function if you want your code to be executed (see Listing 3-2).

***Listing 3-2.*** Ch3_01.html

```
$(document).ready(function(){
    // Insert all jqPlot code here.
});
```

Then, to create the actual plot, you must call the $.jqplot plug-in with the id of the target in which you want to draw the chart. This call is executed by the following jQuery function:

```
$.jqplot(target, data, options);
```

The jqplot() function has three arguments; **target**, which is the ID of the target element in which the plot is to be rendered—the ID attribute that you specify in the plot container; **data**, consisting of an array for data series; and **options**, the main feature of jqPlot. Within options, you will enter the customization settings necessary to make your chart more suitable to your needs and tastes.

If you do not define any options (yes, it is optional!), you can produce a chart following the settings for standard options. In fact, many options are already defined, and it is not necessary to change the all settings every time you develop a chart. If the standard options meet your requirements, you do not need to define them. This will save you a lot of time and avoids having to write many lines of code. For example, let us write the function in Listing 3-3.

***Listing 3-3.*** Ch3_01.html

```
$(document).ready(function(){
    $.jqplot ('myChart', [[100, 110, 140, 130, 80, 75, 120, 130, 100]]);
});
```

With only a few lines of code, you can produce charts like the one in Figure 3-1.

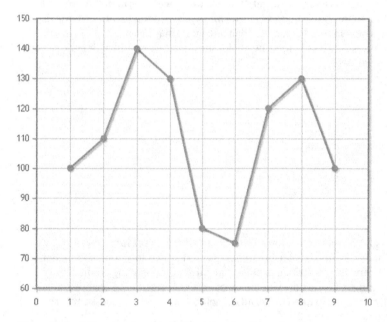

***Figure 3-1.*** *A line chart created with only a few lines of code*

From what you have just seen, you can surmise that if you do not specify any options, the default outcome will be a line chart, and the data that you have added will be interpreted as such. The values in the array are, therefore, the y values, and the indexes of their sequence are reported on the x axis. In later chapters, you will learn how these values are interpreted and how to get different types of charts from the linear one.

# Using jqPlot Plug-ins

The most recent jqPlot distribution offers approximately thirty plug-ins (for a list of all the jqPlot plug-ins, see Appendix B). Each is specialized to perform a specific task, and the name is often indicative of function. You will be looking at many of these plug-ins in the following chapters—at their uses and their main options.

Let us take, for instance, *BarRenderer*. This plug-in is necessary if you want the input data to be interpreted as a bar chart:

```
$.jqplot ('myChart', [[100, 110, 140, 130, 80, 75, 120, 130, 100]],
{
    series:[{renderer: $.jqplot.BarRenderer}]
});
```

In jqPlot, we often refer to a plug-in as a renderer. This is because the architecture of the framework specifies that each plug-in must cover a specific task. If the developer deems it necessary, then he or she will include it. In addition, real renderer should be as independent as possible from one another. In fact, you can add as many plug-ins as you wish, and generally their order is not important. Some plug-ins do not require that you specify any extra option or setup; they are already defined and are directly activated just by virtue of being included. One such plug-in is *Highlighter*, which highlights data points near the mouse. However, if you are not satisfied with the default settings, you can always define the properties with new values; these plug-ins also contain additional, settable properties. Other plug-ins provide functionalities that have to be specified in the options argument in order to be activated.

Thus, both the basic elements of the jqPlot library and the additional components, which are introduced gradually by the included plug-ins, can be characterized by a series of attributes (in a manner very similar to that seen with the CSS style). The jqPlot library calls these attributes **options**.

# Understanding jqPlot Options

The key to using jqPlot effectively is to understand jqPlot's options. The properties of any object in a chart are defined by attributes, which can take different values. It is very important to understand how to set and use these attributes through object types that I will refer to as **options**.

## Inserting Options

So far, you have seen how the jqPlot() function is called within the JavaScript code and how to include the plug-ins and data, but you have not yet observed how to enter options. You can customize the default line chart by passing different attributes to the $.jqplot() function in this way:

```
$(document).ready(function(){
    $.jqplot ('myChart', [[100, 110, 140, 130, 80, 75, 120, 130, 100]],
    {
        //All the attributes here.
    });
});
```

The first thing to note is that it is not possible to set properties directly in the chart object after you call $.jqplot(). At best, this will not do anything. You have to pass all the attributes in the options argument.

The options argument represents the jqPlot object in each of its properties. Everything that characterizes a chart is expressed by a number of properties, which are set to certain values. These values differentiate a bar chart from a line chart, regulate the stroke of a line or the length of an axis, indicate whether to display a legend and where, and so on. Usually, when including the various plug-ins, it is not necessary to specify values for all properties; they are already set to a default value. It is because of these default values that, in adding a plug-in, you can realize a nice chart without adding a single line of code. If you specify a property explicitly, you are actually overwriting the value of a property already defined with a default value.

Because our aim is to set the `jqPlot` object, and because this is made up of a series of components, it will be necessary to build the `options` object with a structure that perfectly reflects these components by defining a whole series of objects with their properties. Recalling the object corresponding to the component and assigning a value to one of its properties inside the `options` object, you are going to overlay the default value and change the property of the respective component of the `jqPlot` object. The most commonly used objects you can define inside the `options` object are

- `seriesColors`
- `stackSeries`
- `title`
- `axesDefaults`
- `axes`
- `seriesDefaults`
- `series`
- `legend`
- `grid`
- `cursor`
- `highlighter`

Each name reflects the component of the chart that will be affected by a change in its property value. These objects are built by a whole series of well-defined properties, each with its own default value.

This is the structure of the `jqPlot` object:

*jqplot object* ➤ *component objects* ➤ *object properties* ➤ *default value*

In Listing 3-4, you can see the corresponding structure that you need to follow when defining the options object.

***Listing 3-4.*** Ch3_02c.html

```
var options = {
    axes:{
        yaxis:{
            min: 70,
            max: 150
        },
        ...
    },
    ...
};
```

I believe that the easiest object to add to a chart is the `title`. It does not contain any property, and can often be considered a property itself of the `jqPlot` object. Moreover, it is possible to set a text value directly on it, text that will be the title of your chart. Given its simplicity, the `title` is a good starting point for understanding how to use options (Listing 3-5).

*Listing 3-5.* Ch3_02a.html

```
$(document).ready(function(){
    $.jqplot ('myChart', [[100, 110, 140, 130, 80, 75, 120, 130, 100]],
    {
        title: 'My first jqPlot chart'
    });
});
```

If you prefer, you can also define the properties of objects externally, with the jqplot() function, assigning properties to a variable. This variable will then be passed as an argument in the jqPlot() function, as shown in Listing 3-6. This variable is actually the options object.

*Listing 3-6.* Ch3_02a.html

```
var options = { title: 'My first jqPlot chart' };
$.jqplot ('myChart', [[100, 110, 140, 130, 80, 75, 120, 130, 100]], options);
```

In both cases, you now have a chart with a title at the top (see Figure 3-2).

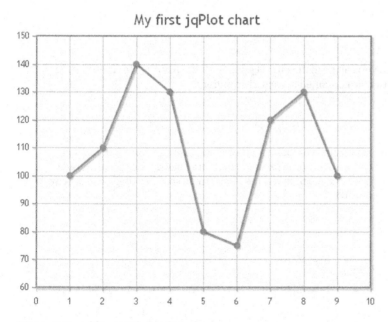

*Figure 3-2.* *Adding a title to a line chart*

To better understand how to set the jqPlot properties within the options object, let us take an example, referring to the API Documentation section of the jqPlot web site (www.jqplot.com/docs/files/jqplot-core-js.html). Let us say you want to hide the grid lines in your chart. In the list of properties belonging to the grid object, you will find what you are looking for:

```
this.drawGridlines = true.
```

this is the instance of the grid, and `true` is the default value assigned to the `jqplot` object at the time of its creation. Because you want the grid to be hidden (a behavior different from that of default), you will need to replace the value `true` with the value `false` within the `jqPlot` object. To do this, you have to add the `drawGridlines` property within the `options` object definition, maintaining the structure object:{property:attribute}.

```
options = {grid:{drawGridlines: false}};
```

Now, you have a chart without grid lines (see Figure 3-3).

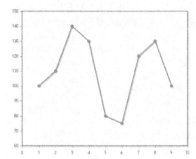

**Figure 3-3.** *Hiding the grid lines in a line chart*

For a full list of attributes that can be set, you can go to the official jqPlot web site (`www.jqplot.com/docs/index/General.html`) or read the `jqPlotOptions.txt` file contained in each distribution.

## Handling Options on Axes

Axes are handled a little differently from the other normal component objects, because they have four distinct children, namely, `xaxis`, `yaxis`, `x2axis`, and `y2axis`. To illustrate axes, we therefore need a more deeply nested example. Let us say you want to specify the `min` and `max` attributes on the y axis. To do so, you will need to specify the `options` object with the structure shown in Listing 3-7.

*Listing 3-7.* Ch3_02c.html

```
var options = {
    axes:{
        yaxis:{
            min: 70,
            max: 150
        }
    }
};
```

Now, the range on the y axis is between the `max` and `min` properties that you defined in `options` (see Figure 3-4).

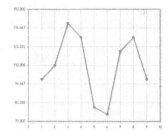

**Figure 3-4.** *A line chart focused on a specific range on the y axis*

To make things easier, jqPlot provides a handy shortcut that enables us to assign the same value to the properties of all axes in one go: the axesDefaults object. If you want to set the same value to both x and y (or x2 and y2), you need to specify these properties only for the axesDefaults option object, assigning the value once (see Listing 3-8).

**Listing 3-8.** Ch3_02d.html

```
$(document).ready(function(){

    var options = {
        axesDefaults:{
            min: 0,
            max: 20
        }
    };
    $.jqplot ('myChart', [[1,4,8,13,8,7,12,10,5]], options);
});
```

# Inserting Series of Data

Earlier, you saw how to produce a simple line chart, using the settings for standard options (see the section "Creating the Plot"). In this example the array of data was passed directly as the second argument in the function $.jqplot(). However, you can also define an array of data as a variable externally and then pass it as the second argument.

```
$(document).ready(function(){
    var data = [[100,110,140,130,80,75,120,130,100]];
    $.jqplot ('myChart', data);
});
```

Here, you find a single series of data corresponding to the values on the y axis. But, as you will see, it is possible to pass data as (x, y) pairs of values and also to pass multiple series of data at once. These input modes vary, depending on the chart you are designing and the requirements of the various plug-ins used. For example, if you want to input multiple data series, you need to declare four different arrays, as shown in Listing 3-9.

**Listing 3-9.** Ch3_03a.html

```
$(document).ready(function(){
    var series1 = [1, 2, 3, 2, 3, 4];
    var series2 = [3, 4, 5, 6, 5, 7];
    var series3 = [5, 6, 8, 9, 7, 9];
    var series4 = [7, 8, 9, 11, 10, 11];
    $.jqplot ('myChart', [series1, series2, series3, series4]);
});
```

51

jqPlot is able to manage multiple series without having to specify any property in options. In fact, the browser will display a line chart with as many lines as there are data series, each in a different color, as shown in Figure 3-5.

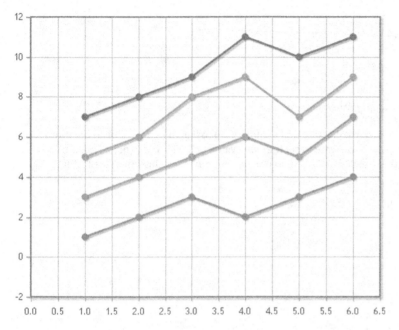

**Figure 3-5.** *A multiseries line chart with different colors for each series*

As you can see, as well as making the code more readable and tidy, the externally defined series of data can also assist in the future extension and manipulation of the data. Using all the tools that JavaScript makes available, you can create, manipulate, sort, calculate, and compute an infinite variety of data.

It is possible to change the properties of the options object even for series of data. The series are inserted in a particular order into an array passed as a second argument in the $.jqplot() function. This order will be reflected in the creation of the series objects inside the jqPlot object. For instance, if you want only the second series not to show its marker points, it will be necessary to leave empty the space for the properties of the first series (not to overwrite its attributes) and then set the showMarker property to 'false' in the second space. In so doing, jqPlot will overwrite only the values of the property of the second series. To accomplish this, you must write the options object as shown in Listing 3-10.

**Listing 3-10.** Ch3_03b.html

```
$(document).ready(function(){
    var series1 = [1, 2, 3, 2, 3, 4];
    var series2 = [3, 4, 5, 6, 5, 7];
    var series3 = [5, 6, 8, 9, 7, 9];
    var series4 = [7, 8, 9, 11, 10, 11];
    var options = {
      series: [ {},
```

```
        {
          showMarker: false
        }]
    }

    $.jqplot ('myChart', [series1, series2, series3, series4], options);
});
```

The result of these settings is the chart with four series in Figure 3-6. Note that the third series from the top has no marker point.

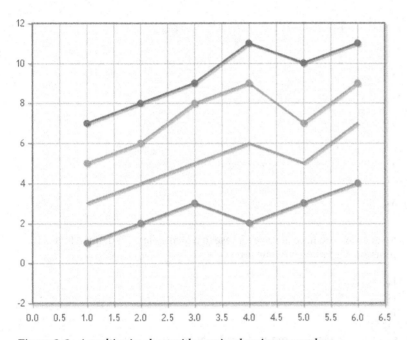

***Figure 3-6.*** *A multiseries chart with a series showing no markers*

If you decide to set the showMarker property in axesDefaults, instead of in the axes object, you will assign the same value for all the series at once (see Listing 3-11).

***Listing 3-11.*** Ch3_03c.html

```
$(document).ready(function(){
    var series1 = [1, 2, 3, 2, 3, 4];
    var series2 = [3, 4, 5, 6, 5, 7];
    var series3 = [5, 6, 8, 9, 7, 9];
    var series4 = [7, 8, 9, 11, 10, 11];
    var options = {
        seriesDefaults: { showMarker: false }
    };
    $.jqplot ('myChart', [series1, series2, series3, series4], options);
});
```

Now, none of the series in the chart show any marker points (see Figure 3-7).

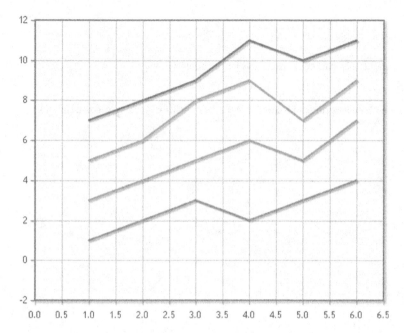

**Figure 3-7.** *A multiseries chart with no markers*

There is a third way to enter the data as an array. You have just seen a case in which an array is defined for each series and then passed to the $.jqplot() function, all gathered in one array:

```
var series1 = [1, 2, 3, 2, 3, 4];
var series2 = [3, 4, 5, 6, 5, 7];
var series3 = [5, 6, 8, 9, 7, 9];
var series4 = [7, 8, 9, 11, 10, 11];
$.jqplot ('myChart', [series1, series2, series3, series4], options);
```

But, it is also possible to define all the series in a single variable, which you call dataSets:

```
var dataSets = {
    data1: [[1,1], [2,2], [3,3], [4,2],  [5,3],  [6,4]],
    data2: [[1,3], [2,4], [3,5], [4,6],  [5,5],  [6,7]],
    data3: [[1,5], [2,6], [3,8], [4,9],  [5,7],  [6,9]],
    data4: [[1,7], [2,8], [3,9], [4,11], [5,10], [6,11]]
};
```

Once you have declared the dataSets variable, in order to access the values, you have to specify the series inside it, with dataSets. as a prefix. Thus, when you need to pass the four series individually as a second argument of the jqplot() function, you must do so in this way:

```
$.jqplot ('myChart', [dataSets.data1, dataSets.data2, dataSets.data3, dataSets.data4], options);
```

Although, at the moment, this whole operation may seem too laborious, later you will see that gathering all the data in a data set can be useful in special cases.

# Renderers and Plug-ins: A Further Clarification

Normally, a renderer is an object that is attached to something in the plot in order to draw it. A plug-in, as well as adding drawing functionality, can perform other functions, such as event handling; making calculations; and handling the format of strings and values, such as dates. So, it is possible to consider a renderer a drawing plug-in, but the converse is not always true.

Let us examine this slight difference in more detail with the help of some examples. You have seen, for instance, that by entering only a single data series, you can obtain a line chart by default (see the section "Creating the Plot"). If you want to render this series as a bar chart, you need to attach the *barRenderer* plugin to the seriesDefaults object in options. Moreover, when switching from a line chart to a bar chart, it is necessary to create categories on the x axis in order to have the bars well separated from each other. To do this, you need to attach the CategoryAxisRenderer to the axes object in options (see Listing 3-12).

*Listing 3-12.* Ch3_04a.html

```
$(document).ready(function(){
    var data = [[100, 110, 140, 130, 80, 75, 120, 130, 100]];
    var options = {
        seriesDefaults: {
            renderer: $.jqplot.BarRenderer
        },
        axes:{
            xaxis:{
                renderer: $.jqplot.CategoryAxisRenderer
            }
        }
    }
    $.jqplot ('myChart', data, options);
});
```

However, calling the two renderers in options is not enough. You must also load them in the page, so you have to include the corresponding plug-ins, as shown in Listings 3-13 and 3-14 (CDN service).

*Listing 3-13.* Ch3_04a.html

```
<script type="text/javascript" src="../src/jquery.min.js"></script>
<script type="text/javascript" src="../src/jquery.jqplot.min.js"></script>
<link rel="stylesheet" type="text/css" href="../src/jquery.jqplot.min.css"/>
<script type="text/javascript" src="../src/plugins/jqplot.barRenderer.min.js"></script>
<script type="text/javascript" src="../src/plugins/jqplot.categoryAxisRenderer.min.js"></script>
```

*Listing 3-14.* Ch3_04a.html

```
<script src="http://code.jquery.com/jquery-1.9.1.min.js"></script>
<script type="text/javascript" src="http://cdn.jsdelivr.net/jqplot/1.0.8/
jquery.jqplot.min.js"></script>
<link rel="stylesheet" type="text/css" href="http://cdn.jsdelivr.net/jqplot/1.0.8/
jquery.jqplot.min.css"/>
<script type="text/javascript" src="http://cdn.jsdelivr.net/jqplot/1.0.8/plugins/
jqplot.barRenderer.min.js"></script>
<script type="text/javascript" src="http://cdn.jsdelivr.net/jqplot/1.0.8/plugins/
jqplot.categoryAxisRenderer.min.js"></script>
```

If you reload your page in the browser, the line chart has just become a bar chart, as shown in Figure 3-8.

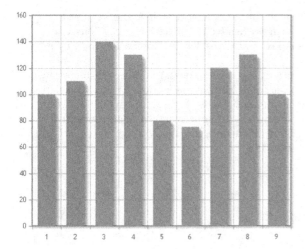

**Figure 3-8.** *A bar chart*

By calling these two renderers to options, you replace the default renderer valid for all series in the plot with these category renderers. The latter have in turn several properties set on default values, which may be modified as well. Many of these properties may be specific to that particular renderer, and so they will be added to those already defined in the jqplot object in order to introduce new features to the plot.

Even for this class of additional properties, you can change the default values through the options object. First, assign the desired renderer to the renderer property. Then, specify all the properties you want to set inside the rendererOptions property. All these properties will be specified in the component object on which you want to act. For example, if you want each bar of a given series to have a different color, you need to change the varyBarColor property, replacing the default value false with true (see Listing 3-15).

**Listing 3-15.** Ch3_04b.html

```
var options = {
    seriesDefaults: {
        renderer: $.jqplot.BarRenderer,
        rendererOptions: {
            varyBarColor: true
        }
    },
    axes:{
       xaxis:{
           renderer: $.jqplot.CategoryAxisRenderer
       }
    }
}
```

With the changes you have just made, the *BarRenderer* plugin will automatically assign a different color to each bar (see Figure 3-9).

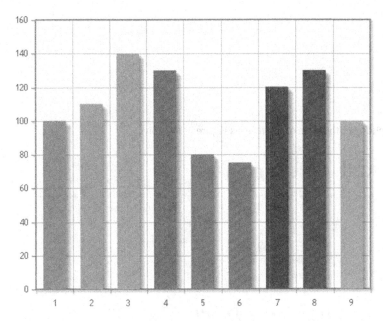

**Figure 3-9.** *A bar chart with different colors*

Plug-ins also have specific properties that can be set inside the options object. As mentioned earlier, not all jqPlot plug-ins are renderers, and those that are not are easily recognizable in the jqPlot distribution, because they do not contain the term *renderer* in their file names. These plug-ins perform specific functions that are not directly related to a particular type of component in the plot. Such features enhance the capability of jqPlot in general. *Highlighter*, for instance, is a plug-in that highlights data points when they are moused over. As you will see, this plug-in has a series of tools within it that handles formatting specifiers for data values and that can show tool tip content with an HTML structure. Other notable plug-ins include *Trendline*, which automatically computes and draws trend lines for plotted data; *Cursor*, which represents the cursor, as displayed in the plot; and *PointLabels*, which places labels at the data points.

# CSS Customization

Much of the styling of jqPlot charts is done through CSS. The jquery.jqplot.css file is available in every distribution, and it is one of the three fundamental files to be included in your web page in order to obtain a jqPlot chart.

All the components that make up the chart can be customized through CSS without having to set any of their properties in the options object. This is to maintain consistency with all other objects in the web page: the style of the chart, and all that is in it (inside the canvas), must be managed by CSS files, like any other HTML object. The names of the CSS classes ruling the style of jqPlot objects begin with the prefix .jqplot-*. For example, the style class that affects all axes is .jqplot-axis.

To illustrate how it is possible to modify some elements of the chart using CSS, let us look at how to change the font and font size of the chart title. As with any HTML element, you simply have to recall the CSS selector of the jqPlot element and modify the attributes. So, in this case, you add the CSS style setting in Listing 3-16.

***Listing 3-16.*** Ch3_02e.html

```
<style>
    .jqplot-title {
        font: italic bold 22px arial, sans-serif;
    }
</style>
```

With this new CSS statement, you have changed the style of the title, as Figure 3-10 shows.

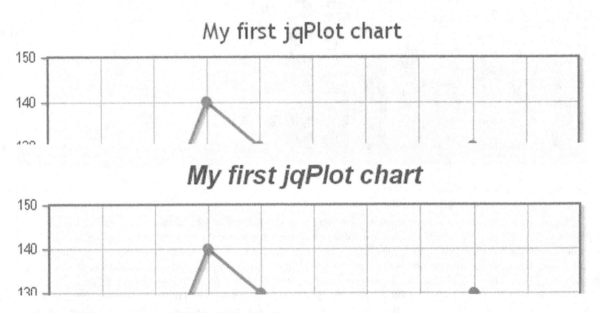

***Figure 3-10.*** *Two different CSS styles applied to the title*

# Thinking in Modules

When things get increasingly complex, and the lines to add to your web site become many, it is best to think in terms of modules. As well as providing better visibility and ease of maintenance, creating separate modules also promotes the reusability of what you have just created. Let us analyze the current situation with your web page in Listing 3-17.

***Listing 3-17.*** Ch3_05a.html

```
<HTML>
<HEAD>
<TITLE>My first chart</TITLE>
<script type="text/javascript" src="../src/jquery.min.js"></script>
<script type="text/javascript" src="../src/jquery.jqplot.min.js"></script>
<link rel="stylesheet" type="text/css" href="../src/jquery.jqplot.min.css"/>
<style>
    .jqplot-title {
        font: italic bold 22px arial, sans-serif;
    }
</style>
```

```
<script class="code" type="text/javascript">
$(document).ready(function(){
    var data = [[100, 110, 140, 130, 80, 75, 120, 130, 100]];
    $(document).ready(function(){
        $.jqplot ('myChart', data,
        {
            title: 'My first jqPlot chart'
        });
    });
});
</script>
</HEAD>
<BODY>
    <div id="myChart" style="height:400px; width:500px;"></div>
</BODY>
</HTML>
```

If you load this web page in the browser, you obtain the line chart in Figure 3-11.

*Figure 3-11.* *A simple line chart*

As is evident, the part that regulates the style of the page is contained within the <style></style> pair of tags, whereas JavaScript, or the jqPlot code, is within the <script></script> pair of tags. These are the two main areas in which we add lines of code. But, it is interesting to note that these two sections can be copied and pasted into two separate external files. The style section will be copied in a file that we will call myCss.css (see Listing 3-18).

*Listing 3-18.* myCss.css

```
.jqplot-title {
    font: italic bold 22px arial, sans-serif;
}
```

The JavaScript code will be copied in a file that we will name myJS.js (see Listing 3-19).

**Listing 3-19.** myJS.js

```
$(document).ready(function(){
    var data = [[100, 110, 140, 130, 80, 75, 120, 130, 100]];
    $.jqplot ('myChart', data,
    {
        title: 'My first jqPlot chart'
    });
});
```

Now, you can change your HTML page by removing the copied parts and including the two newly created files (see Listing 3-20).

**Listing 3-20.** Ch3_05b.html

```
<HTML>
<HEAD>
    <TITLE>My first chart</TITLE>
    <script type="text/javascript" src="../src/jquery.min.js"></script>
    <script type="text/javascript" src="../src/jquery.jqplot.min.js"></script>
    <link rel="stylesheet" type="text/css" href="../src/jquery.jqplot.min.css"/>
    <script type="text/javascript" src="myJS.js"></script>
    <link rel="stylesheet" type="text/css" href="myCss.css"/>
</HEAD>
<BODY>
    <div id="myChart" style="height:400px; width:500px;"></div>
</BODY>
</HTML>
```

If you now load the page in your browser, you will not see any difference, compared with the initial case, in which the JavaScript code and CSS styles were on the same page (see Figure 3-11).

Being aware of the possibility of working in modules will enable you to write a code that can be reused by multiple charts. This can be very useful when you want to create, for example, a standard set of CSS styles that assigns a graphic theme that will be common to all your charts. Or, if you have developed methods in JavaScript the application of which can be valuable in many other cases, then you can include these methods externally in each HTML page of your personal library.

# Summary

In this chapter, you took your first steps with the jqPlot library. In particular, you looked at how the library is designed and at key concepts, such as plug-ins and options. With a series of examples, you gradually learned how to use the three different arguments passed to the function $.jqPlot(): the **target**, which is the jqPlot library canvas; input **data**—their format and the various input modes; and, especially, the options object, through which the settings of all the components of the library are performed. options will constitute the core of all implementations that you will be looking at in later chapters.

In the following chapters, you will be using the jqPlot library more specifically, implementing all the most common chart types. In the next chapter, you will begin with **line charts**.

■ ■ ■

# CHAPTER 4

# Line Charts with jqPlot

In the previous chapter, you observed the most basic use of jqPlot, in which a series of data serves to plot a line, with no need for any additional options. You saw that in order to create the most basic type of chart, a line chart, you do not need to include plug-ins.

In this chapter, you will begin to examine in more detail the possibilities that the jqPlot library affords by exploring the various plug-ins and their functionality. First, because the line chart is represented on the Cartesian axes, you will be introduced to the use of pairs of values (x, y) as input data. You will then move on to the study the axes and how to create them, using the appropriate plug-ins. You will also analyze in detail how to implement the various elements connected to the axes as ticks, axis labels, and grid. A discussion of logarithmic scale (log scale) follows.

Next, you will learn how to realize multiseries line charts through the treatment of multiple series of data at the same time. You will discover how, by setting the lines and markers, you can modify patterns, shapes, and even colors. In addition, you will view how to create an animation by adjusting the speed at which the browser draws the chart.

Moreover, you will investigate the way in which the jqPlot library lets you manipulate different formats of date and time values. You will also see how it is possible to customize some elements, using the HTML format, along with the highlighting of data points. In the final part of the chapter, you will deal with more complex cases, such as generating a trend line and working with band charts.

## Using (x, y) Pairs as Input Data

So far, for simplicity's sake, the input data have been passed in as an array of y values (see Listing 4-1). If jqPlot finds y values only, x values are assigned as 1, 2, 3, and so on, following their order in the array.

*Listing 4-1.* Ch4_01.html

```
$(document).ready(function(){
    var plot1 = $.jqplot ('myChart', [[100,110,140,130,80,75,120,130,100]]);
});
```

In Figure 4-1, you can see along the x axis a sequence of integer numbers, which are the indexes of the array passed as data.

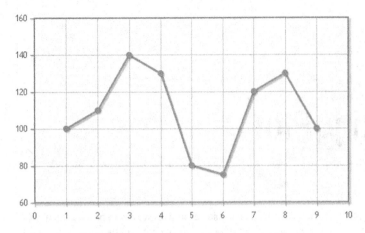

**Figure 4-1.** *The x axis reports the indexes of the values inserted*

When you are working with a linear plot, it is better to use arrays with pairs of values (x, y), as this avoids many complications, such as the need to enter the data in a particular order, which is not always possible or correct. In fact, using pairs of values, the data should not be listed in order of increasing x value; jqPlot will do that for you. Furthermore, the values of x need not be equidistant, but can follow any distribution. In Listing 4-2, pairs of values (x, y) have been inserted in which the x values are neither sorted nor evenly distributed.

**Listing 4-2.** Ch4_02.html

```
$(document).ready(function(){
    var data = [[[10,100], [80,130], [65,75], [40,130],
                [60,80], [30,140], [70,120], [20,110], [95,100]]];
    $.jqplot ('myChart', data);
});
```

In Figure 4-2, you can see how jqPlot sorts all the points in the chart, regardless of the order in which they were entered and whether they have been uniformly distributed along the x axis.

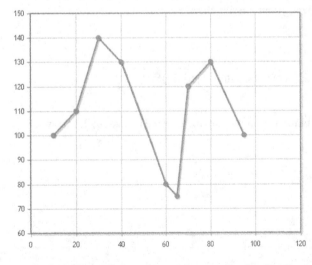

**Figure 4-2.** *A simple line chart with nonuniformly distributed points on the x axis*

# First Steps in the Development of a Line Chart: The Axes

Before looking at the more complex aspects of the line chart in detail, let us first examine the basis on which this kind of chart is represented: the axes. Proper management of the axes is crucial if you want to develop a chart that effects a perfect visualization of data. To this end, you need a good understanding of the modes of action that the jqPlot library offers through the use of specific properties in the `options` object.

## Add a Title and Axis Labels

When developing a chart, the first step is to add a title and to manage the axis labels, using the *CanvasAxisLabelRenderer* plug-in.

But, in order to function properly, this plug-in requires another plug-in, one that provides the writing functionality: *CanvasTextRenderer*. With this plug-in, you can render label text directly on canvas elements. This allows you to treat the text like any other graphic element, giving you the ability to rotate the text as you wish. By default the axis label on the y axis is now rotated by 90 degrees, as shown in Figure 4-3.

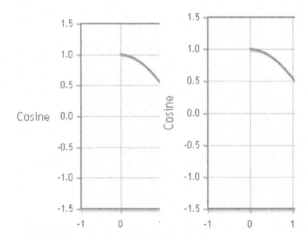

***Figure 4-3.*** *Without including the CanvasAxisLabelRenderer plug-in, the y axis label is horizontal. When the plug-in is included, the y axis label is rotated vertically*

To integrate this new functionality, you need to add the two plug-ins to the basic set of plug-ins:

```
<script type="text/javascript" src="../src/plugins/jqplot.canvasTextRenderer.min.js">
</script>
<script type="text/javascript"
    src="../src/plugins/jqplot.canvasAxisLabelRenderer.min.js"></script>
```

Or, if you prefer to use a content delivery network (CDN) service, you can do so as follows:

```
<script type="text/javascript" src="http://cdn.jsdelivr.net/jqplot/1.0.8/plugins
    /jqplot.canvasTextRenderer.min.js"></script>
<script type="text/javascript" src="http://cdn.jsdelivr.net/jqplot/1.0.8/plugins↵
    /jqplot.canvasAxisLabelRenderer.min.js"></script>
```

Having created the `options` variable, you must then specify some properties inside, as shown in Listing 4-3. You have already seen how to add a title by assigning a string to the `title` object. Then, have to make an explicit call to the `canvasAxisLabelRenderer` object in order to activate its functionality, and by doing so inside the `axesDefaults` object, it will be valid for all axes. To assign the text in both the x axis and y axis labels, you have to set the `label` properties in the `xaxis` and `yaxis` child objects of the `axes` object. Its tree structure will allow you to carry out different changes at the level of each individual axis.

*Listing 4-3.* ch9_03a.html

```
$(document).ready(function(){
    var data = [[100, 110, 140, 130, 80, 75, 120, 130, 100]] ;
    var options = {
        title: 'My Line Chart',
        axesDefaults: {
            labelRenderer: $.jqplot.CanvasAxisLabelRenderer
        },
        axes: {
            xaxis: {
                label: "X Axis"
            },
            yaxis: {
                label: "Y Axis"
            }
        }
    };
    $.jqplot ('myChart', data, options);
});
```

Figure 4-4 illustrates the chart the listing code produces.

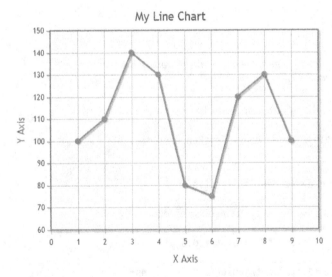

*Figure 4-4.* A line chart with the y axis label vertically oriented

## Axis Properties

As with axis labels, there are several properties that can be specified within the axes object. For example, looking at the chart (see Figure 9.4), you can see that the line starts from the x value 1, whereas the x axis starts from the value 0, thus leaving an empty space. Another space is seen at the end of the x range (between 9 and 10).If you want to act on these distances (between the limits of the axes and the end points of your data set), you have to use the pad properties. You apply the padding to extend the range above and below the data bounds. The data range is multiplied by this factor to determine minimum and maximum axis bounds. A value of 0 will be interpreted to mean no padding, and pad will be set to 1. Thus, by adding the pad properties to the xaxis object and setting pad to 1 (see Listing 4-4), you get the chart in Figure 4-5.

***Listing 4-4.*** Ch4_03b.html

```
xaxis: {
    label: "X Axis",
    pad: 1
},
```

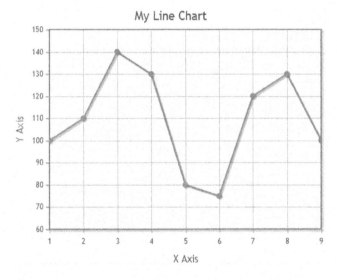

***Figure 4-5.*** *The same line chart as in Figure 4-4, with pad set to 1 on the x axis*

Now, the x axis starts from value 1 and ends with 9, as does the line representing the data series. To better understand the concept of padding, you will now set the pad property to 2 (see Listing 4-5). This means that you want to extend the current range (which is 10) two times. As a result, you will have a chart with an x axis that goes from –4 to 14, as demonstrated in Figure 4-6. This is because jqPlot tends to keep the data in a symmetrical manner, showing it in the middle.

***Listing 4-5.*** Ch4_03c.html

```
xaxis: {
label: "X Axis",
pad: 2
},
```

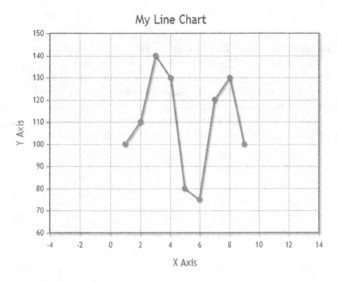

**Figure 4-6.** *The same line chart, with pad set to 2 on the x axis*

Another way to control the range in which you can display your data is by using the min and max properties (see Listing 4-6).

**Listing 4-6.** Ch4_03d.html

```
xaxis: {
    label: "X Axis",
    min: 1,
    max: 9
},
```

Figure 4-7 shows the x axis with the new range.

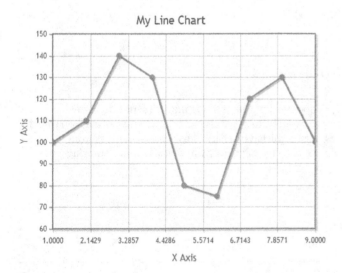

**Figure 4-7.** *The same line chart, with defined max and min on the x axis*

Other useful properties are those that control subdivisions (split axes) and their underlying numeric term: the ticks properties. As their use is not limited to simple options under the axes object—they are themselves an object and require a renderer plug-in in order to work—their treatment deserves a separate section.

## Axes Ticks

A **tick** is a component that shows the value of a tick or grid line in the plot. A tick's behavior in the plot can be specified inside axes objects in options, and, being an object itself, a tick has several properties that can be set inside the tickOption property. For example, you may need to set a specific number of grid lines for each axis. This can be done in different ways. The most simple entails directly specifying the numberTicks property (see Listing 4-7). If you set its value to 5, you will get five ticks on the x axis: 0, 3, 6, 9, and 12 (see Figure 4-8).

***Listing 4-7.*** Ch4_03e.html

```
xaxis: {
    label: "X Axis",
    numberTicks: 5
},
```

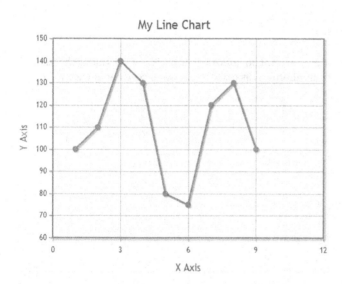

***Figure 4-8.*** *A line chart with a prefixed number of ticks on the x axis*

This can be applied to the y axis, too. In that case, you need to set the same properties in the yaxis object. From what you can see, the intervals at which the x axis is divided are uniform, and so the ticks are equidistant. Another way to do this is to define the ticks you want displayed on the chart directly, as shown in Listing 4-8.

***Listing 4-8.*** Ch4_03f.html

```
xaxis: {
    label: "X Axis",
    ticks: [0,3,6,9,12]
},
```

This produces the same chart (see Figure 4-9).

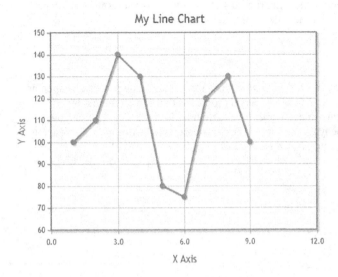

***Figure 4-9.*** *A line chart with directly defined ticks on the x axis*

But, it is generally preferable to use this approach when you want an uneven distribution of ticks along the axis, as in Listing 4-9. The line of the grid will also follow this nonuniformity, as it will be drawn in correspondence with each tick (see Figure 4-10).

***Listing 4-9.*** Ch4_03g.html

```
xaxis: {
    label: "X Axis",
    ticks: [1,2,3,7,9]
},
```

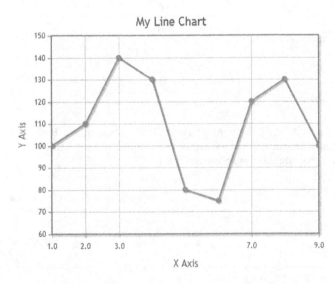

***Figure 4-10.*** *A line chart with nonuniform, prefixed ticks on the x axis*

Ticks are so important in a chart that they have a plug-in that is dedicated specifically to them: *CanvasAxisTickRenderer*.

If you want to create a chart without grid lines while keeping the values on ticks, you can set the showGridLine property to 'false'. Before that, however, you need to include the plug-in in the web page:

```
<link rel="stylesheet" type="text/css" href="../src/jquery.jqplot.min.css" />
<script type="text/javascript"
    src="../src/plugins/jqplot.canvasTextRenderer.min.js"></script>
<script type="text/javascript"
    src="../src/plugins/jqplot.canvasAxisLabelRenderer.min.js"></script>
<script type="text/javascript"
    src="../src/plugins/jqplot.canvasAxisTickRenderer.min.js"></script>
```

Or, if you prefer to use a CDN service, you can do so as follows:

```
<script type="text/javascript" src="http://cdn.jsdelivr.net/jqplot/1.0.8/plugins↵
    /jqplot.canvasTextRenderer.min.js"></script>
<script type="text/javascript" src="http://cdn.jsdelivr.net/jqplot/1.0.8/plugins↵
    /jqplot.canvasAxisLabelRenderer.min.js"></script>
<script type="text/javascript" src="http://cdn.jsdelivr.net/jqplot/1.0.8/plugins↵
    /jqplot.canvasAxisTickRenderer.min.js"></script>
```

You must then make the settings inside the axesDefaults object, because you want to hide the grid lines for both axes. Remember to call the plug-in just included with the tickRenderer property (see Listing 4-10). Furthermore, you must not forget to delete the **ticks** property defined within the **xaxis** object.

***Listing 4-10.*** Ch4_04a.html

```
axesDefaults: {
    labelRenderer: $.jqplot.CanvasAxisLabelRenderer,
    tickRenderer: $.jqplot.AxisTickRenderer,
    tickOptions: {
        showGridline: false
    }
},
axes: {
    xaxis: {
        label: "X Axis"  //remove the comma here
    },
```

As in Figure 4-11, you get a chart without a grid.

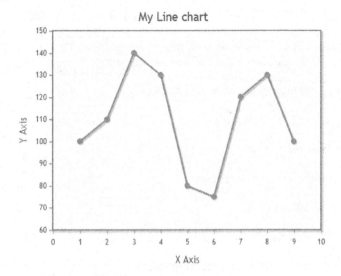

**Figure 4-11.** *A line chart without grid lines*

Sometimes, you need to hide the grid lines only for one axis, for example, the x axis (see Figure 4-12). In this case, you have to call the renderer inside only the xaxis object. In Listing 4-11, you can see the rows of code that must be removed from axesDefaults and then written within the xaxis object.

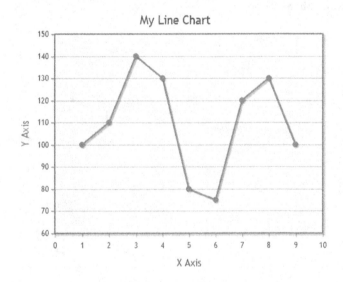

**Figure 4-12.** *A line chart with only horizontal grid lines*

*Listing 4-11.* ch9_04b.html

```
axesDefaults: {
    labelRenderer: $.jqplot.CanvasAxisLabelRenderer
    //delete all this lines
    //tickRenderer: $.jqplot.AxisTickRenderer,
    //tickOptions: {
    //showGridline: false
    //}
},
axes: {
    xaxis: {
        label: "X Axis",
        tickRenderer: $.jqplot.AxisTickRenderer,
        tickOptions: {
            showGridline: false
        }
    },
    ...
```

Another possible functionality you may want to add is one that allows you to handle the format of the numeric values as strings. The most common situation in which this could be useful is when you want to show percentage values on the y axis. To accomplish this, you need to add the char '%' after the numeric value, as shown in Listing 4-12.

*Listing 4-12.* Ch4_04c.html

```
yaxis: {
    label: "Y Axis",
    tickRenderer: $.jqplot.AxisTickRenderer,
    tickOptions: {
        formatString:'%d%'
    }
}
```

As Figure 4-13 illustrates, the chart now reports percentage values on the y axis.

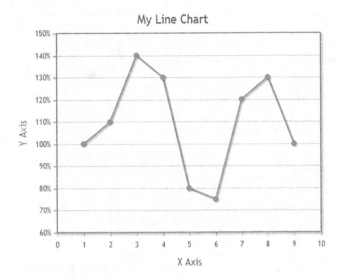

**Figure 4-13.** *A line chart reporting percentages on the y axis*

Later, you will see other cases in which this kind of string formatting proves to be a very powerful tool (see the section "Handling Date Values").

## Using the Log Scale

Depending on the trend of the data that you want to represent in a chart, it is sometimes necessary to use a log scale on one, or even both, of the axes. jqPlot supports the log scale, including the *LogAxisRenderer* plug-in in your web page.

```
<script type="text/javascript"
    src="../src/plugins/jqplot.logAxisRenderer.min.js"></script>
```

---

### LOG SCALE

---

The log scale uses intervals corresponding to orders of magnitude (generally ten) rather than a standard linear scale. This allows you to represent a large range of values (v) on an axis.

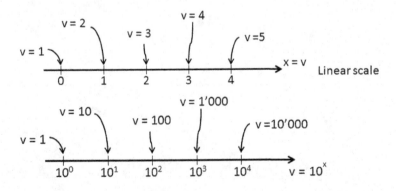

The logarithm is another way of writing exponentials, and you can use it to separate the exponent (x) and place it on an axis.

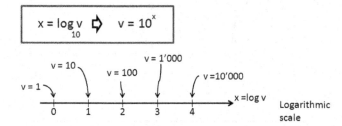

For example, an increase of one point on a log scale corresponds to an increase of 10 times that value. Similarly, an increase of two points corresponds to an increase of 100 times that value. And so on.

On the axis on which you want to represent the data in log scale, it is only necessary to add the renderer property with the plug-in reference. In this case, you need to create a data array that follows an exponential trend approximately. So, you use the array of [x, y] pairs in Listing 4-13.

**Listing 4-13.** Ch4_11.html

```
var data = [[0,1.2],[10,2.4],[20,5.6],[30,12],[40,23],
            [50,60],[60,120],[70,270],[80,800]];
```

Next, you put the y axis on log scale, as shown in Listing 4-14.

**Listing 4-14.** Ch4_11.html

```
$.jqplot ('myChart', [data],{
    axes:{
    xaxis:{},
    yaxis:{ renderer: $.jqplot.LogAxisRenderer }
    }
});
```

In Figure 4-14, you can see how the data assume, in a semilog scale (log scale on one axis), a shape approximating to a straight line.

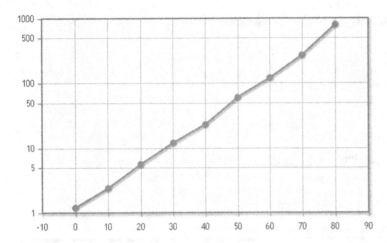

***Figure 4-14.*** *A line chart on a semilog scale on the y axis*

# The Multiseries Line Chart

Now that the axes on which you will represent your line chart have been well specified, the time has come to address the multiseries line chart. Typically, you will need to display more than a single series of data in the same chart. Indeed, very often the purpose of a chart is precisely the comparison of different data series.

The jqPlot library provides us with the tools needed to manage multiseries charts. By acting on the patterns, shapes, and colors of lines and markers, it is possible to introduce graphic effects that can aid in the representation of different data series.

## Multiple Series of Data

So far, you have been working with only a single set of data. Sometimes, however, you want to represent more than one data set at once. In Chapter 1, you saw that in jqPlot, multiple series are handled in the same way as a single set. Each series must first be defined separately by assigning it to a variable and then combined with the other series in an array. This array is then passed as the second argument to the jqPlot() function (see Listing 4-15).

***Listing 4-15.*** Ch4_05a.html

```
$(document).ready(function(){
    var data1 = [1, 2, 3, 2, 3, 4];
    var data2 = [3, 4, 5, 6, 5, 7];
    var data3 = [5, 6, 8, 8, 7, 9];
    var data4 = [7, 8, 9, 9, 10, 11];
    var options = {
        title:'Multiple Data Arrays'
    };
    $.jqplot ('myChart', [data1, data2, data3, data4], options);
});
```

Figure 4-15 shows the resulting multiseries chart from Listing 4-15.

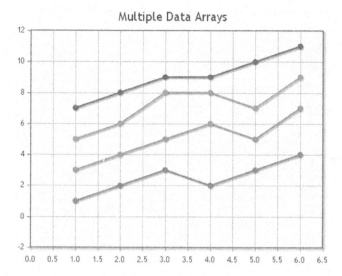

***Figure 4-15.*** *A multiseries line chart*

The system automatically gives each series a different color. This sequence of colors is defined within jqPlot as the default. Here are the colors that jqPlot will assign to the series, in order:

```
seriesColors: [   "#4bb2c5", "#c5b47f", "#EAA228", "#579575",
                  "#839557", "#958c12", "#953579", "#4b5de4",
                  "#d8b83f", "#ff5800", "#0085cc"]
```

These values stand for '#rrggbb', where *rr*, *gg,* and *bb* are the hexadecimal values for red, green, and blue. The browser combines these values to generate all the colors needed for the series.

When there are more than 11 series, jqPlot starts the sequence again from the beginning. If you do not want this or simply need to do things differently, you can define an array with a different sequence of colors in the seriesColors property, such as the series given in Listing 4-16. Figure 4-16 shows a variation of gray, but run the example, and see the difference for yourself (the colors ranging from blue to violet).

***Listing 4-16.*** Ch4_05b.html

```
var options = {
    seriesColors: ["#105567","#805567","#bb5567","#ff5567"],
    title:'Multiple Data Arrays'
};
```

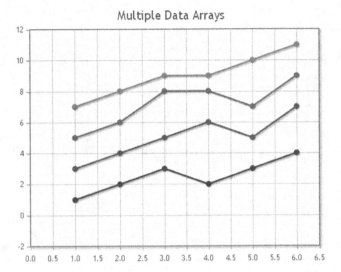

**Figure 4-16.** *A multiseries line chart with a customized color set*

---

■ **Note**   To check the color codes, I suggest visiting the web site HTML Color Codes (`http://html-color-codes.info`).

---

You can also attribute a specific color, using two functions: $rgba(r,g,b,a)$ and $rgb(r,g,b)$. You insert these functions directly in each value of the array to be allocated to the seriesColors property, as shown in Listing 4-17.

*Listing 4-17.* Ch4_05c.html

```
seriesColors: ["rgba(16,85,103,0.2)", "rgba(128,85,103,0.6)",
               "rgb(187,85,103)", "rgb(250,85,103)"],
```

Whereas you have been specifying colors through the combination of red, green, and blue light required to achieve a given color, with the rgba() function, a new variable, a, is introduced. This a (for "alpha") stands for the level of opacity/transparency of a color. As Figure 4-17 demonstrates, defining low alpha values lets you see what lies behind the colored object.

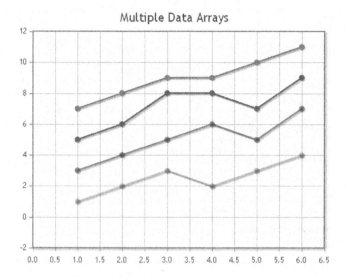

***Figure 4-17.*** *A multiseries line chart with different levels of transparency*

## Smooth-Line Chart

In addition to choosing whether to represent dot markers and the straight lines linking them, often you will decide that you want to get a smooth curve progress, as presented in Figure 4-18. This can be done simply by using the `smooth` property and setting it to `'true'` (see Listing 4-18).

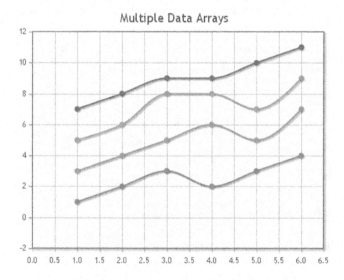

***Figure 4-18.*** *A multiseries line chart with smoothed lines*

*Listing 4-18.* Ch4_06.html

```
$(document).ready(function(){
    var data1 = [1, 2, 3, 2, 3, 4];
    var data2 = [3, 4, 5, 6, 5, 7];
    var data3 = [5, 6, 8, 8, 7, 9];
    var data4 = [7, 8, 9, 9, 10, 11];
    var options = {
        title:'Multiple Data Arrays',
        seriesDefaults: {
            rendererOptions: {
                smooth: true
            }
        }
    };
    $.jqplot ('myChart', [data1, data2, data3, data4], options);
});
```

## Line and Marker Style

Another key aspect that you need to take into account while designing your line chart is how lines and markers are displayed. You can represent a chart using a line, a sequence of markers, or both. By default, jqPlot shows each series with dot markers for every point corresponding to the [x, y] pairs and a line joining them in sequence.

All this can be controlled using two key properties belonging to the series objects: linePattern and lineWidth; while adding the markerOptions property, it is also possible to act on two other properties affecting marker components: style and size. Listing 4-19 is an example of these settings.

*Listing 4-19.* Ch4_07a.html

```
$(document).ready(function(){
    var data1 = [1, 2, 3, 2, 3, 4];
    var data2 = [3, 4, 5, 6, 5, 7];
    var data3 = [5, 6, 8, 9, 7, 9];
    var data4 = [7, 8, 9, 11, 10, 11];
    var options = {
        title: 'Multiple Data Arrays',
        series:[{
            linePattern: 'dashed',
            lineWidth:2,
            markerOptions: { style: 'diamond' }
        },
        {
            showLine:false,
            markerOptions: { size: 7, style: 'x' }
        },
        {
            markerOptions: { style: 'circle' }
        },
```

```
    {
        lineWidth:5,
        linePattern: 'dotted',
        markerOptions: { style: 'filledSquare', size: 10 }
    }]
}
$.jqplot ('myChart', [data1, data2, data3, data4], options);
});
```

Figure 4-19 illustrates the result of the settings in Listing 4-19.

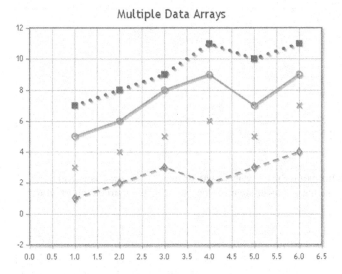

***Figure 4-19.*** *In a line chart it is possible to set different markers and patterns*

The lines on a chart can be drawn as solid, dashed, or dotted with the linePattern property. By default every line drawn is solid, so if you want a line to have a different style, it is necessary to specify it in options. You saw in Listing 4-19 that it is possible to set the linePattern property to 'dotted' or 'dashed' in order to obtain a dotted or dashed line, respectively. In Listing 4-20, you can see that it is also possible to obtain a customized line pattern, defining the format as an array ([dash length, gap length, and so on]). A line looks best when the array assigned to the linePattern property has an even number of elements, such that the line begins with a dash and ends with a gap. The linePattern property can also create a customized pattern, using a shorthand string notation of dash (-) and dot (.) characters. Listing 4-20 provides examples.

***Listing 4-20.*** Ch4_07b.html

```
var options = {
    title: 'Multiple Data Arrays',
    seriesDefaults: {
        showMarker: false
    },
    series: [{ linePattern: 'dashed'},
            { linePattern: 'dotted'},
            { linePattern: [4, 3, 1, 3, 1, 3]},
            { linePattern: '-.'}]
};
```

Figure 4-20 shows the examples of customized line patterns used in Listing 4-20.

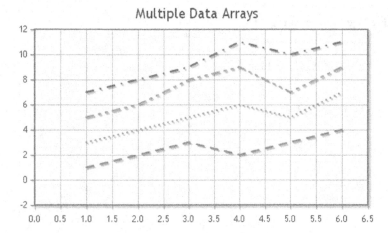

***Figure 4-20.*** *A multiseries line chart with different patterns*

## Animated Charts

When you load your web page in the browser, you will note that the chart is drawn almost instantaneously. You can slow down the drawing speed, adjusting it to your preference; a slower speed gives a floating effect to the chart while its elements are being drawn (see Listing 4-21).

***Listing 4-21.*** Ch4_23.html

```
var options = {
    title: 'Multiple Data Arrays',
    seriesDefaults: {
        showMarker: false,
        rendererOptions: {
            smooth: true,
            animation: { show: true  }
        }
    }
};
```

Figure 4-21 shows the sequence in which the chart is drawn, giving it an animated look.

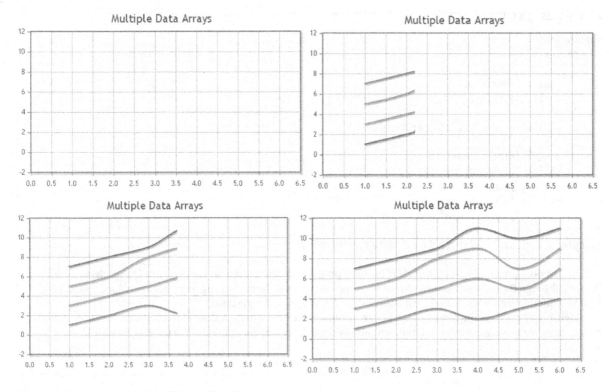

**Figure 4-21.** *An animated multiseries line chart*

## More Than One y Axis

jqPlot supports multiple y axes in relation to the same x axis. This can be useful when, in a single chart, you want to display different series distributed on different y scales, but with the same x values. In such cases, it is wise to set the y axes with the color of the corresponding series so that you can determine the correct y value of any given point. As input data, let us create three data arrays containing the same x values but with y values distributed on different ranges, as shown in Listing 4-22. Using the same x values is not mandatory, but it is smart to do so.

*Listing 4-22.* Ch4_12.html

```
var data1 = [[10, 200], [20, 230], [30, 214], [40, 212], [50, 225], [60, 234]];
var data2 = [[10, 455], [20, 470], [30, 465], [40, 432], [50, 455], [60, 464]];
var data3 = [[10, 40], [20, 60], [30, 54], [40, 52], [50, 65], [60, 54]];
```

It is very important to specify the correct range of values for each y axis in order to be able to compare the different series of values easily (see Listing 4-23). In the series object, you need to specify explicitly three values, each of which assigns a series to a different y axis. If you want to keep the default setting for a particular series, that is, representation along the default y axis, you must still assign an empty object {} in the position corresponding to that series. In fact, in this example the first element of the series array is just an empty object {}.

***Listing 4-23.*** Ch4_12.html

```
var options = {
    series:[
        {},
        {yaxis: 'y2axis'},
        {yaxis: 'y3axis'}
    ],
    axesDefaults:{useSeriesColor: true},
    axes:{
        xaxis: {min: 0, max: 70},
        yaxis: {min: 190, max: 240},
        y2axis: {min: 430, max: 480},
        y3axis: {min: 35, max: 80}
    }
};
$.jqplot ('myChart', [data1, data2, data3], options);
```

In addition, you need to set the useSeriesColor property for the axesDefaults object to 'true'. In so doing, jqPlot will assign the color of the series to the corresponding y axis. Thus, by using three default colors, you will get light blue for the first series, orange for the second, and gray-brown for the third.

Figure 4-22 presents the three series, each represented in relation to the values of its y axis. The axes are shown here in different grayscale shades, but they actually assume the colors corresponding to the related series.

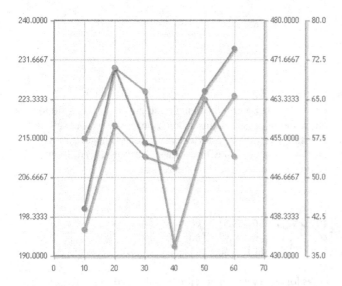

***Figure 4-22.*** *A multiseries line chart with multiple y axes*

# Data with JavaScript

As discussed previously, it is preferable to define data arrays separately and outside the jqPlot function. You have seen how to create an array containing numeric values that are either y values or [x, y] pairs. Yet, because jqPlot belongs to the world of JavaScript, there is another approach that often proves to be very useful: generating data series through JavaScript methods.

# Generating Data, Using Math Functions

The jqPlot library is based on JavaScript, and, as with all programming languages, it allows you to implement functions that generate sequences of values to use as input data. For example, Listing 4-24 takes three of the most used and best-known mathematical functions (sine, cosine, power) and creates an array of data through them.

*Listing 4-24.* Ch4_08a.html

```
$(document).ready(function(){
    var options = {
        title:'Math function Arrays'
    };

    varcosPoints = [];
    for (vari=0; i< 2 * Math.PI; i += 0.1){
        cosPoints.push([i, Math.cos(i)]);
    }

    varsinPoints = [];
    for (vari=0; i< 2 * Math.PI; i += 0.1){
        sinPoints.push([i, 2 * Math.sin(i-.8)]);
    }

    varpowPoints = [];
    for (vari=0; i< 2 * Math.PI; i += 0.1) {
        powPoints.push([i, 2.5 + Math.pow(i/4, 2)]);
    }

    $.jqplot ('myChart', [cosPoints, sinPoints, powPoints], options);
});
```

Figure 4-23 illustrates how the points generated by the three functions in the listing form, on a line chart, the characteristic trends of the three mathematical functions.

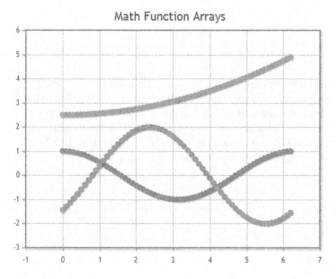

*Figure 4-23.* *A line chart reporting three different series of data generated from mathematical functions*

Because this is a function with a high density of points, and because the objective here is to highlight trends, it is best not to display the marker points (see Figure 4-24). It is also preferable to enable smoothing in options, as shown in Listing 4-25.

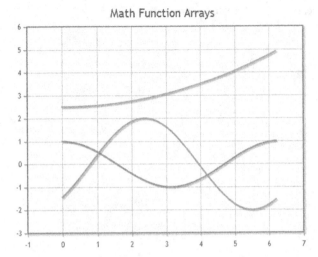

**Figure 4-24.** *The same line chart, but rendered more legibly*

**Listing 4-25.** Ch4_08b.html

```
var options = {
    title: 'Math function Arrays',
    seriesDefaults: {
      rendererOptions: {
          smooth: true
      },
      markerOptions: { show: false }
    }
};
```

## Generating Random Data

You have just seen how to generate input data by using mathematical functions. Similarly, it is sometimes necessary to generate random data. For instance, let us say you have just finished writing your jqPlot chart and would like to try inputting dummy data. To this end, the use randomly generated data is best. The function in Listing 4-26 generates random data, with every point generated according to the value of the previous one. At each step, the new value is determined by a random number that is added to or subtracted from the preceding number. This results in a continuous series of data, starting from a value passed as an argument to the function.

**Listing 4-26.** Ch4_09.html

```
function generateRandomData(npts, start, delta) {
    var data = [];
    if (delta == null) {
        delta = start;
        start = (Math.random() - 0.5) * 2 * delta;
    }
```

```
for (j=0; j<npts; j++) {
    data.push([j, start]);
    start += (Math.random() - 0.5) * 2 * delta;
}
return data;
}
```

You are using three arguments: npts is the number of points to generate, start is the starting value, and delta is the maximum value to add or subtract randomly at every step. The function returns an array that will be passed as input data to the chart. You can define it externally:

```
var data = generateRandomData(30, 100, 1);
$.jqplot('myChart', [data]);
```

Or, you can pass it directly:

```
$.jqplot ('myChart', [makeContinuousData(30, 100, 1)]);
```

As a result, you get a chart like the one in Figure 4-25 (it will be different every time).

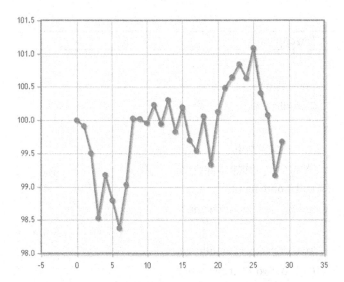

***Figure 4-25.*** *A line chart representing a random series of data*

# Handling Date Values

A kind of value that is used, especially in other charts (e.g., bar charts), is date type. These specialized values are not so easy to deal with, and jqPlot has a plug-in for them: *DateAxisRenderer*. This plug-in expands JavaScript's native date-handling capabilities, allowing you to represent date values in any unambiguous form, not just in milliseconds.

# The *DateAxisRenderer* Plug-in

A date can be represented in many ways, and its format varies, depending on country and use. A date consists of day, month, and year indicators. These can be ordered differently, and with one, two, or four digits; or, you may even want to use only one or two of the indicators (e.g., month, year). Furthermore, various characters act as separators. Let us take, for example, 04/07/2012: "4" stands for the fourth month (April), "7" is the seventh day of the month, and "2012" is the year. Such a date can be shown in numerous ways: `'07/04/2012'`, `'07/04/12'`, `'04/07/12'`, `'7-Apr-12'`, `'7-Apr'`, `'Apr-12'`, `'7 April'`, `'2012'`, and so on.

The standard format for date values is as follows:

`'YYYY-MM-DD HH:MM<PM or AM>'`

This string contains all the necessary information—a bit too much, perhaps. In fact, you will often require only a part of the date information: sometimes, you may need to report only day and month, or, if you refer to time, you may need to handle only hours and minutes, and so on.

Once the *DateAxisRenderer* plug-in is included, jqPlot accepts almost any recognizable value. After the value has been internally parsed, it will be rendered on the axis on which you made the call to the plug-in, represented in the format specified in `tickOptions.formatString`.

Table 4-1 shows the acceptable format codes.

***Table 4-1.*** *Date and Time Formats Accepted by jqPlot*

| Code | Result | Description |
|------|--------|-------------|
| **Years** | | |
| %Y | 2008 | Four-digit year |
| %y | 08 | Two-digit year |
| **Months** | | |
| %m | 09 | Two-digit month |
| %#m | 9 | One- or two-digit month |
| %B | September | Full month name |
| %b | Sep | Abbreviated month name |
| **Days** | | |
| %d | 05 | Two-digit day of month |
| %#d | 5 | One- or two-digit day of month |
| %e | 5 | One- or two-digit day of month |
| %A | Sunday | Full name of day of the week |
| %a | Sun | Abbreviated name of day of the week |
| %w | 0 | Number of day of the week (0 = Sunday, 6 = Saturday) |
| %o | th | Ordinal suffix string following day of the month |

*(continued)*

***Table 4-1.*** (*continued*)

| Code | Result | Description |
|------|--------|-------------|
| **Hours** | | |
| %H | 23 | Hours in 24-hour format (two digits) |
| %#H | 3 | Hours in 24-hour integer format (one or two digits) |
| %I | 11 | Hours in 12-hour format (two digits) |
| %#I | 3 | Hours in 12-hour integer format (one or two digits) |
| %p | PM | AM or PM |
| **Minutes** | | |
| %M | 09 | Minutes (two digits) |
| %#M | 9 | Minutes (one or two digits) |
| **Seconds** | | |
| %S | 02 | Seconds (two digits) |
| %#S | 2 | Seconds (one or two digits) |
| %s | 1206567625723 | Unix timestamp (seconds past 1970-01-01 00:00:00) |
| **Milliseconds** | | |
| %N | 008 | Milliseconds (three digits) |
| %#N | 8 | Milliseconds (one to three digits) |
| **Time zone** | | |
| %O | 360 | Difference in minutes between local time and Greenwich mean time (GMT) |
| %Z | Mountain Standard Time (MST) | Name of time zone, as reported by browser |
| %G | –06:00 | Hours and minutes between GMT |
| **Shortcuts** | | |
| %F | 2008-03-26 | %Y-%m-%d |
| %T | 05:06:30 | %H:%M:%S |
| %X | 05:06:30 | %H:%M:%S |
| %x | 03/26/08 | %m/%d/%y |
| %D | 03/26/08 | %m/%d/%y |
| %#c | Wed Mar 26 15:31:00 2008 | %a %b %e %H:%M:%S %Y |
| %v | 3-Sep-2008 | %e-%b-%Y |
| %R | 15:31 | %H:%M |
| %r | 3:31:00 PM | %I:%M:%S %p |
| **Characters** | | |
| %n | \n | New line |
| %t | \t | Tab |
| %% | % | Percent symbol |

To get a clearer idea of how jqPlot handles date values, let us look at a series of examples illustrating various formats. Regardless of the format, however, you must always include the *DateAxisRenderer* plug-in in the <head> section of the web page.

```
<script type="text/javascript"
    src="../src/plugins/jqplot.dateAxisRenderer.min.js"></script>
```

## Handling Date Values in Different Formats

This first example deals with the exchange rate over a period of time, with day-by-day point values. To this end, the input data array should have a sequence of [x, y] values inside it, where x is a date value. The sequence of x values does not comply with the temporal order; jqPlot will sort those points along the x- axis. In Listing 4-27, you use a series of x input values, with different formats for the first five.

*Listing 4-27.* Ch4_13a.html

```
var line1 = [['14-Oct-2012', 1300.41], ['2012-10-15', 1310.50],
             ['2012/10/16', 1322.88], ['17 Oct 2012', 1312.41],
             ['10/18/2012', 1308.16], ['19-Oct-2012', 1310.71],
             ['20-Oct-2012', 1305.01],['21-Oct-2012', 1300.85],
             ['22-Oct-2012', 1290.67]];
```

Next, you have to call the renderer inside the xaxis object in options in order to activate it. You want to represent the days of the month in which you follow the trend of the exchange values, so you will set the output format without including the year, which remains unchanged. In addition, at the beginning, you want to show the day of the month in numerical form and then the month written with the first three characters, separated by a space. Simply put, in Listing 4-28 the format will be '%d %b', where %d stands for day, in digits, and %b, for the first three characters of month. The y values are dollars, so you need to add the dollar sign ($) as a prefix for the ticks of the y axis. To accomplish this, you must use the formatString property for the y ticks as well.

*Listing 4-28.* Ch4_13a.html

```
var options = {
    title: 'Handling Date Values',
    axes:{
        xaxis:{
            renderer: $.jqplot.DateAxisRenderer,
            tickOptions:{
                formatString:'%d %b'
            }
        },
        yaxis:{
            tickOptions:{
                formatString:'$%d'
            }
        }
    }
};
$.jqplot('myChart', [line1], options);
```

Figure 4-26 shows the dollar value, with the prefix $, on the y axis and the day and month on the x axis. This is only one of the several formats you can set to represent values on ticks.

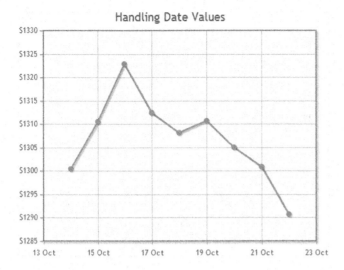

**Figure 4-26.** *A line chart with date values on the x axis*

## Handling Time Values

Let us say you want to draw a chart representing visits to a museum. It is possible to make time explicit in the input data (hours, minutes, seconds). This allows you to handle these time values in the same manner as in previous example (see Listing 4-27), for instance, by creating a chart containing data collected on a given day. Here, too, the date can be set with any of the previously discussed formats. You can express time in various ways: in a 12-hour format, with AM or PM suffixes, or directly, in a 24-hour format, either including or ignoring seconds and minutes. Listing 4-29 illustrates an array with a sequence of time values at 2-hour intervals.

**Listing 4-29.** Ch4_13b.html

```
var line1 = [['2012-10-14 08:00AM', 30],['2012-10-14 10:00AM', 60],
             ['2012-10-14 00:00PM', 120], ['2012-10-14 02:00PM', 60],
             ['2012-10-14 04:00PM', 100], ['2012-10-14 06:00PM', 40]];
```

With regard to the output format, you must remember to manage the time format as well; because you are interested only in the hours of the day, you set '%R' as 'formatString' (see Listing 4-30).

**Listing 4-30.** Ch4_13b.html

```
var options = {
    title: 'Museum Visitors',
    axes:{
        xaxis:{
            label: 'time',
            renderer:$.jqplot.DateAxisRenderer,
            tickOptions:{
                formatString: '%R'
            }
        },
```

```
    yaxis:{
        label: 'visitors'
    }
  }
};
$.jqplot('myChart', [line1], options);
```

The browser will show the chart presented in Figure 4-27.

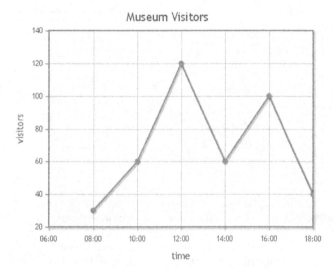

**Figure 4-27.** *A bar chart with time values on the x axis*

# Highlighting

An eye-catching effect that you can add to your chart is highlighting (i.e., having your plot react to mouseover. For example, the *Highlighter* plug-in will highlight data points near the mouse, with a nice dynamic effect. This can be enhanced by displaying a tool tip with the data point value.

## Cursor Highlighter

The following example will serve to familiarize you with highlighting. This functionality is very important and consists in activation of an event when you mouse over particular elements in the chart. Generally, these are elements that represent the data and that, in a line chart, for example, are represented by a point (or, more precisely, by the marker; you will see that this applies to other types of chart as well: a bar in a bar chart, a slice in a pie chart, and so on).

By default the triggered event is just one highlight of the data, represented by a tool tip showing its (x, y) values.

To add these functionalities to your charts, you have to include a set of plug-ins:

```
<script type="text/javascript" src="../src/plugins/jqplot.highlighter.min.js">
</script>
<script type="text/javascript" src="../src/plugins/jqplot.cursor.min.js">
</script>
```

In Listing 4-31, as input data, you use a series of [x, y] pairs with date values on the x axis and numeric values on the y axis.

*Listing 4-31.* Ch4_14a.html

```
var line1 = [['14-Oct-12', 1300.41], ['15-Oct-12', 1310.50],['16-Oct-12', 1322.88],
             ['17-Oct-12', 1312.41],['18-Oct-12', 1308.16],['19-Oct-12', 1310.71],
             ['20-Oct-12', 1305.01],['21-Oct-12', 1300.85],['22-Oct-12', 1290.67]];
```

As you have already seen, in order to handle date values, you need to include the *DateAxisRenderer* plug-in.

```
<script type="text/javascript"
    src="../src/plugins/jqplot.dateAxisRenderer.min.js"></script>
```

In Listing 4-32, you see the options object, containing two new objects: highlighter and cursor.

*Listing 4-32.* Ch4_14a.html

```
var options = {
    title: 'Data Point Highlighting',
    axes:{
        xaxis:{
            renderer: $.jqplot.DateAxisRenderer,
            tickOptions:{
                formatString: '%b %#d'
            }
        },
        yaxis:{
            tickOptions:{
                formatString: '$%d'
            }
        }
    },
    highlighter:{
        show: true,
        sizeAdjust: 7.5
    },
    cursor:{
        show: false
    }
};
```

In Figure 4-28 a tool tip appears when the cursor moves over a data point on the chart. By default this tool tip reports both x and y values, separated by a comma, using the axis formatters, but this can be customized with a different format string.

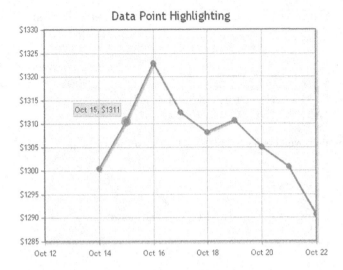

**Figure 4-28.** *Data point highlighting on a line chart*

In Listing 4-32, you will note that the cursor has been disabled, by setting its show property to 'false' (it is enabled by default). Enabling it, as in Listing 4-33, you will see the mouse cursor changing when it enters the graph area and displaying an optional tool tip in the bottom-right corner, reporting the mouse position. The tool tip can be in a fixed location, or it can follow the mouse. The pointer style, set to 'crosshair' by default, can also be customized.

**Listing 4-33.** Ch4_14b.html

```
...
highlighter: {
    show: true,
    sizeAdjust: 7.5
},
cursor: {
    show: true,
    tooltipLocation:'ne'
}
});
```

Figures 4-29 shows a tool tip reporting the cursor coordinates. Note that the cursor is represented by a black cross in the middle of the chart.

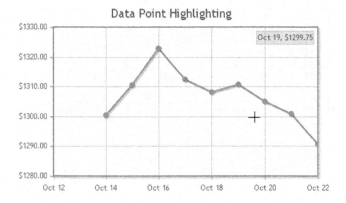

**Figure 4-29.** *A line chart showing the cursor coordinates*

# Highlighting with HTML Format

You can change the content of a tool tip, using HTML tags as format. This makes the possibilities of customization almost unlimited. In fact, you can think of the tool tip as a little web page in which to add any type of element, such as an image or an anchor link (for more details, see Chapter 5). For example, you can use the settings shown in Listing 4-34 with an HTML format string assigned to the formatString property.

*Listing 4-34.* Ch4_14c.html

```
highlighter: {
    show: true,
    sizeAdjust: 7.5,
    showMarker: false,
    tooltipAxes: 'xy',
    yvalues: 4,
    formatString:'<table class="jqplot-highlighter"> \
                <tr><td>date:</td><td>%s</td></tr> \
                <tr><td>value:</td><td>%s</td></tr></table>'
},
```

As a result, the tool tip with the content will behave like a small HTML page, as shown in Figure 4-30.

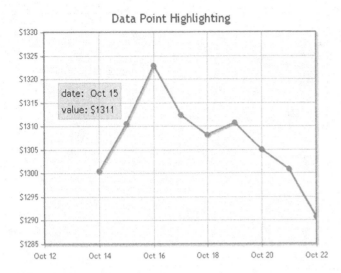

**Figure 4-30.** *A line chart with an HTML tool tip*

# Interacting with the Chart: Limit Lines and Zooming

Once you have a line chart with its graphics and elements well set, the next step is to introduce interactive elements. For instance, it may be necessary for the user to employ threshold values in order to see which data are external to these values. The user mayalso need to vary this threshold to determine which data lie inside and which lie outside it. Often, a lot of data are represented. In this case, the user may need to analyze only a detail.

The jqPlot library provides a solution for both cases with limit lines and zooming. Let us look at some examples addressing these issues in detail.

## Drawing a Limit Line on the Chart

Another feature that can be very useful is the *CanvasOverlay* plug-in. It enables you to draw horizontal and vertical lines on your charts, with the purpose of indicating a limit, a threshold, or a deadline or of delimiting a particular range. This can be done by including the *CanvasOverlay* plug-in in the web page:

```
<script type="text/javascript"
    src="../src/plugins/jqplot.canvasOverlay.min.js"></script>
```

By including this plug-in, you have a new object in options: canvasOverlay. Within this object, you will define an array of objects with their properties. Each of these objects will be represented by a line drawn on the canvas on which jqPlot creates your chart. Five types of objects are already defined in canvasOverlay:

- horizontalLine
- verticalLine
- dashedHorizontalLine
- dashedVerticalLine
- Line (generic)

To see how to insert these limit lines in your charts, let us start from a simple line chart in which you want to show two horizontal limit lines with different colors: a red line marking the upper limit, and a dashed blue line, the lower limit.

In Listing 4-35, you define the two objects: a horizontalLine for the lower limit and a dashedHorizontalLine for the upper limit. Once you have defined the two lines, you must specify their attributes. The meaning of their attributes, such as y values, lineWidth, and color, is evident. The lineCap property specifies the type of ending placed on the line; it can be round, butt, or square.

*Listing 4-35.* Ch4_15.html

```
$(document).ready(function(){
    var data = [100, 110, 140, 130, 80, 75, 120, 130, 100];
    var options = {
        canvasOverlay: {
            show: true,
            objects: [
            {horizontalLine: {
                y: 70,
                lineWidth: 3,
                color: 'rgb(255, 0, 0)',
                shadow: true,
                lineCap: 'butt'
            }},
            {dashedHorizontalLine: {
                y: 145,
                lineWidth: 4,
                color: 'rgb(0, 0, 255)',
                shadow: false,
                dashPattern: [8, 16],
                lineCap: 'round'
            }}
            ]
        }
    };
    $.jqplot('myChart', [data], options);
});
```

Figure 4-31 displays the two limit lines delimiting the line chart between the values 70 and 145.

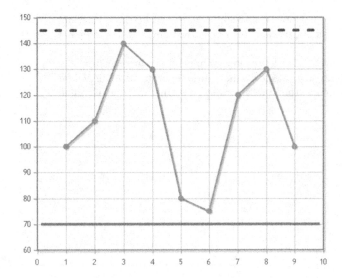

**Figure 4-31.** *A line chart with lower and upper limits*

You have just seen how to delimit line chart between two limit lines, In more complex cases (but not in this case, which is less common), it may be convenient to vary the value of these limits, and thus be able to move them at will, for instance, by clicking a series of buttons. In the next example, you will continue to implement the current chart by adding buttons that serve to slide the limit lines on the surface of the chart.

## Adding Buttons to Your Charts

Using the previous example (see Listing 4-35), you will now see how to add buttons to a chart. Buttons can be placed in any part of a web page, as they are outside the canvas. Here, their function is to allow you to shift the limit lines as you wish, just by clicking them.

For this purpose, you will need four buttons: two to move the limit lines upward and two to move them downward, labeled as follows:

- Low Limit Up

- Low Limit Down

- High Limit Up

- High Limit Down

You can add the four buttons defined in Listing 4-36 anywhere in the <body> section of the web page.

**Listing 4-36.** Ch4_16.html

```html
<div>
    <button onclick="lineup(myPlot, 'lowlimit')">Low Limit Up</button>
    <button onclick="linedown(myPlot, 'lowlimit')">Low Limit Down</button>
</div>
<div>
    <button onclick="lineup(myPlot, 'hilimit')">High Limit Up</button>
    <button onclick="linedown(myPlot, 'hilimit')">High Limit Down</button>
</div>
```

These rows will generate the four buttons shown in Figure 4-32.

*Figure 4-32.* *The buttons added to the chart in order to move the limit lines*

In Chapter 2, you were introduced to JQuery User Interface library (jQuery UI) widgets that can be used as controls. Given the potential of this type of control, it is advisable to use the button widget provided by the library (for further information on how to use these widgets, see Chapter 10).If you want to use jQuery UI widgets to replace the four buttons, you need to include the following plug-ins:

```
<link rel="stylesheet" href="http://code.jquery.com/ui/1.10.3/themes/smoothness⏎
    /jquery-ui.css" />
<script src="http://code.jquery.com/ui/1.10.3/jquery-ui.min.js"></script>
```

If, however, you would rather refer to the libraries installed locally (see Appendix A), you have to include the following code:

```
<link rel="stylesheet" href="../src/css/smoothness/jquery-ui-1.10.3.custom.min.css" />
<script src="../src/js/jquery-ui-1.10.3.custom.min.js"></script>
```

And, in the <body> section of the HTML page, you add code in Listing 4-37.

*Listing 4-37.* Ch4_16.html

```
<script>
$(function() {
    $('button')
        .button()
        .click(function( event ) {
            event.preventDefault();
        });
});
</script>
```

The buttons are now displayed in jQuery UI style (or, more precisely, with the "smoothness" theme, one of many), as you can see in Figure 4-33.

*Figure 4-33.* *The same four buttons, but displayed using the jQuery UI*

At this point, these buttons are totally inactive. You need to develop two JavaScript functions; these will be executed when the buttons are pressed. The first function, lineup(),will increase the y value of the line passed as argument (high limit or low limit) and then force a new drawing of the chart. The second function, linedown(), will decrease the y value. These two functions must be external to the jQuery function $(document).ready() (see Listing 4-38).

*Listing 4-38.* Ch4_16.html

```
function lineup(plot, name) {
    var co = plot.plugins.canvasOverlay;
    var line = co.get(name);
    line.options.y += 5;
    co.draw(plot);
}

functionlinedown(plot, name) {
    var co = plot.plugins.canvasOverlay;
    var line = co.get(name);
    line.options.y -= 5;
    co.draw(plot);
}
```

The next step consists in assigning the object returned by the $.jqplot()function to a variable:

```
myPlot = $.jqplot('myChart', [data], options);
```

---

■ **Note**   Take care not to write varmyPlot, or you will not see any changes in the chart when you press the buttons.

---

The last step is to name the two lines inside the canvasOverlay object, as demonstrated in Listing 4-39.

*Listing 4-39.* Ch4_16.html

```
objects: [
    {horizontalLine: {
        name: 'lowlimit',
        y: 70,
        lineWidth: 3,
        color: 'rgb(255, 0, 0)',
        shadow: true,
        lineCap: 'butt'
    }},
    {dashedHorizontalLine: {
        name: 'hilimit',
        y: 145,
        lineWidth: 4,
        color: 'rgb(0, 0, 255)',
        shadow: false,
        dashPattern: [8, 16],
        lineCap: 'round'
    }}
]
```

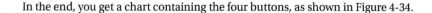

In the end, you get a chart containing the four buttons, as shown in Figure 4-34.

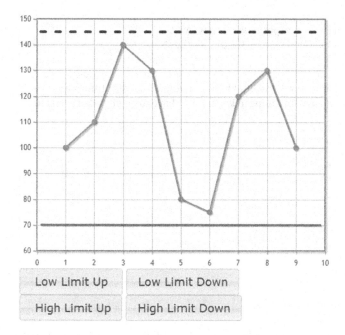

**Figure 4-34.** *A line chart with a set of buttons that vary the lower and upper thresholds*

Sometimes, you need to add vertical lines to your chart, especially when you have to mark a deadline. In this case we shall work as before, but with some differences. For example, let us say you want to place a single vertical line representing a deadline in your line chart. In this case, you use the code in Listing 4-40.

**Listing 4-40.** Ch4_17.html

```
$(document).ready(function(){
    var data = [100, 110, 140, 130, 80, 75, 120, 130, 100];
    var options = {
        canvasOverlay: {
            show: true,
            objects: [
            {verticalLine: {
                name: 'lowlimit',
                x: 5,
                lineWidth: 3,
                color: 'rgb(50, 200, 50)',
                shadow: true,
                lineCap: 'butt',
                yOffset: 0
            }}
            ]
        }
    };
    myPlot = $.jqplot('myChart', [data], options);
});
```

This time, you will need only two buttons.

```
<div>
    <button onclick="lineright(myPlot, 'lowlimit')">Postpone Deadline</button>
    <button onclick="lineleft(myPlot, 'lowlimit')">Anticipate Deadline</button>
</div>
```

Now, you must develop two JavaScript functions that will shift the limit lines horizontally as the buttons are pressed. Like the JavaScript functions seen previously, the two functions in Listing 4-41 have to be placed external to the jQuery function $(document).ready().

***Listing 4-41.*** Ch4_17.html

```
functionlineright(plot, name) {
    var co = plot.plugins.canvasOverlay;
    var line = co.get(name);
    line.options.x += 1;
    co.draw(plot);
}

functionlineleft(plot, name) {
    var co = plot.plugins.canvasOverlay;
    var line = co.get(name);
    line.options.x -= 1;
    co.draw(plot);
}
```

The result is the chart in Figure 4-35, with a green vertical line in the middle. By clicking the two buttons, the line will move to the left if you want to anticipate, or to the right if you want to postpone, the deadline.

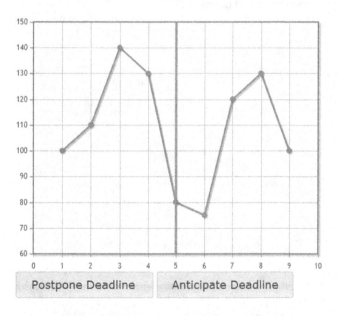

***Figure 4-35.*** *A line chart with a green horizontal limit line*

# Zooming

Often, when you are dealing with a large amount of data, you end up with a line made up of thousands of points on your chart. It is precisely in such a case that the zooming function can be indispensable. Starting from a macroscopic view, you can zoom in on part of the line to get a microscopic view of the data.

The *Cursor* plug-in also enables a plot-zooming function. By clicking and dragging the cursor on the plot, you can zoom in on and scroll small sections of your chart. If you double-click, you can reset all and go back to the macroscopic view. Thus, you need to include the *Cursor* plug-in in your web page, and because you have date values on the x axis, the *DateAxisRenderer* plug-in must be included as well:

```
<script type="text/javascript"
    src="../src/plugins/jqplot.dateAxisRenderer.min.js"></script>
<script type="text/javascript" src="../src/plugins/jqplot.cursor.min.js"></script>
```

Or, if you prefer to use a CDN service, you can do so as follows:

```
<script type="text/javascript" src="http://cdn.jsdelivr.net/jqplot/1.0.8/plugins↵
    /jqplot.dateAxisRenderer.min.js"></script>
<script type="text/javascript"
    src="http://cdn.jsdelivr.net/jqplot/1.0.8/plugins/jqplot.cursor.min.js"></script>
```

Listing 4-42 illustrates the availability of a large amount of incoming data.

***Listing 4-42.*** Ch4_18.html

```
var data = [["6/22/2012 10:00:00", 110.32], ["6/8/2012 10:00:00", 115.84],
            ["5/26/2012 10:00:00", 121.23], ["5/11/2012 10:00:00", 122.12],
            ["4/27/2012 10:00:00", 120.69], ["4/13/2012 10:00:00",123.24],
            ["3/30/2012 10:00:00", 116.78], ["3/16/2012 10:00:00", 115.16],
            ["3/2/2012 10:00:00", 113.57], ["2/17/2012 10:00:00", 120.45],
            ["2/2/2012 10:00:00", 121.28], ["1/20/2012 10:00:00", 124.7],
            ["1/5/2012 10:00:00", 130.07], ["12/22/2011 10:00:00", 129.36],
            ["12/8/2011 10:00:00", 130.76], ["11/24/2011 10:00:00", 133.96],
            ["11/10/2011 10:00:00", 140.02] ,["10/27/2011 10:00:00", 138.36],
            ["10/13/2011 10:00:00", 140.54], ["9/29/2011 10:00:00", 140.91],
            ["9/15/2011 10:00:00", 140.15], ["9/2/2011 10:00:00", 138.25],
            ["8/25/2011 10:00:00", 137.29], ["8/11/2011 10:00:00", 139.15],
            ["7/28/2011 10:00:00", 144.86], ["7/14/2011 10:00:00", 145.32],
            ["6/30/2011 10:00:00", 148.12], ["6/16/2011 10:00:00", 146.43],
            ["6/2/2011 10:00:00", 147], ["5/19/2011 10:00:00", 144.62],
            ["5/5/2011 10:00:00", 143.2], ["4/21/2011 10:00:00", 144.06],
            ["4/7/2011 10:00:00", 137.45], ["3/24/2011 10:00:00", 138.08],
            ["3/10/2011 10:00:00", 137.92], ["2/25/2011 10:00:00", 131.18],
            ["2/11/2011 10:00:00", 129.64], ["1/28/2011 10:00:00", 133.9],
            ["1/14/2011 10:00:00", 134.25], ["12/31/2010 10:00:00", 137],
            ["12/17/2010 10:00:00", 136.69], ["12/3/2010 10:00:00", 144.87],
            ["11/19/2010 10:00:00", 146.7], ["11/5/2010 10:00:00", 143.97],
            ["10/22/2010 10:00:00", 139.6], ["10/8/2010 10:00:00", 133.39],
            ["9/24/2010 10:00:00", 130.27], ["9/10/2010 10:00:00", 132.75],
            ["8/27/2010 10:00:00", 130.25]];
```

It is very simple to enable the zooming function. Simply set the zoom property to 'true' in options, as shown in Listing 4-43.

***Listing 4-43.*** Ch4_18.html

```
var options = {
    series: [{
        neighborThreshold: -1
    }],
    axes:{
        xaxis:{
            renderer: $.jqplot.DateAxisRenderer,
            min:'August 1, 2010 16:00:00',
            tickInterval: '6 months',
            tickOptions: {formatString: '%#m/%#d/%Y'}
        }
    },
    cursor:{
        show: true,
        zoom: true,
        showTooltip: false
    }
};
myPlot = $.jqplot('myChart', [data], options);
```

Or, if you prefer, you can disable the double-clicking that resets the zoom. The *Cursor* plug-in also extends the plot object (the value returned by the $.jqplot() function) by using the resetZoom() method externally. Moreover, this method can be called from the user code or another HTML element, such as a button, to reset the plot zoom.

You can define this function inside the jQuery ready() function:

```
$('.button-reset').click(function() { myPlot.resetZoom() });
```

Then, insert the following row anywhere you want to in order to place the button in the <body> section of the web page:

```
<button class="button-reset">Reset Zoom</button>
```

Figure 4-36 offers a sequence of pictures representing the line chart at different moments. The first picture is the line chart as displayed from the browser, without any zooming. The second picture shows an area of the chart selected by the user, with the intention of zooming. The final picture illustrates the result of this zooming. If the user clicks the Reset Zoom button, the browser will display the first picture again.

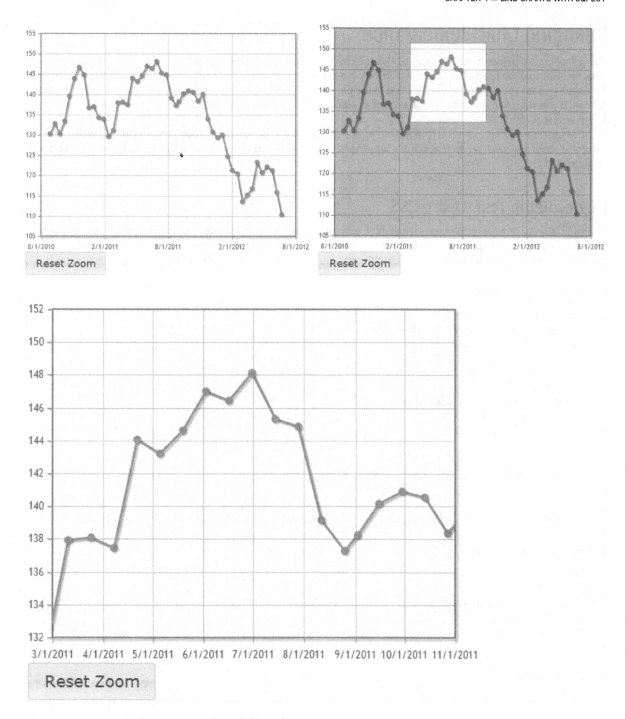

**Figure 4-36.** *A detail of the line chart extracted by zooming*

# Changing Chart Appearance

Thanks to its several plug-ins, jqPlot can render the chart components, including the text, directly on canvas. By now it must be clear that the highlight of the jqPlot library is the potential to change the look of any chart element by varying the default values of the jqPlot properties and of the plug-ins added. But, this is not the only method for effecting such change. If you want to modify the appearance of an element in an HTML page, you have recourse to the CSS style. This is true even for jqPlot elements.

It is possible to refer to several (but not all) jqPlot objects with CSS classes in order to change the style of these objects without having to set their attributes in options. The objects can be customized by CSS, using a CSS class such as .jqplot-*.

## Customizing Text, Using CSS

The jqPlot library provides CSS classes with which you can change some properties without referring to the options object. By way of an example, you will use some of these classes to change the text inside a chart. Let us start by implementing a simple multiseries line chart with only a title and an axis label defined in options (see listing 4-44).

***Listing 4-44.*** Ch4_10a.html

```
$(document).ready(function(){
    var data1 = [1, 2, 3, 2, 3, 4];
    var data2 = [3, 4, 5, 6, 5, 7];
    var data3 = [5, 6, 8, 9, 7, 9];
    var data4 = [7, 8, 9, 11, 10, 11];
    var options = {
        title: 'Multiseries Line Chart,
        axesDefaults: {
            label: 'Axis Label'
        }
    };
    $.jqplot('myChart',[data1, data2, data3, data4], options);
});
```

You add the <style> section in Listing 4-45, which can be extracted as a CSS file.

***Listing 4-45.*** Ch4_10a.html

```
<style>
.jqplot-title {
    font-family: "Arial Black";
    font-size: 24px;
    color: lightblue;
}

.jqplot-xaxis-label {
    font-size: 24px;
}

.jqplot-axis {
    font-family: "Arial";
    font-size: 16px;
}
```

```
.jqplot-xaxis {
    color: green;
}

.jqplot-yaxis {
    color: orange;
    font-weight: bold;
}
</style>
```

Figure 4-37 shows the situation before and after the settings of CSS style in Listing 4-45, allowing us to see the changes made.

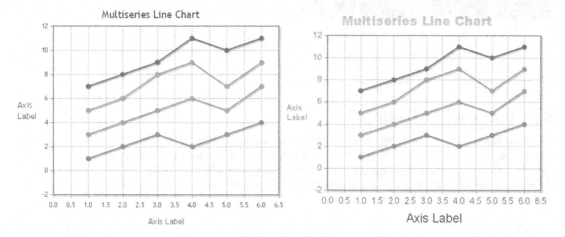

***Figure 4-37.*** *Some CSS styles applied to the tick labels and title*

## Changing the Background Color

Continuing with the previous example (see Listing 4-45), you now discover that by simply adding a single property to options (highlighted in Listing 4-46), you can obtain a black background. as demonstrated in Figure 4-38.

***Listing 4-46.*** Ch4_10b.html

```
var options = {
    title: 'Multiple Data Arrays',
    axesDefaults: {
        label: 'Axis Label'
    },
    grid: {
        background: '#000000'
    }
};
```

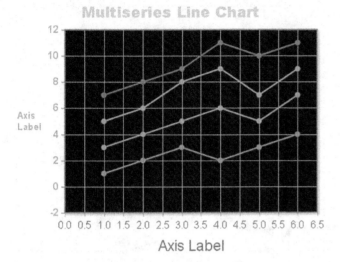

**Figure 4-38.** *A line chart with a black background*

# Further Customization, Using CSS

This time, you will change not only the background to the grid, but also the space that surrounds your chart, making it even more attractive. You will accomplish this by applying CSS styles directly to the chart elements.

For example, counter to the default setting (gray grid, white background), let us say you decide to place your chart on a completely black background. In this case, you need to create a container with a <div> element incorporated inside the myChart target (another<div> element):

```
<div class="chart-container">
    <div id="myChart" style="height:400px; width:500px;"></div>
</div>
```

This container serves to extend the area on which the black background will be placed; we refer to the container by setting its class with chart-container.

At this point, the most important thing to keep in mind is that the two <div> elements, the container and the target, can now be suitably characterized by changing their CSS styles. This can be done by specifying attributes for the .chart-container, as shown in Listing 4-47 (as for the elements of the target, these have already been set, using the .jqplot-* classes). In the .chart-container class, you set the background property to 'black'; the size of the container is established with the width and height properties. You also use the padding property in order to better center the target inside the container. The padding clears an area around the content of an element, extending its background color. The four values are, respectively, top, right, bottom, and left padding.

**Listing 4-47.** Ch4_20.html

```
<style type="text/css">
.chart-container {
    background : #000000;
    padding: 30px 0px 80px 30px;
    width: 560px;
    height: 330px;
}
...
</style>
```

The combined result emerging from the CSS customization of the container and the target is the chart shown in Figure 4-39.

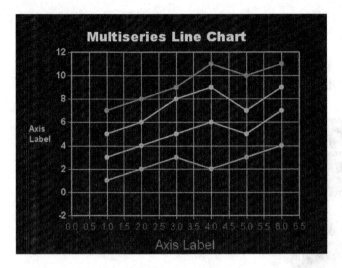

**Figure 4-39.** *A multiseries line chart with a black background*

## Setting the Grid

By default, the grids of your charts are gray. In the previous example (see Listing 4-47), however, you saw how you can change the grid by setting the properties within the grid object in options. In this example, you continue to modify the same multiseries line chart, but this time, you will focus on the grid properties.

You can change both the grid color and thickness. For instance, you might want a black grid, with increased thickness, in which case you must define the gridLineColor and gridLineWidth properties. Moreover, sometimes, by default, jqPlot might display your chart with a grid that is too thick and that could hinder rather than aid in readability. In such instances, you will need to reduce the number of ticks. This can be done very easily, by setting the numberTicks property in a specific way for each axis within the axes object in options. Listing 4-48 includes all these changes.

*Listing 4-48.* Ch4_10d.html

```
var options = {
    title: 'Multiseries Line Chart',
    axesDefaults: {
        label: 'AxisLabel'
    },
    grid: {
        background: '#000000',
        gridLineColor: '#ffffff',
        gridLineWidth: 2
    },
    axes: {
        xaxis: {
            numberTicks: 5,
            min: 0,
            max: 8
        },
```

```
        yaxis: {
            numberTicks: 3,
            min: 0,
            max: 12
        }
    }
};
```

In the end, you get a new chart with the desired grid (see Figure 4-40).

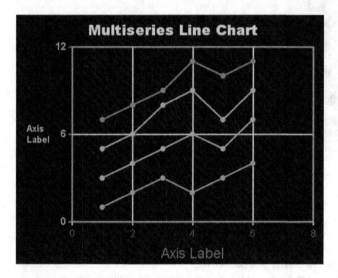

*Figure 4-40. A multiseries line chart with a customized grid*

Note that there is a gray outline delimiting the chart: the border. You can change that as well, or disable it, as in Listing 4-49. You can set the drawBorder property to 'false' and disable the shadow, too.

*Listing 4-49.* Ch4_20e.html

```
grid: {
    drawBorder: false,
    shadow: false,
    gridLineColor: '#000000',
    gridLineWidth: 2,
},
```

Following these changes, you obtain a more readable grid, such as the one in Figure 4-41, which has a border the same color as the grid (white).

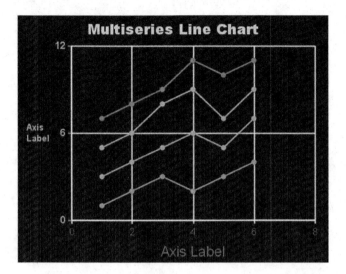

*Figure 4-41.* *A more readable multiseries line chart, with a customized grid*

# Working with Areas on Line Charts

So far, you have seen that the line chart basically consists of sets of points connected by lines, describing trends of a certain size. Now, you may find that such a view is somewhat limited. Often, the most interesting part of a line chart is the area that a line (or several lines) delimits in some way.

## Area Charts

A line chart can be converted into an area chart. In this example, you will use the multiseries line chart you have already created (see Listing 4-50), effecting changes in order to get a new chart mixing areas and lines. Here, you will see that very few changes need to be made to achieve the desired effect.

*Listing 4-50.* Ch4_22a.html

```
$(document).ready(function(){
    var data1 = [1, 2, 3, 2, 3, 4];
    var data2 = [3, 4, 5, 6, 5, 7];
    var data3 = [5, 6, 8, 9, 7, 9];
    var data4 = [7, 8, 9, 11, 10, 11];
    var options = {
        title:'Multiple Data Arrays'
    };
    $.jqplot ('myChart', [data1, data2, data3, data4], options);
});
```

First, in options you have to insert the fill attribute in the series that you want to represent as an area. This time, you choose seriesDefaults to apply the representation by area to all series. In this way, you obtain an area chart. To make the chart nicer, you can add other options, such as smoothing (see Listing 4-51).

*Listing 4-51.* Ch4_22a.html

```
var options = {
    title: 'Multiple Data Arrays',
    seriesDefaults: {
        showMarker: false,
        rendererOptions: {
            smooth: true
        },
        fill: true
    }
};
```

But, when running the web page, you immediately find that something is wrong: the area of the last series is covering the others (see Figure 4-42).

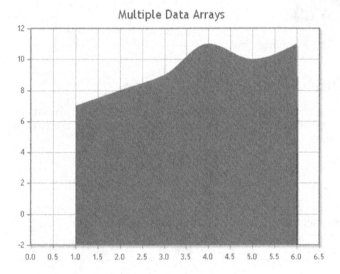

*Figure 4-42.* An area chart with one series covering the others

Before applying the fill attribute to series, you need to consider the order in which the corresponding areas of the series should be represented. In this case, it is only necessary to order the sequence of series in a different way:

```
$.jqplot ('myChart', [data4, data3, data2, data1], options);
```

The result is an accurate area chart, as seen in Figure 4-43.

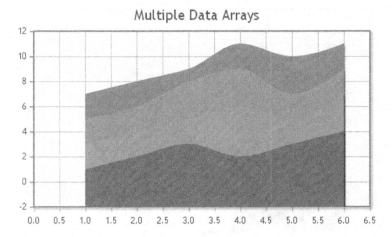

**Figure 4-43.** *A multiseries area chart rendered correctly*

## Line and Area Charts

Mixing lines and areas in the same chart can also create a very nice effect. Continuing with the previous example (see Listing 4-51), instead of setting the `fill` property in `seriesDefaults` and therefore applying the fill for all the series, you can decide to do so series by series in order to choose which series must be represented as area and which as line, as shown in Listing 4-52.

**Listing 4-52.** Ch4_22b.html

```
var options = {
    title:'Multiple Data Arrays',
    seriesDefaults: {
        showMarker: false,
        rendererOptions: {
            smooth: true
        }
    },
    series: [{}, {fill: true}, {}, {fill: true}]
};
```

Figure 4-44 shows how is possible to combine line and area charts.

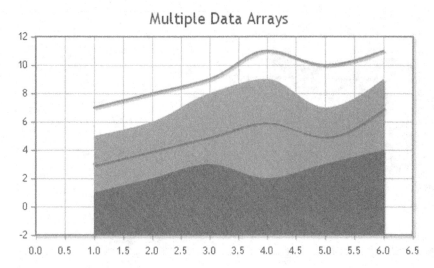

**Figure 4-44.** *A combined line and area chart*

# Band Charts

Band charts (also called high-low line charts or range charts) are a type of chart that combines the features of an area chart with those of a line chart.

A band chart is a line chart enhanced with an underlying shaded area (see Figure 4-45). This area represents the upper and lower boundaries of a range of values on the y axis. This range varies with the x, such that, in the end, you have a band.

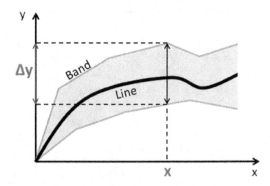

**Figure 4-45.** *A band chart*

You can use a band to indicate a particular interval on the y axis, which varies with the value on the x axis, correlated with the trend of a line inside it, illustrating, for example, confidence intervals or error bands. Another use might be to highlight a distribution that varies with time and the line showing the arithmetic mean.

Using jqPlot, the bands can be automatically computed or manually assigned. If assigned manually, the bounds of the band must be supplied as two arrays of [x, y] values. The first array delimits the lower bound line; the second array, the upper bound line. These two arrays are joined as the two elements of another array that is passed to the bandData property inside options.

First, let us define a data array with pairs of [x, y] values and the band array bdata, containing the two arrays: lower bound line and upper bound line (see Listing 4-53).

**Listing 4-53.** Ch4_24a.html

```
var data =[ [10,100],[20,110],[30,140],[40,130],
            [50,80],[60,75],[70,120],[80,130],[90,100]];
varbdata =[ [[10,90],[20,100],[30,130],[40,120],
            [50,70],[60,65],[70,110],[80,120],[90,90]],
            [[10,110],[20,120],[30,150],[40,140],
            [50,90],[60,85],[70,130],[80,140],[90,110]]];
```

Then, in options, use the code shown in Listing 4-54. Figure 4-46 presents the resulting banded-line chart.

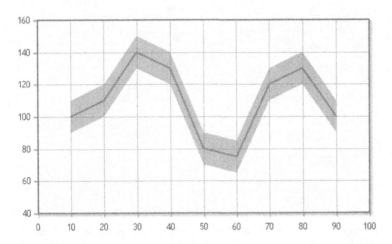

**Figure 4-46.** *A banded-line chart*

**Listing 4-54.** Ch4_24a.html

```
var options = {
    series: [{
        rendererOptions: { bandData: bdata }
    }],
    seriesDefaults: {
        shadow: false,
        showMarker: false
    }
};
$.jqplot ('myChart', [data], options);
```

If you choose to draw a smooth-line chart, the band will be smoothed out as well. Listing 4-55 gives the code, and Figure 4-47, the outcome.

***Listing 4-55.*** Ch4_24b.html

```
rendererOptions: {
    bandData: bdata,
    smooth: true
}
```

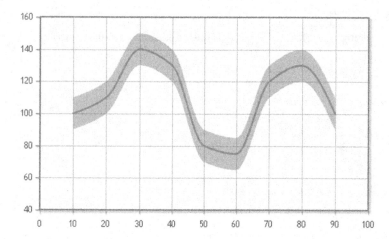

***Figure 4-47.*** *A smooth-banded-line chart*

The number of points in the band data arrays does not have to correspond to the number of points in the data series. Also, band data will be drawn as smoothed lines if the data series is smoothed. The band does not have to be symmetrical, with respect to the main line. The band can be made asymmetrical by inserting an array with asymmetrical y values in the bdata array, as demonstrated in Listing 4-56.

***Listing 4-56.*** Ch4_24c.html

```
varbdata =[ [[10,90],[30,100],[40,100],[50,70],
            [60,65], [70,110],[80,120],[90,90]],
            [[10,110],[30,150],[40,140],[50,120],
            [60,85], [70,130],[80,140],[90,110]] ];
```

Now, the band in Figure 4-48 is not symmetrical, with respect to the main line.

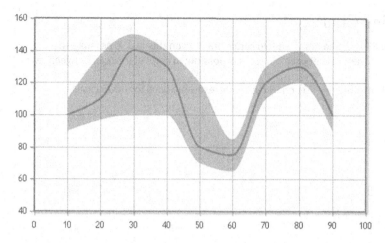

***Figure 4-48.*** *A nonuniform banded-line chart*

But, providing band data is not mandatory; they can be automatically computed by jqPlot. To activate this feature without using any arrays, you have to set the bands object's show property to 'true' in rendererOptions, as in Listing 4-57. As you can see in Figure 4-49, by default the band interval covers +/-3 percent of the y value of the main line.

***Listing 4-57.*** Ch4_24d.html

```
series: [{
    rendererOptions: {
        bands: { show: true},
        smooth: true
    }
}],
```

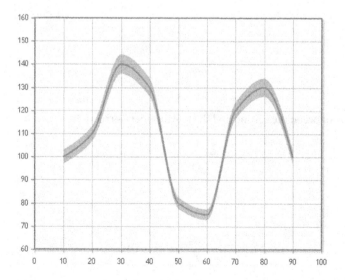

***Figure 4-49.*** *A banded-line chart with a band interval of +/-3 percent*

# Filling Between Lines in a Line Chart

You have just learned about bands. Why not fill the area between two series lines? Even this task is possible with jqPlot, as well. By setting the properties within the fillBetween object, it is possible to control the area between two lines on a plot.

Here, you are starting with a very simple multiseries line chart (the same example used for other cases), described in Listing 4-58.

***Listing 4-58.*** Ch4_5a.html

```
$(document).ready(function(){
    var data1 = [1, 2, 3, 2, 3, 4];
    var data2 = [3, 4, 5, 6, 5, 7];
    var data3 = [5, 6, 8, 9, 7, 9];
    var data4 = [7, 8, 9, 11, 10, 11];
    var options = {
        title:'Multiple Data Arrays',
    };
    $.jqplot('myChart', [data1, data2, data3, data4], options);
});
```

Using this multiseries line chart, you can consider every series, with an index starting from 0, for the first series; 1, for the second series; 2, for the third; and so on.

So, if you want to fill the area between two lines, you need to specify in the series1 and series2 attributes the two indexes corresponding to them. For instance, if you want to fill the area between the second and the fourth series, you have to set series1 to 1 (second series) and series 2 to 3 (fourth series), as shown in Listing 4-59. Optionally, you can set the color of the delimited area by using the color attribute or, better, with an rgba() function.

***Listing 4-59.*** Ch4_25.html

```
var options = {
    title: 'Multiple Data Arrays',
    fillBetween: {
        series1: 1,    //second series
        series2: 3,    //fourth series
        color: "rgba(10, 120, 130, 0.7)"
    }
});
```

In Figure 4-50, you can see that the selected area, between the second and the fourth series, is colored.

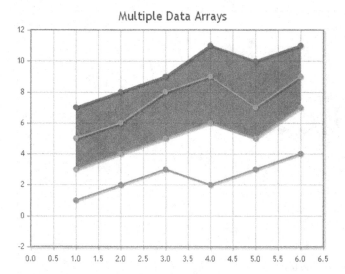

**Figure 4-50.** *A multiseries line chart with a colored area between two lines*

You can bind a JavaScript function to a button that serves to update the plot's settings for each series and then replot everything. To do this, let us add the function in Listing 4-60 inside the jQuery ready() function.

**Listing 4-60.** Ch4_26.html

```
$("button[name=changeFill]").click(function(e) {
    plot1.fillBetween.series1 = parseInt($("input[name=series1]").val());
    plot1.fillBetween.series2 = parseInt($("input[name=series2]").val());
    plot1.replot();
});
```

For the previous JavaScript function to work, you need to assign the variable plot1 with the value returned by the function $.jqplot():

```
plot1 = $.jqplot ('myChart', [data1, data2, data3, data4], options);
```

And, in the <body> section of the web page, you must add two input text areas and a button, as shown in Listing 4-61.

**Listing 4-61.** Ch4_26.html

```
<label for="series1">First Series: </label>
<input type="text" name="series1" value="1" />
<label for="series2"> Second Series: </label>
<input type="text" name="series2" value="3" />
<button name="changeFill">Change Fill</button>
```

The result is given in Figure 4-51.

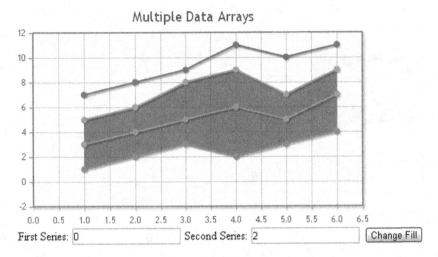

**Figure 4-51.** *A multiseries line chart with a selectable colored area*

To replace the simple HTML controls with a jQuery UI widget, you have to make some changes to the code in order to integrate it, as reported in Listing 4-62.

**Listing 4-62.** Ch4_26ui.html

```
<link rel="stylesheet" href="../src/css/smoothness/jquery-ui-1.10.3.custom.min.css" />
<script src="../src/js/jquery-ui-1.10.3.custom.min.js"></script>
...
$("button[name=changeFill]").click(function(e) {
    plot1.fillBetween.series1 = parseInt($("#combobox").val());
    plot1.fillBetween.series2 = parseInt($("#combobox2").val());
    plot1.replot();
});
...
<div class="ui-widget">
<label>First Series : </label>
<select id="combobox">
    <option value="0">1</option>
    <option value="1">2</option>
    <option value="2">3</option>
    <option value="3">4</option>
</select>
</div>
<div class="ui-widget">
<label>Second Series : </label>
<select id="combobox2">
    <option value="0">1</option>
    <option value="1">2</option>
    <option value="2">3</option>
    <option value="3">4</option>
</select>
</div>
<button name="changeFill">Change Fill</button>
```

```
<script>
$(function() {
    $( 'button')
        .button()
        .click(function( event ) {
            event.preventDefault();
        });
});
</script>
```

The result is the chart shown in Figure 4-52.

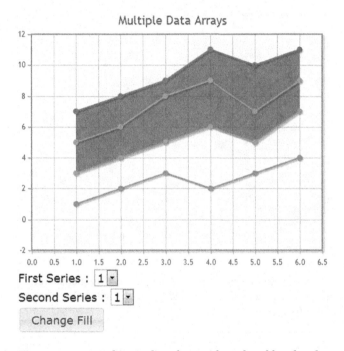

**Figure 4-52.** *A multiseries line chart with a selectable colored area*

# Trend Lines

jqPlot is really full of surprises. In addition to all the things you have already seen regarding the line chart, jqPlot can calculate and represent trend lines. These are generally straight lines drawn in a chart, but sometimes they can be exponential (if they are linear in a log scale). A trend line indicates the general pattern or direction of the series data plotted in a chart. The line is drawn by using statistical techniques. This function is performed by another plug-in: *Trendline.*

To enable this function, you need to include the plug-in in the web page:

```
<script type="text/javascript" src="../src/plugins/jqplot.trendline.min.js"></script>
```

After that, you need only activate the plug-in, adding the row that enables it, as in Listing 4-63.

**Listing 4-63.** Ch4_27a.html

```
$(document).ready(function(){
    var data = [100, 110, 140, 130, 135, 132, 140, 135, 142]
    $.jqplot.config.enablePlugins = true;
    $.jqplot ('myChart', [data]);
});
```

With these few lines it is possible to obtain a trend line, as in Figure 4-53.

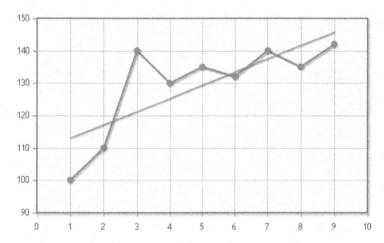

**Figure 4-53.** The linear trend line of a line chart

But, if you prefer to express the properties explicitly, you can do so through the use of options. This enables you to handle the trend line in the same way as other objects in the chart. Let us say you would like to change the line's color and increase its thickness to make it stand out (see Listing 4-64).

**Listing 4-64.** Ch4_27b.html

```
var options = {
    seriesDefaults: {
        trendline: {
            show:true,
            color: '#ff0000',
            lineWidth: 4
        }
    }
}
$.jqplot ('myChart', [data], options);
```

You now gain more control of the trend line. Figure 4-54 shows a line with property settings in the `trendline` object (the trend line is thicker and is displayed with a deep red color on the browser).

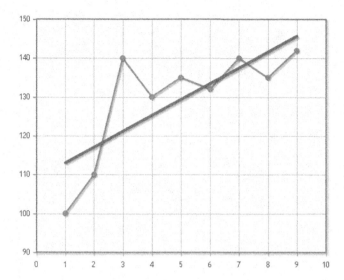

**Figure 4-54.** *A customized linear trend line in a line chart*

As mentioned earlier, it is possible to use trend line curves, which indicate an exponential trend followed by the points of the chart. Let examine this in the next example, in Listing 4-65.

**Listing 4-65.** Ch4_28.html

```
$(document).ready(function(){
    var data = [[10, 1.44], [30, 6.98], [50, 10.7], [70, 37.5], [90, 78.1]];
    var options = {
        seriesDefaults: {
            trendline: {
                show:true,
                color: '#ff0000',
                lineWidth: 4,
                type: 'exponential'
            }
        }
    }
    $.jqplot ('myChart', [data], options);
});
```

Figure 4-55 presents a line chart in which you have plotted a series of points following an exponential trend. You can, therefore, highlight this with an exponential trend line.

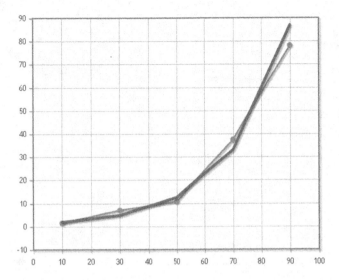

***Figure 4-55.*** *A customized exponential trend in a line chart*

# Summary

In this rich chapter, you have become well versed in the jqPlot world. You looked at the many possibilities that this library provides, enabling you to implement line charts to the best of your ability. You learned how to manipulate the basic elements on which to plot your chart, such as **axes** and **ticks**. In particular, you saw how to manage multiple data series in the same chart (**multiseries charts**), adding various graphic effects. You also explored the way in which the jqPlot library allows you to manipulate different formats of **date and time values**. Moreover, you saw how it is possible to customize some elements, using the **HTML format**, along with the **highlighting** of data points. In the final part of the chapter, you dealt with more complex cases, such as generating a **trend line** and working with **band charts**.

In the next chapter, one that is full of arguments, you will face other new concepts, applied this time to bar charts.

■ ■ ■

# CHAPTER 5

# Bar Charts with jqPlot

In this chapter, you will deal with another large class of charts: bar charts. In the previous chapter, you were shown ways to characterize line charts, the default chart type in jqPlot. Now, using the *BarRenderer* plug-in, you will discover how the structure of the main jqPlot object is gradually enriched with new properties and objects. Through practical examples, you will see how to change the values of property and object attributes with rendererOptions.

Sometimes, it is possible to obtain different representations using the same set of data. Learning how to choose which representation is most suitable to your needs is one of the fundamental objectives of this book. To this end, using one set of data, you will see how to switch from a grouped bar chart to a stacked bar chart, in both cases choosing between a vertical and a horizontal representation.

In addition, you will learn how it is possible to represent a combined chart with the jqPlot library, for example, how to represent a line chart and a bar chart at the same time, and how, simply by slowing down the speed of drawing, you can get a simple but eye-catching animation., You will also become acquainted with a particular type of bar chart, the Marimekko chart, which is implemented by the jqPlot library in a very satisfactory way.

In the last part of the chapter, I will introduce the use of events in jqPlot. This is a complex subject, but thanks to special jQuery functions, you can achieve significant interactive effects with only a few lines of code. The chapter concludes with a typical example in this regard: how to customize tool tips.

## Using the *BarRenderer* Plug-In to Create Bar Charts

When you have a set of data that is divided into various categories, and there is a need to compare these categories with one another, then a bar chart may be the representation that is best suited to your needs. You have seen that without including any plug-ins, by default the incoming data are interpreted as points joined to form a line. To tell jqPlot that the incoming data must be used to draw a bar chart, you have to place a set of plug-ins in the <head> section of the HTML page:

```
<script type="text/javascript" src="../src/plugins/jqplot.dateAxisRenderer.min.js"></script>
<script type="text/javascript"
    src="../src/plugins/jqplot.canvasAxisTickRenderer.min.js"></script>
<script type="text/javascript" src="../src/plugins/jqplot.categoryAxisRenderer.min.js"></script>
<script type="text/javascript" src="../src/plugins/jqplot.barRenderer.min.js"></script>
```

Or, if you prefer to use a content delivery network (CDN) service, you may do so as follows:

```
<script type="text/javascript" src="http://cdn.jsdelivr.net/jqplot/1.0.8/plugins/
jqplot.dateAxisRenderer.min.js"></script>
<script type="text/javascript" src="http://cdn.jsdelivr.net/jqplot/1.0.8/plugins/
jqplot.canvasAxisTickRenderer.min.js"></script>
<script type="text/javascript" src="http://cdn.jsdelivr.net/jqplot/1.0.8/plugins/
jqplot.categoryAxisRenderer.min.js"></script>
<script type="text/javascript" src="http://cdn.jsdelivr.net/jqplot/1.0.8/plugins/
jqplot.barRenderer.min.js"></script>
```

To set the input data so that it may be used in a bar chart, you must insert an array in the format [label, y], where x is no longer present, but an indicative label takes its place. This label is often a string value. In fact, when we talk about bar charts, we are no longer interested in following the trend of a variable (y values) in relation to another variable (x values), but rather, are interested in comparing categories, or groups, of data (labels). For this example, you will use five groups, each of which represents a state, reported as a label:

```
var data = [['Germany', 12], ['Italy', 8], ['Spain', 6], ['France', 10], ['UK', 7]];
```

Once you have included the *BarRenderer* plug-in,, you have to activate it, assigning its reference to the renderer property within the series object (see Listing 5-1). You will do the same thing with the second plug-in, *CategoryAxisRenderer*, specifying it only for the xaxis object.

***Listing 5-1.*** Ch5_01a.html

```
var options = {
    title: 'Foreign Customers',
    series:[{renderer:$.jqplot.BarRenderer}],
    axes: {
       xaxis: {
           renderer: $.jqplot.CategoryAxisRenderer
       }
    }
};
$.jqplot ('myChart', [data], options);
```

Next, in the <body> section of the HTML page, you add the following row:

```
<div id="myChart" style="height:300px; width:500px;"></div>
```

In this way, you get a simple bar chart, as shown in Figure 5-1. Every state contained in the data array is represented by a blue bar, with the height corresponding to the y value.

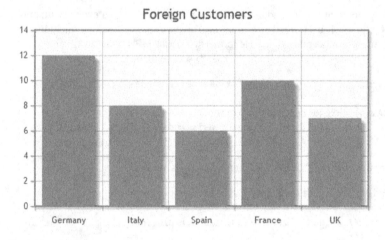

***Figure 5-1.*** *A simple bar chart*

# Rotate Axis Tick Labels

Often, it may be necessary or desirable to rotate the tick labels reported on the x axis. For instance, the text may be too long to be reported, and in order to maintain the readability of the labels, you need to write them so that they incline at a certain angle. This rotation is achieved by including the *CanvasTextRenderer* plug-in:

```
<script type="text/javascript" src="../src/plugins/jqplot.canvasTextRenderer.min.js"></script>
```

Or, if you prefer to use a CDN service, you may do so as follows:

```
<script type="text/javascript" src="http://cdn.jsdelivr.net/jqplot/1.0.8/plugins↵
    /jqplot.canvasTextRenderer.min.js"></script>
```

Here, too, simply including the plug-in will not be enough; you must also activate it by passing its reference to the tickRenderer property, as demonstrated in Listing 5-2. Then, you need to specify certain properties in tickOptions: you set the angle property to –30 degrees. With this value, you are indicating the degrees of inclination of the text, with respect to the x axis. If the value is positive, the text will rotate in a clockwise direction; if negative (as in Listing 5-2), counterclockwise.

*Listing 5-2.* Ch5_01b.html

```
var options = {
    title: 'Foreign customers',
    series:[{ renderer: $.jqplot.BarRenderer }],
    axes: {
       xaxis: {
          renderer: $.jqplot.CategoryAxisRenderer,
          tickRenderer: $.jqplot.CanvasAxisTickRenderer,
          tickOptions: {
             angle: -30,
             fontSize: '10pt'
          }
       }
    }
};
$.jqplot ('myChart', [data], options);
```

If you now load the web page in your browser, at the bottom of your chart, you will see that all the labels are rotated counterclockwise, with respect to the x axis (see Figure 5-2).

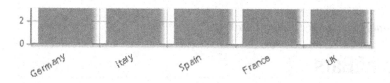

*Figure 5-2.* A bar chart with rotated labels on the x axis

# Modify the Space Between the Bars

Working with bar charts, perhaps the most common requirement is to vary the amount of space between bars. This space can be adjusted directly, by setting the `barMargin` property with different values. Because this property does not belong to the `jqplot` object, but is specific to the *BarRenderer* plug-in, you have to specify it within `rendererOptions`. Whenever you include a renderer plug-in, you also include a whole new set of properties not belonging to the original `jqplot` object. So, if you want a value that is different from the default of one of these properties, you will need to write this property in `rendererOptions`, setting the new value. For instance, let us apply a space of 30 pixels between bars, as illustrated in Listing 5-3.

*Listing 5-3.* Ch5_02.html

```
var options = {
    title: 'Foreign Customers',
    seriesDefaults:{
        renderer:$.jqplot.BarRenderer,
        rendererOptions: {
            barMargin: 30
        },
    },
    axes: {
```

Because the width of the chart remains the same, as a consequence of increasing the `barMargin` property to 30, all bars are narrower than before (see Figure 5-3).

*Figure 5-3.* *The space between bars is adjustable with a new property introduced by the plug-in*

# Adding Values at the Top of Bars

The jqPlot library allows you to handle even point labels. Although you can use them in line charts, as well, point labels are an important component of bar charts. Point labels, if activated, explicitly show the y value above the bars, enhancing the readability of values, especially for the stacked bar chart. To activate this functionality, you need to include another plug-in:

```
<script type="text/javascript" src="../src/plugins/jqplot.pointLabels.min.js"></script>
```

Or, if you prefer to use a CDN service, you may do so as follows:

```
<script type="text/javascript"
    src="http://cdn.jsdelivr.net/jqplot/1.0.8/plugins/jqplot.pointLabels.min.js"></script>
```

You may have noticed that *PointLabels* is not a renderer plug-in and that it is therefore already active. This time, there will be no need to pass a reference in the renderer property. The process is very simple and quick: in options, you set the show property of the pointLabels object to 'true' (see Listing 5-4).

**Listing 5-4.** Ch5_03.html

```
seriesDefaults:{
    renderer:$.jqplot.BarRenderer,
    pointLabels: { show: true }
},
```

As shown in Figure 5-4, with the point labels activated, the y value will appear above each bar.

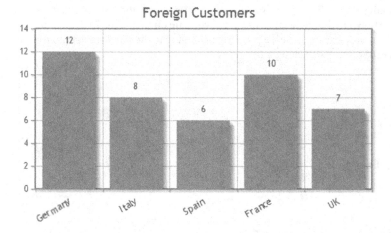

**Figure 5-4.** *A bar chart reporting the y value above each bar*

# Bars with Negative Values

Generally, we are accustomed to seeing bar charts with all positive y values, but this is not always the case. If you want to represent negative values on a bar chart, however, you must be careful. If you try to use an input data array containing negative values, as in the following example

```
var data = [['Germany', -12], ['Italy', -8], ['Spain', -6], ['France', -10], ['UK', -7]];
```

you get the bar chart in Figure 5-5.

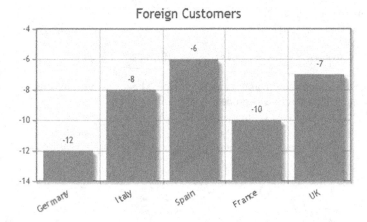

**Figure 5-5.** *This bar chart has interpreted the negative values badly*

This is not what you really wanted. The bars are drawn as if they were still positive. Only the point labels show the values of y properly. Furthermore, the values reported on the y axis are not correlated with the representation of the bars, which should start at the top and go down to the corresponding negative value on the y axis. To overcome all these issues, you need to set the fillToZero property to 'true', a property belonging to the *BarRenderer* plug-in; therefore, you have to specify this in rendererOptions (see Listing 5-5).

**Listing 5-5.** ch10_04a.html

```
var options = {
    title: 'Foreign Customers',
    seriesDefaults:{
        renderer:$.jqplot.BarRenderer,
        rendererOptions: { fillToZero: true },
        pointLabels: { show: true }
    },
    ...
```

Now, jqPlot can represent the negative bars correctly (see Figure 5-6).

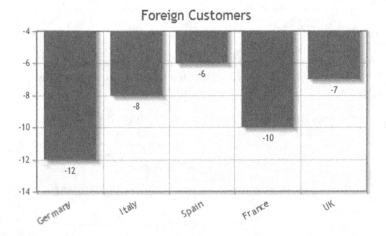

**Figure 5-6.** *A simple bar chart with negative values*

128

This functionality is better appreciated when both positive and negative values are represented in the same bar chart:

```
var data = [['Germany', -12], ['Italy', 8], ['Spain', -6], ['France', 10], ['UK', -7]];
```

As you can see in Figure 5-7, a slightly darker color distinguishes the bars with negative values.

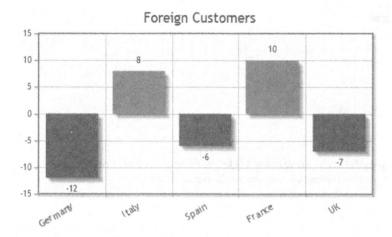

***Figure 5-7.*** *A simple bar chart with positive and negative values*

# Bar Charts with More Than One Set of Data

You have seen how line charts manage multiple series, and so you might expect bar charts to afford the same possibility. In the transition from single series to multiple series, you need to make some changes in the way input data are organized. Hence, you start from the format for the input data array for a single series:

```
var data = [['Germany', 12], ['Italy', 8], ['Spain', 6], ['France', 10], ['UK', 7]];
```

First, you have to specify a customized `ticks` array, which must contain the names of the groups, or categories, of data (the values you want to report on the x axis). The number of ticks should match the number of y values in each series.

```
var ticks = ['Germany', 'Italy', 'Spain', 'France', 'UK'];
```

Because you are working with more than one series, you can specify at least three series of data. Each series represents a further classification of the data, so you can distinguish one from the other by means of a label reporting the group the data belong to. Now, you have to insert only y values for each series (from the `ticks` array), as in Listing 5-6, given that the x values are the same for each.

***Listing 5-6.*** Ch5_05.html

```
var data = [12, 8, 6, 10, 7];        // Electronics customers
var data2 = [14, 12, 4, 14, 11];     // Software customers
var data3 = [18, 10, 5, 9, 9];       // Mechanics customers
```

With regard to the names indicating the series, you must specify these within the `series` object (see Listing 5-7), assigning them one by one to the `label` property of each series.

***Listing 5-7.*** Ch5_05.html

```
var options = {
        title: 'Foreign Customers',
        seriesDefaults:{
            renderer:$.jqplot.BarRenderer,
        },
    series:[
       {label: 'Electronics'},
       {label: 'Software'},
       {label: 'Mechanics'}
    ],
    axes: {
    ...
```

Now, as always within `options`, you assign the `ticks` array to the `ticks` property of the `xaxis` object (see Listing 5-8). In so doing , you have assigned each tick generated on the x axis to a string contained in the array.

***Listing 5-8.*** ch10_05.html

```
axes: {
    xaxis: {
        renderer: $.jqplot.CategoryAxisRenderer,
        ticks: ticks
    }
},
```

You have just seen that working with multiple series simply adds a further categorization of data. In addition to being divided into categories represented on the x axis, the data are divided into multiple series, each representing a different group. To distinguish one series from another, it is necessary to draw the corresponding bars with different colors. But, if you were to stop there, the user observing this chart would not have any information regarding which group is indicated by which color. The introduction of a legend is therefore required (see Listing 5-9).

***Listing 5-9.*** Ch5_05.html

```
var options = {
    title: 'Foreign Customers',
    seriesDefaults: {
        renderer: $.jqplot.BarRenderer,
    },
    series:[
        {label: 'Electronics'},
        {label: 'Software'},
        {label: 'Mechanics'}
    ],
```

```
    axes: {
      xaxis: {
        renderer: $.jqplot.CategoryAxisRenderer,
        ticks: ticks
      }
    },
    legend: {
      show: true,
      placement: 'outsideGrid',
      location: 'e'
    }
};
$.jqplot ('myChart', [data, data2, data3], options);
```

You thus obtain a multiseries bar chart, as illustrated in Figure 5-8. As you can see, when you use multiple series, you must use different colors in order to distinguish between them.

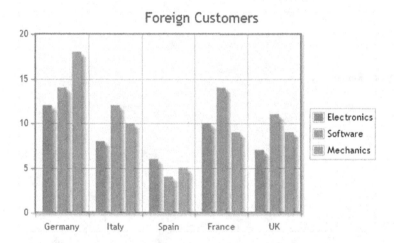

**Figure 5-8.** *A multiseries bar chart containing a legend*

## Vertical and Horizontal Bar Charts

Looking at the chart in Figure 5-8, you will note that each group is represented by a color. The assigned colors follow the sequence specified internally to jqPlot by default, and that sequence is reflected in the line chart. Each country has three columns represented in its segment on the x- axis, with every segment bounded by grid lines.

This kind of bar chart is generally defined as a vertical bar chart. Nothing prevents us from representing the same input data with bars oriented horizontally, but here, too, you will need to make changes in the format of the input data arrays. In this case, it is necessary to use [y, n] pairs, where n is an integer value that is assigned to a string (see Listing 5-10). The strings are the label descriptions contained in the ticks array, and n is its index.

**Listing 5-10.** Ch5_06.html

```
var data =  [[12, 1], [8, 2], [6, 3], [10, 4], [7, 5]];
var data2 = [[14, 1], [12, 2], [4, 3], [14, 4], [11, 5]];
var data3 = [[18, 1], [10, 2], [5, 3], [9, 4], [9, 5]];
var ticks = ['Germany', 'Italy', 'Spain', 'France', 'UK'];
```

After you have changed the format of the input data arrays, you must set the barDirection property to 'horizontal' ('vertical' is the default value). As shown in Listing 5-11, you have to do so in seriesDefaults in order to apply the horizontal orientation to all series. This time, it is necessary to assign the ticks array to the ticks property in the yaxis object, instead of the xaxis object, as before.

***Listing 5-11.*** Ch5_06.html

```
var options = {
    title: 'Foreign Customers',
    seriesDefaults:{
        renderer: $.jqplot.BarRenderer,
        rendererOptions: {
            barDirection: 'horizontal'
        }
    },
    series:[
        {label: 'Electronics'},
        {label: 'Software'},
        {label: 'Mechanics'}
    ],
    axes: {
        yaxis: {
            renderer: $.jqplot.CategoryAxisRenderer,
            ticks: ticks
        }
    },
    legend: {
        show: true,
        placement: 'outsideGrid',
        location: 'e'
    }
};
$.jqplot ('myChart', [data, data2, data3], options);
```

Now, you get the horizontal multiseries bar chart shown in Figure 5-9.

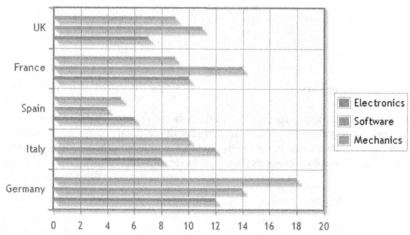

**Figure 5-9.** *A horizontal multiseries bar chart*

## Vertical Stacked Bars

When you need to break down data series into their constituent parts, while retaining the ability to compare these data series as a whole, you have to use a stacked chart. jqPlot library supports such charts. With stacked bar charts, it is especially appropriate to add point labels, to make the chart more readable. The values reported are cumulative, that is, the sum of the underlying bars in the stack, as in Listing 5-12.

**Listing 5-12.** Ch5_07.html

```
var data = [12, 8, 6, 10, 7];
var data2 = [14, 12, 4, 14, 11];
var data3 = [18, 10, 5, 9, 9];
var ticks = ['Germany', 'Italy', 'Spain', 'France', 'UK'];

 var options = {
   title: 'Foreign Customers',
   stackSeries: true,
   seriesDefaults:{
      renderer:$.jqplot.BarRenderer,
      pointLabels: { show: true,location: 's' }
   },
   series:[
      {label: 'Electronics'},
      {label: 'Software'},
      {label: 'Mechanics'}
   ],
   axes: {
      xaxis: {
         renderer: $.jqplot.CategoryAxisRenderer,
         ticks: ticks
      }
   },
```

```
    legend: {
        show: true,
        placement: 'outsideGrid',
        location: 'e'
    }
};

$.jqplot ('myChart', [data, data2, data3], options);
```

By setting values for the pointLabels property, you can specify the location where the point labels are shown: 'n', 's',' e', 'w', 'ne', 'nw', 'se', or 'sw'. These values should be interpreted as the cardinal points indicating the direction in which to draw the point label, with respect to the top of the bar. In this example, you choose 's' (south) to display the value just below the top of the bar, in the colored area, as presented in Figure 5-10.

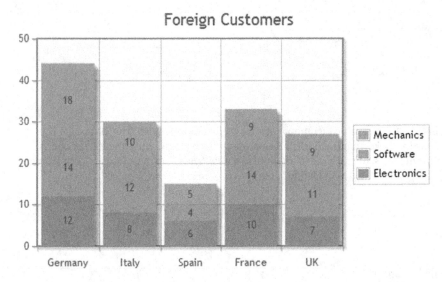

**Figure 5-10.** *A vertical multiseries stacked bar chart*

## Horizontal Stacked Bars

In the same way, you can create a horizontal stacked bar chart. In this case, in order to represent the point labels inside the segments, you need to set them to 'w' (west) (see Listing 5-13).

***Listing 5-13.*** ch10_08.html

```
var data  =  [[12, 1], [8, 2], [6, 3], [10, 4], [7, 5]];
var data2 =  [[14, 1], [12, 2], [4, 3], [14, 4], [11, 5]];
var data3 =  [[18, 1], [10, 2], [5, 3], [9, 4], [9, 5]];
var ticks = ['Germany', 'Italy', 'Spain', 'France', 'UK'];

var options = {
    title: 'Foreign Customers',
    stackSeries: true,
    seriesDefaults:{
        renderer: $.jqplot.BarRenderer,
```

```
        rendererOptions: {
            barDirection: 'horizontal'
        },
        pointLabels: { show: true, location: 'w' }
    },
    series:[
        {label: 'Electronics'},
        {label: 'Software'},
        {label: 'Mechanics'}
    ],
    axes: {
        yaxis: {
            renderer: $.jqplot.CategoryAxisRenderer,
            ticks: ticks
        }
    },
    legend: {
    show: true,
    placement: 'outsideGrid',
    location: 'e'
    }
};
$.jqplot ('myChart', [data, data2, data3], options);
```

In Figure 5-11, you can see how the values are shown near the end of the bar (west), in the colored area.

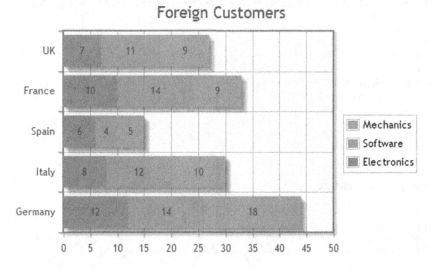

***Figure 5-11.*** *A horizontal multiseries stacked bar chart*

# Combination Charts: Lines in Bar Charts

A combination chart is a chart that combines two or more chart types in a single chart. In the following example, you will consider a bar chart series and a line chart series represented at the same time in one chart. For this kind of representation, you need to use a dual y axis. Each series has its own unit and magnitude and so must conform to one of these axes. Therefore, you have to use primary and secondary axes. You have to activate the autoscale functionality, too, in order to force the y axes to line up tick marks, thus obtaining consistent grid lines.

Let us, therefore, define the two input series (see Listing 5-14). The array data contains the [label1, y1] pairs of values to be presented as a bar chart. The array line contains the [label2, y2] pairs of values to be presented as a line chart.

**Listing 5-14.** Ch5_09.html

```
var data = [['Germany', 12], ['Italy', 8], ['Spain' ,6], ['France', 10], ['UK', 7]];
var line = [['BMW', 45], ['AlfaRomeo', 30], ['Seat', 24],['Renault', 36], ['Mini', 30]];
```

This case is useful for understanding the utility of having multiple y axes to work on (jqPlot supports up to nine y axes and two x axes). Here, you have two series, the sequences of which are defined by the order in which you pass them as a second argument in the function $.jqplot():

```
$.jqplot ('myChart', [data, line], options);
```

The array data, the series intended for the bar chart, is first, and the array line, intended for the line chart, is second. This is very important. Having established this order, in options, you need to specify two elements within the series object, as shown in Listing 5-15. In the first element only, you activate the *BarRenderer* plug-in, whereas in the second, you define two supplementary axes: x2axis and y2axis. Now, you have four axes to work with, and, consequently, you have to specify them within the axes object. On yaxis and y2axis, you must activate autoscale.

**Listing 5-15.** Ch5_09.html

```
var options = {
    title: 'Foreign customers',
    series:[{renderer: $.jqplot.BarRenderer},
        {
            xaxis: 'x2axis',
            yaxis: 'y2axis'
        }],
    axes: {
        xaxis: {
            renderer: $.jqplot.CategoryAxisRenderer
        },
        x2axis: {
            renderer: $.jqplot.CategoryAxisRenderer
        },
        yaxis: {
            autoscale: true
        },
```

```
        y2axis: {
            autoscale: true,
            renderOptions: {
                alignTicks: true
            }
        }
    }
};
```

The result is the chart in Figure 5-12, containing bars and lines at the same time.

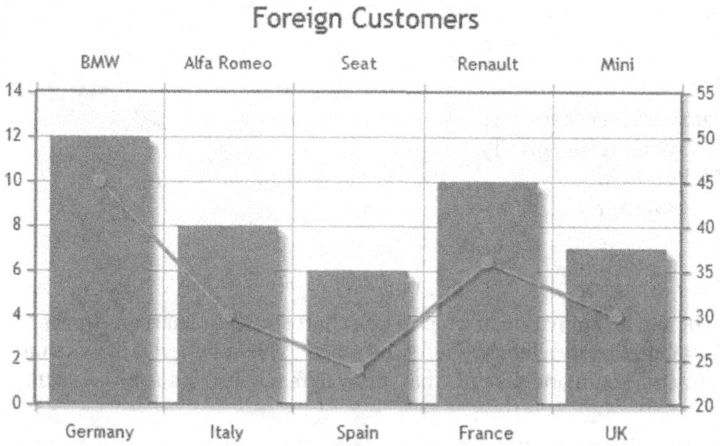

**Figure 5-12.**  *A line chart combined with a bar chart*

# Animated Plot

The jqPlot library also provides you with the ability to animate your charts. To this end, you do not need any further plug-ins. Starting from the previous example, the combination chart (see Listing 5-15), you can assign a different speed for each series. In defining a drawing speed, it is as though you were slowing down the creation of an element of the chart by the browser. This produces a dynamic effect during the drawing process, thus creating an animation. Furthermore, by assigning different speeds to different parts, you can obtain very nice effects.

As we can see in Listing 5-16, in options, you have to activate the animation functionality by setting to 'true' the animate and the animateReplot properties. Then, you define a different speed for each series, using a numeric value (number of milliseconds).

**Listing 5-16.**  Ch5_10.html

```
var options = {
    animate: true,
    animateReplot: true,
    title: 'Foreign Customers',
    series:[{
        renderer: $.jqplot.BarRenderer,
```

```
      rendererOptions: {
         animation: {
            speed: 2500
         },
      }
   },{
      xaxis: 'x2axis',
      yaxis: 'y2axis',
      rendererOptions: {
         animation: {
            speed: 2500
         },
      }
   }],
   axes: {
      xaxis: { renderer: $.jqplot.CategoryAxisRenderer  },
      x2axis: {renderer: $.jqplot.CategoryAxisRenderer  },
      yaxis: { autoscale:true, numberTicks: 6 },
      y2axis: { autoscale:true, numberTicks: 6 }
   }
};
```

When you load this chart in a browser, you obtain an animation in which a line chart and a bar chart are drawn slowly and smoothly. Figure 5-13 shows how the animation develops in successive stages. The line chart is drawn from left to right, following the order of the data points, and, simultaneously, the bars grow to reach their respective y values.

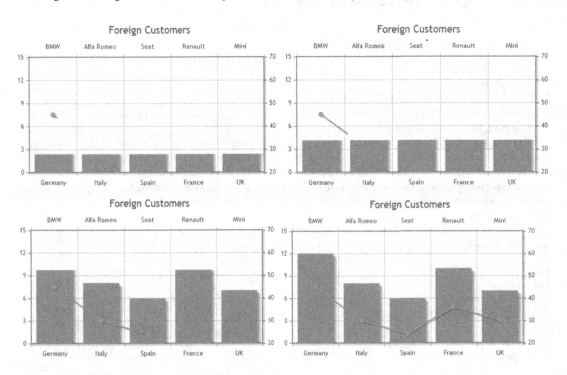

**Figure 5-13.** *An animated combined line-bar chart*

# Marimekko Chart

A kind of chart that can be derived from the bar chart is the so-called Marimekko chart (also called Mekko chart), named for its resemblance to a Marimekko print. This type of chart has been adopted in the business world. Marimekko charts are essentially stacked column charts. Here, however, all the bars are of equal height. Moreover, there are no spaces between the bars, and the bars are divided into several segments, the height of which is correlated to a percentage (see Figure 5-14).

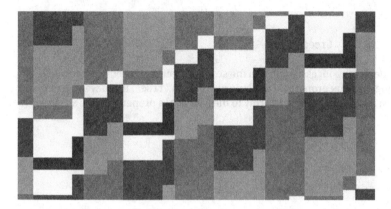

***Figure 5-14.*** *A Marimekko pattern*

Marimekko charts are designed to report percentage values on both axes: the percentage covered by each category along the x axis, where each bar is placed, and the percentage covered by each category along the y axis, represented by the segments into which each bar is divided.

jqPlot allows you to develop this kind of chart, using two specific plug-ins: *MekkoRenderer* and *MekkoAxisRenderer*:

```
<script class="include" type="text/javascript"
    src="../src/plugins/jqplot.mekkoRenderer.min.js"></script>
<script class="include" type="text/javascript"
    src="../src/plugins/jqplot.mekkoAxisRenderer.min.js"></script>
<script class="include" type="text/javascript"
    src="../src/plugins/jqplot.canvasTextRenderer.min.js"></script>
<script class="include" type="text/javascript"
    src="../src/plugins/jqplot.canvasAxisLabelRenderer.min.js"></script>
```

Or, if you prefer to use a CDN service, you may do so as follows:

```
<script type="text/javascript" src="http://cdn.jsdelivr.net/jqplot/1.0.8/plugins↵
    /jqplot.mekkoRenderer.min.js"></script>
<script type="text/javascript" src="http://cdn.jsdelivr.net/jqplot/1.0.8/plugins↵
    /jqplot.mekkoAxisRenderer.min.js"></script>
<script type="text/javascript" src="http://cdn.jsdelivr.net/jqplot/1.0.8/plugins↵
    /jqplot.canvasTextRenderer.min.js"></script>
<script type="text/javascript" src="http://cdn.jsdelivr.net/jqplot/1.0.8/plugins↵
    /jqplot.canvasAxisLabelRenderer.min.js"></script>
```

Along with these two plug-ins, you need to include *CanvasTextRenderer* and *CanvasAxisLabelRenderer*. Data are specified for each bar in the chart. You can specify data as an array of y values or as an array of [label, value] pairs. In Listing 5-17, note that labels are used only for the first series; labels for subsequent series will be ignored.

***Listing 5-17.*** Ch5_11.html

```
var bar1 = [['bananas', 10],['apples', 7],['pears', 4],
            ['peaches', 8],['lemons', 7],['oranges',5]];
var bar2 = [9, 5, 8, 11, 9, 4];
var bar3 = [11, 4, 7, 3, 8, 7];
var bar4 = [5, 8, 11, 4, 12, 3];
var barLabels = ['Italy', 'Spain', 'France', 'Greece'];
```

In options, you activate the *MekkoRenderer* plug-in, assigning it to the seriesDefaults object. You can add a legend on the right side of the chart by setting the show property of the legend object to 'true'. If you want to place labels for each bar below the x axis, you must assign the barLabels array to the barLabels property on the x axis.

***Listing 5-18.*** Ch5_11.html [no callout]

```
var options = {
    title: 'Fruit Consumption in 2012',
    seriesDefaults:{renderer: $.jqplot.MekkoRenderer},
    legend:{show: true},
    axesDefaults:{
        renderer: $.jqplot.MekkoAxisRenderer
    },
    axes:{
        xaxis:{
            barLabels: barLabels,
            tickOptions:{formatString: '%d'}
        }
    }
};

$.jqplot('myChart', [bar1, bar2, bar3, bar4], options);
```

Now, you get the Mekko chart illustrated in Figure 5-15.

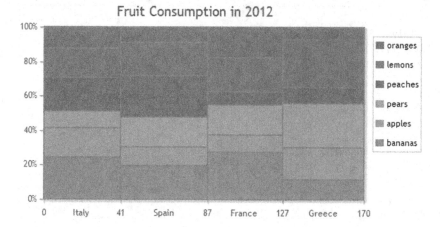

**Figure 5-15.** *A Mekko chart*

# Bar Chart Events

In a bar chart, if you move the cursor over a bar, it will be highlighted by default. Events are triggered when you mouse over a bar and also when you click a bar. The ability to capture these events and to manage them is very important, and the jqPlot library allows you to do so. You can implement a specific response action for different types of events, thus making your chart much more interactive. The response you obtain can depend on where you find the mouse pointer or which targets you click.

Table 5-1 reports events that, owing to their wealth of elements, lend themselves to application in a bar chart. Let us take a look at such events one by one.

**Table 5-1.** *Handling Events with the jqPlot Library*

| Event | When Triggered |
|---|---|
| jqplotDataClick | You click with the left mouse button on the data point. |
| jqplotRightClick | You click with the right mouse button on the data point. |
| jqplotDataMouseOver | You mouse over the data point. |
| jqplotDataHighlight | The data point is highlighted. |
| jqplotDataUnhighlight | The data point is unhighlighted. |

## The jqplotDataClick Event

This example presents the jqplotDataClick event—the clicked series index, the point, and its data values.
Let us start by considering the first example, the simple bar chart (see Listing 5-19).

**Listing 5-19.** Ch5_12.html

```
var data = [['Germany', 12], ['Italy', 8], ['Spain', 6],
            ['France', 10], ['UK', 7]];

var options = {
   title: 'Foreign Customers',
   series:[{renderer: $.jqplot.BarRenderer}],
   axes: {
      xaxis: {
         renderer: $.jqplot.CategoryAxisRenderer
      }
   }
};
$.jqplot ('myChart', [data], options);
```

Inside the jQuery ready() function, you add the function in Listing 5-20. This is a jQuery function in which you bind the jqplotDataClick event with the execution of a function. As argument, this event takes some values of attributes of the jqPlot object, such as seriesIndex, pointIndex, and data. These values will be converted into a string and concatenated with the jQuery html() function. This HTML text will be sent to the info1 element in the web page.

**Listing 5-20.** Ch5_12.html

```
$('#myChart').bind('jqplotDataClick',
    function (ev, seriesIndex, pointIndex, data) {
       $('#info1').html('series: ' + seriesIndex +
       ', point: '+pointIndex+', data: '+data);
    }
);
```

Now, you add a <span> element where you want to show the text with values. This element will show a "Nothing yet" message until you click a bar. Then, a new text will replace the message with values, depending on the point clicked:

```
<div><span>You clicked: </span><span id="info1">Nothing yet</span></div>
```

Figure 5-16 shows the message corresponding to the event triggered when the user clicks the "France" bar.

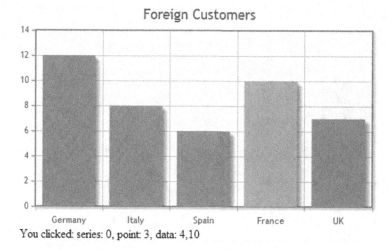

You clicked: series: 0, point: 3, data: 4,10

**Figure 5-16.** *By clicking a bar, you can obtain its values*

## The jqplotRightClick Event

This example covers another event that jqPlot provides: `jqplotRightClick`. This event requires an explicit activation in `options` (see Listing 5-21). This causes jqPlot to fire a `jqplotRightClick` event when the user right-clicks a bar.

**Listing 5-21.** Ch5_13.html

```
var options = {
    title: 'Foreign Customers',
    captureRightClick: true,
    series:[{renderer: $.jqplot.BarRenderer}],
    axes: {
      xaxis: {
          renderer: $.jqplot.CategoryAxisRenderer
      }
    }
};
```

Next, you need to replace the previous jqPlot function with the one in Listing 5-22.

**Listing 5-22.** Ch5_13.html

```
$('#myChart').bind('jqplotDataRightClick',
    function (ev, seriesIndex, pointIndex, data) {
        $('#info1').html('series: ' + seriesIndex +
        ', point: '+pointIndex+', data: '+data);
    }
);
```

The general effect is the same, but this time you have to right-click instead of left-click. Right-clicking the "Spain" bar gives you the result in Figure 5-17.

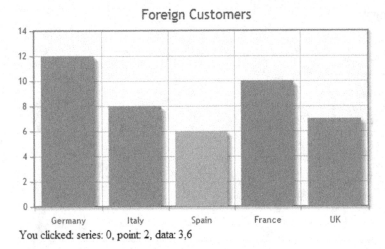

You clicked: series: 0, point: 2, data: 3,6

**Figure 5-17.** *By right-clicking a bar, you obtain its values*

## Other Bar Chart Events

Often, you may want to capture another event: when the cursor is moused over a bar, jqPlot fires a jqplotDataMouseOver event. This event is also generated when you have explicitly disabled the highlighting. The event will fire continuously as the user passes the mouse over the bar. In contrast, another event, jqplotDataHighlight, fires only once, when the user first passes the mouse over the bar. When the user moves out of a bar, jqPlot fires a third event: jqplotDataUnhighlight. These last two events are generated only if highlighting is enabled.

Continuing from the previous example (see Listing 5-22), you replace the jQuery function that captures the jqplotDataClick event with two other functions (see Listing 5-23). The first will send an HTML text to the info1 element with the same values as before as soon as you mouse over a bar. The second will replace the previous string in the info1 element with 'Nothing' just as you move out of the bar.

**Listing 5-23.** Ch5_14a.html

```
$('#myChart').bind('jqplotDataHighlight',
    function (ev, seriesIndex, pointIndex, data) {
        $('#info1').html('series: ' + seriesIndex +
        ', point: '+pointIndex+', data: '+data);
    }
);

$('#myChart').bind('jqplotDataUnhighlight',
    function (ev) {
        $('#info1').html('Nothing');
    }
);
```

Now, you want to see the difference in behavior between the jqplotDataMouseOver event and the jqPlotDataHighlight event. There is no better way to understand this difference than with an example that allows you to compare them. This time, you will count the number of events fired when you mouse over a bar. To do this, you define a counter, nEvents, initializing it to 0. As expected, with the jqPlotDataHighlight event, the counter is set to 1 whenever you mouse over a bar and assumes the value 0 when you move out of the bar. With the jqplotDataMouseOver event the behavior is very different: the counter increases continuously, keeping the cursor over the same bar. In both cases, you use the jqplotDataUnhighlight event to reset the counter every time you move out of a bar.

First, you need to change the info1 HTML element:

```
<div><span>Events: </span><span id="info1">Nothing yet</span></div>
```

Then, to study the behavior of the jqplotDataHighlight event, you replace the two jQuery functions with the two in Listing 5-24.

***Listing 5-24.*** Ch5_14b.html

```
nEvents = 0;
$('#myChart').bind('jqplotDataHighlight',
    function (ev, seriesIndex, pointIndex, data) {
        nEvents = nEvents + 1;
        $('#info1').html(nEvents);
    }
);

$('#myChart').bind('jqplotDataUnhighlight',
    function (ev) {
        $('#info1').html('Nothing');
        nEvents = 0;
    }
);
```

As presented in Figure 5-18, while keeping the mouse on the "Spain" bar, the counter gives a steady 1.

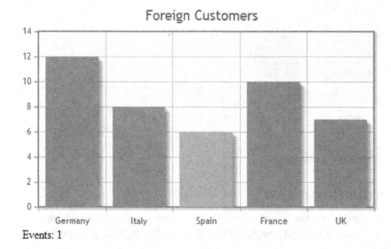

Events: 1

***Figure 5-18.*** *Counting how many jqPlotDataHighlight events occur*

To study the behavior of the jqplotDataMouseOver event, you replace the two jQuery functions with the two in Listing 5-25.

**Listing 5-25.** Ch5_14c.html

```
nEvents = 0;
$('#myChart').bind('jqplotDataMouseOver',
    function (ev, seriesIndex, pointIndex, data) {
        nEvents = nEvents + 1;
        $('#info1').html(nEvents);
    }
);

$('#myChart').bind('jqplotDataUnhighlight',
    function (ev) {
        $('#info1').html('Nothing');
        nEvents = 0;
    }
);
```

As shown in Figure 5-19, while keeping the mouse on the "Spain" bar, the counter continuously increases its value.

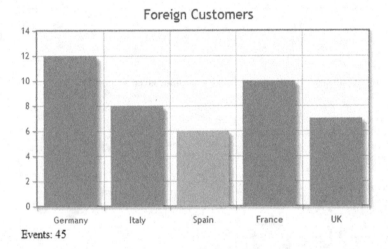

Events: 45

**Figure 5-19.** Counting how many jqplotDataMouseOver events occur

## Clicking the Bar to Show Information in Text

Because of jqPlot's potential in managing events, let us take the opportunity to look at a common case. By clicking a bar, you can get information about that bar and show it in a text box on the HTML page. This is made possible by binding a listener to the jqlotDataClick event.

For this example, you start with the code used to generate the horizontal stacked bar chart (see Listing 5-26).

***Listing 5-26.*** Ch5_15.html

```
var data = [12, 8, 6, 10, 7];
var data2 = [14, 12, 4, 14, 11];
var data3 = [18, 10, 5, 9, 9];
var ticks = ['Germany', 'Italy', 'Spain', 'France', 'UK'];

var options = {
    title: 'Foreign Customers',
    stackSeries: true,
    seriesDefaults:{
        renderer: $.jqplot.BarRenderer,
        pointLabels: { show: true, location: 's' }
    },
    series:[
        {label: 'Electronics'},
        {label: 'Software'},
        {label: 'Mechanics'}
    ],
    axes: {
        xaxis: {
            renderer: $.jqplot.CategoryAxisRenderer,
            ticks: ticks
        }
    },
    legend: {
        show: true,
        placement: 'outsideGrid',
        location: 'e'
    }
};
$.jqplot ('myChart', [data, data2, data3], options);
```

As in the previous examples for events, in the end you add a jQuery function that captures the jqplotDataClick event and that sends a set of information to the info1 element (see Listing 5-27).

***Listing 5-27.*** Ch5_15.html

```
$('#myChart').bind('jqplotDataClick',
    function (ev, seriesIndex, pointIndex, data) {
        $('#info1').html('series: ' + seriesIndex +
        ', point: '+pointIndex+', data: '+data);
    }
);
```

Whenever you click a bar, this function will refresh the information displayed where you have placed the <span> element with 'info1' as id. Here, you add the <span> element to the HTML page:

```
<span id="info1">Information will be provided here </span>
```

Now, by clicking the highlighted area of a bar, you get all the data relative to that bar in the text box, as seen in Figure 5-20.

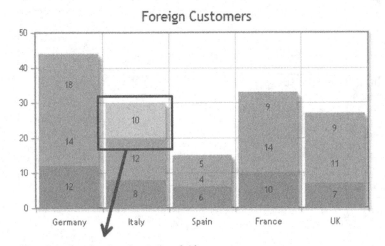

**Figure 5-20.** *By clicking a stacked bar, you obtain its values*

# Handling Legends

Working with bar charts, you made use of the legend, a key component of most charts. The legend is a defined element within jqPlot. Usually, you need only call the `legend` object in `options` to make the legend pop up next to your chart. Here, you will analyze this useful element in more detail.

When does using a legend become necessary? When you are dealing with multiseries data, that is, when you have a grouping of data, often distinguished by different colors. The legend does nothing but report in a small space the relationship that exists between each color and a label distinguishing the elements of the group.

## Adding a Legend

The previous example (see Figure 5-20) is perfect for studying legends. By observing the stacked chart, you can easily see that the bars for each country are made up of three portions, which are characterized by different colors. Thus, you understand that three series are represented in the chart. Furthermore, you also have information about the amount that each series contributes to the overall value, but still you lack crucial information: which categories are represented by which colors. By adding a legend, you will clarify the association between the three colors and these categories: "Mechanics," "Software," and "Electronics."

Therefore, continuing to work using the code from the previous example (see Listings 5-26 and 5-27), let us add the legend definition to the `options` object, as shown in Listing 5-28. To do this, you do not have to include any plug-ins; you need only set the `show` attribute to `'true'`.

**Listing 5-28.** Ch5_15.html

```
var options = {
    ...
    axes: {
        xaxis: {
            renderer: $.jqplot.CategoryAxisRenderer,
            ticks: ticks
        }
    },
```

```
    legend: {
        show: true,
        placement: 'outsideGrid',
        location: 'e'
    }
};
$.jqplot ('myChart', [data,data2,data3],options);
```

Figure 5-21 illustrates the chart with a legend.

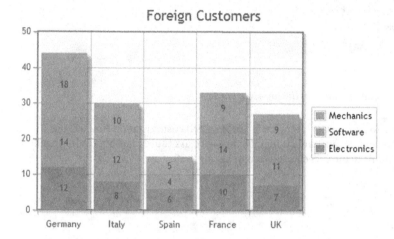

Information will be provided here

***Figure 5-21.*** *A stacked bar chart with a legend*

The placement attribute specifies where you want the legend; omitting it, you get the default behavior: the legend is drawn inside the chart. To avoid covering the bars, you can change the position of the legend by setting the location attribute, as given in Listing 5-29.

***Listing 5-29.*** Ch5_16a.html

```
legend: {
    show: true,
}
```

Thus, as Figure 5-22 shows, the chart is changed, with the legend drawn inside (by default), in the top-right corner ('ne' [northeast]).

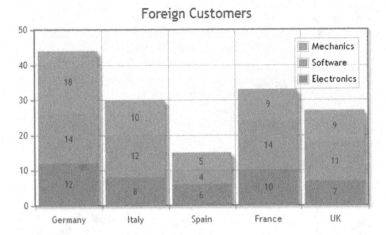

**Figure 5-22.** *The default legend position is inside the chart, in the top-right corner*

For a more thorough approach, it is best to use the Cascading Style Sheets (CSS) customization. You will use some CSS classes for the legend to modify the default attributes—mainly, the CSS class `table.jqplot-table-legend`.

For example, you can add the specifications to the CSS class offered in Listing 5-30.

**Listing 5-30.** Ch5_16b.html

```
<style>
    table.jqplot-table-legend {
        background-color: rgba(175, 175, 175, 1);
        font: "Arial Narrow";
        font-style: italic;
        font-size: 13pt;
        color: white;
    }
</style>
```

And, the legend will change, as demonstrated in Figure 5-23.

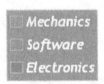

**Figure 5-23.** *The modified legend, using CSS styles*

# The Enhanced Legend

If you look at several plug-ins in the jqPlot distribution, you will find a plug-in related to legends: *EnhancedLegendRenderer*. This plug-in extends the functionalities of the legend: clicking the legend items, you can show or hide the corresponding series. You can see this with a concrete example. First, you include the plug-in in your web page:

```
<script type="text/javascript"
    src="../src/plugins/jqplot.enhancedLegendRenderer.min.js"></script>
```

Or, if you prefer to use a CDN service, you may do so as follows:

```
<script type="text/javascript" src="http://cdn.jsdelivr.net/jqplot/1.0.8/plugins↵
    /jqplot.enhancedLegendRenderer.min.js"></script>
```

Then, you must activate the plug-in in options in the same way you have done with other plug-ins, as presented in Listing 5-31.

***Listing 5-31.*** Ch5_16c.html

```
legend: {
    renderer: $.jqplot.EnhancedLegendRenderer,
    show: true,
    placement: 'outsideGrid',
    location: 'ne'
}
```

After you load the page in your browser, you get the chart in Figure 5-24. If you click an item from the legend, the corresponding series will disappear from the chart, leaving an empty space. This can be useful if you want to analyze only a subset of series, ignoring others. Let us therefore click "Software" in the legend and look at what happens.

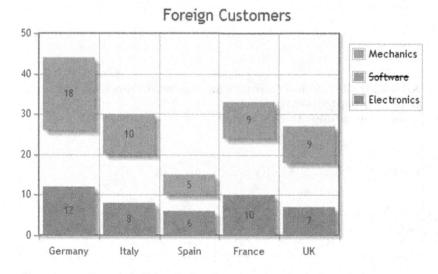

***Figure 5-24.*** *You can hide a series by selecting an item in the legend*

In the legend in Figure 5-24, the orange segments belonging to Software series have disappeared, and the item "Software" is stricken out.

This effect is cumulative, and you can hide all the series, one by one. If you click a strikeout item again, the corresponding series will appear once more in the chart.

## Custom Legend Highlighting

You have just seen how to use the legend that jqPlot provides by default. But, you can create a custom legend by implementing a simple table in HTML and then populating it dynamically, filling it with the labels for your series. Because you must start from scratch to create your own legend, it is first necessary to select a style. You can define the CSS style by using an external CSS file or writing the style directly in the web page, such as the one given in Listing 5-32.

***Listing 5-32.*** Ch5_17.html

```css
<style type="text/css">
table.sample {
    border-width: thin;
    border-spacing: 0px;
    border-style: outset;
    border-color: rgb(221, 221, 221);
    border-collapse: collapse;
}
table.sample th {
    border-width: 1px;
    padding: 1px;
    border-style: inset;
    border-color: gray;
}
table.sample td {
    border-width: 1px;
    padding: 1px;
    border-style: inset;
    border-color: gray;
}
</style>
```

You have used three different CSS classes. The first specifies the style for the entire table. The other two are defined to specify a specific style for the headings and the cells, respectively.

After defining the style, for our purposes, you can use the code of a simple bar chart (see Listing 5-33).

***Listing 5-33.*** Ch5_17.html

```javascript
var data = [['Germany', 12], ['Italy', 8], ['Spain', 6], ['France', 10], ['UK', 7]];

var options = {
    title: 'Foreign Customers',
    series:[{renderer:$.jqplot.BarRenderer}],
```

```
    axes: {
       xaxis: {
          renderer: $.jqplot.CategoryAxisRenderer
       }
    }
};
$.jqplot ('myChart', [data], options);
```

The next step to bind the custom legend to jqplotDataHighlight and jqplotDataUnhighlight events (see Listing 5-34). You have already seen these and how it is possible to bind an object to them using jQuery methods. In this case, you will do a lot more; you will ensure that the whole custom legend is dynamically created with only a few lines of jQuery. These will include the data array. Compared with the default legend offered by jqPlot, here you are able to obtain much more than the labels indicative of the groups' series membership. It is also possible to add summary values (using JavaScript functions) or simply the value of y.

**Listing 5-34.** Ch5_17.html

```
$(document).ready(function(){

    var data = ...
    var options = ...

    $.jqplot ('myChart', [data], options);

    $.each(data, function(index, val) {
       $('#legend1').append('<tr><td>'+val[0]+'</td><td>'+val[1]+'</td></tr>');
    });

    $('#myChart').bind('jqplotDataHighlight',
       function (ev, seriesIndex, pointIndex, data) {
          var color = 'rgb(100%, 90%, 50%)';
          $('#legend1 tr').css('background-color', '#ffffff');
          $('#legend1 tr').eq(pointIndex+1).css('background-color', color);
    });

    $('#myChart').bind('jqplotDataUnhighlight',
       function (ev, seriesIndex, pointIndex, data) {
          $('#legend1 tr').css('background-color', '#ffffff');
    });

});
```

The first jQuery function handles the values of the data array. The other two bind the legend to the highlighting events when you mouse over the legend items. Moreover, these functions also bind a variation in style attributes to these events, in this case, the background color of the item.

Now, you need to define two different areas in which to insert the chart and the legend. You can accomplish this using an HTML table. So, you add the code in Listing 5-35 to the <body> section of the HTML page.

**Listing 5-35.** Ch5_17.html

```
<table style="margin-left:auto; margin-right:auto;">
<tr>
    <td><div id="myChart" style="width:460px; height:340px;"></div></td>
    <td><div style="height:340px;">
        <table id="legend1" class="sample" >
            <tr><th>Nation</th><th>Customers</th></tr>
        </table>
    </div>
    </td>
</tr>
</table>
```

Finally, you can load the new page with the new custom legend (see Figure 5-25).

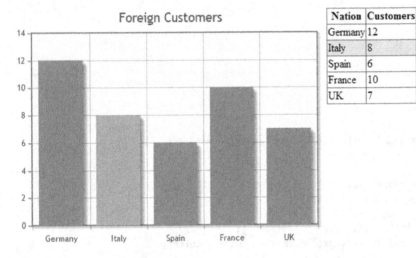

**Figure 5-25.** A custom HTML legend

# Custom Tool Tip

In addition to legends, another very commonly used item in the bar chart is the tool tip. Just as there is the possibility to create a custom legend using code, it is also possible to customize tool tips, creating very original effects. When you mouse over a bar and highlight it, a tool tip will be shown, but, different from the default jqPlot tool tip, this will be totally built in HTML format. This greatly expands your possibilities of artistic expression, giving your chart a touch of personality (using jqPlot, everything risks appearing too "standard jqPlot"). In this example, you would like to show how a small icon image can give a very nice effect to a bar chart.

Before starting to write code, let us create a directory, and name it flags (you can name it as you prefer). In this directory you will store all the portable network graphics (PNG) image files you are going to use. These icons are flags of nations, which you will report on the x axis of the bar chart. It is very easy to find and download these PNG files from the Internet.

■ **Note**    The PNG files required to show the flags in the tool tips are included in the source code accompanying the book, which you will find on the Source Code/Downloads tab of the book's Apress product page (www.apress.com/9781484208632).

When you have finished with the flag images, the first step is to create a custom tool tip. You need to bind tool tips to the jqplotDataHighlight and jqplotDataUnhighlight events. You can create custom tool tips dynamically with a few lines of jQuery.

Here, you start with the bar chart you have already used (see Listing 5-36), as it represents a simple example to understand the way to develop this kind of custom tool tip.

***Listing 5-36.*** Ch5_18.html

```
var data = [['Germany', 12], ['Italy', 8], ['Spain', 6], ['France', 10], ['UK', 7]];

var options = {
    title: 'Foreign Customers',
    series:[{renderer:$.jqplot.BarRenderer}],
    axes: {
      xaxis: {
          renderer: $.jqplot.CategoryAxisRenderer
      }
    }
};

$.jqplot ('myChart', [data], options);
```

You have to add two other arrays of data, containing some strings (see Listing 5-37). You will use these in the dynamically generated tool tip.

***Listing 5-37.*** Ch5_18.html

```
var tick = ['Germany', 'Italy', 'Spain', 'France', 'UK'];
var icon = ['germany.png', 'italy.png', 'spain.png', 'france.png', 'uk.png'];
```

You assign the return value of the jqplot() function to a variable, because you will need to use it later.

```
var myPlot = $.jqplot ('myChart', [data], options);
```

The jQuery code for binding the events to your custom tool tip is in Listing 5-38.

***Listing 5-38.*** Ch5_18.html

```
$('#myChart').bind('jqplotDataHighlight',
    function (ev, seriesIndex, pointIndex, data) {
        var chart_left = $('#myChart').offset().left;
        var chart_top = $('#myChart').offset().top;
        var x = data[0]*95+20;
        var y = myPlot.axes.yaxis.u2p(data[1]);
        var color = 'rgb(30%,50%,60%)';
        $('#tooltip1').css({left:chart_left+x, top:chart_top+y});
```

```
        $('#tooltip1').html('<span style="font-size:16px; font-weight:bold; color:' +
            color + ';">' + tick[data[0] - 1] +
            '</span><br/><img src="flags/'+ icon[data[0] - 1]+
            '" width="30" height="20"><br/> n:' + data[1]);
        $('#tooltip1').show();
    }
);

$('#myChart').bind('jqplotDataUnhighlight',
    function (ev, seriesIndex, pointIndex, data) {
        $('#tooltip1').empty();
        $('#tooltip1').hide();
    }
);
```

Finally, you must create two `<div>` elements in the `<body>` section of the web page, as in Listing 5-39. In the first element, jqPlot will generate your custom tool tip on the canvas; in the second, jqPlot will create the canvas drawing the bar chart.

***Listing 5-39.*** Ch5_18.html

```
<div id="myChart" style="height:300px; width:500px;"></div>
<div id="tooltip1" style="position:absolute; height:0px; width:0px;"></div>
```

Figure 5-26 shows the "Germany" bar highlighted with the customized tool tip beside it. This will happen for all the bars in the bar chart, each showing the corresponding flag in the tool tip, every time the user highlights them by mousing over.

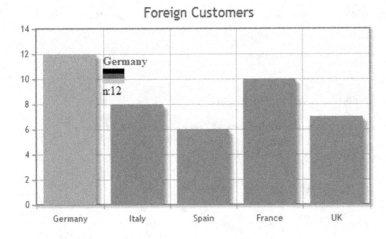

***Figure 5-26.*** *A bar chart with custom tool tips*

# Summary

In this chapter, you have seen how your data can be represented in a bar chart, using the *BarRenderer* plug-in. You began to see how, with the inclusion of this renderer plug-in, the structure of the main jqPlot object is gradually enriched with new properties and objects. Through practical examples, you learned how to change the values of property and object attributes with rendererOptions.

You also learned that it is sometimes possible to obtain different representations, using the same set of data. Knowing how to choose which representation is more suitable to your needs is one of the fundamental objectives of this book. For this purpose, you used the same set of data, both in a **grouped bar chart** and in a **stacked bar chart**. In both cases, you realized data representations with vertical and horizontal bars.

Later in this chapter, you looked at examples that demonstrated how jqPlot allows you to deal with **events**, using special functions. In addition, you further examined the **legend** component and the possibility of customizing legends using HTML code. Then, you applied the same approach to **tool tips**.

Often, the type of data that requires a bar chart representation may also be well represented by means of another type of chart: the **pie chart**. In the next chapter, you will discover how the jqPlot library handles this type of chart.

# CHAPTER 6

■ ■ ■

# Pie Charts and Donut Charts with jqPlot

Pie charts and donut charts are an excellent way to show the breakdown of data into their constituent parts. A pie chart is a circular chart divided into sectors, or "slices," and its main purpose is to illustrate their relative proportions: the arc length of each slice is proportional to the quantity it represents. A donut chart is very similar to a pie chart but has a hole in the center and supports the comparison of multiple series. In this chapter, you will look at both kinds of charts. The chapter concludes with a discussion of multidimentionsional pie charts.

## Pie Charts

In jqPlot, data are interpreted as a line chart by default. If you want to show your data in a pie chart, you need to include the *PieRenderer* plug-in:

```
<script type="text/javascript" src="../src/plugins/jqplot.pieRenderer.min.js">
</script>
```

Or, if you prefer to use a content delivery network (CDN) service, you can do so as follows:

```
<script type="text/javascript" src="http://cdn.jsdelivr.net/jqplot/1.0.8/plugins
    /jqplot.pieRenderer.min.js"></script>
```

To better understand the use of this plug-in, let us take, for example, the amount of food a person consumes in a given period of time. This is a case in which a pie chart proves to be the best choice for data representation. All the food eaten makes up the whole group, and the various types of foods are the components you want to compare. Each type of food will be represented by a slice identified by means of a different color. The size of each slice will give a precise idea of the proportion that food type occupies in the diet of a person. You can start with a data array of [label, amount] pairs of values, as shown in Listing 6-1.

***Listing 6-1.*** Ch6_01a.html

```
var data = [ ['Dairy', 212],['Meat', 140], ['Grains', 276],
            ['Fish', 131],['Vegetables', 510], ['Fruit', 325] ];
```

Now, you can define the options. As you can see in Listing 6-2, you need to activate the plug-in and apply it to the defaultSeries object.

**Listing 6-2.** Ch6_01a.html

```
var options = {
    seriesDefaults: {
        renderer: jQuery.jqplot.PieRenderer,
        rendererOptions: {
          showDataLabels: true
       }
     }
};


$.jqplot ('myChart', [data], options);
```

Figure 6-1 shows a simple pie chart without specification of additional attributes.

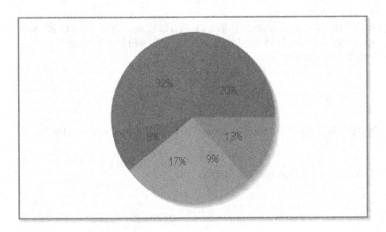

**Figure 6-1.** A simple pie chart

As demonstrated in Figure 6-1, inside its sectors the pie chart reports the percentage by default. If, instead, you want to display the value, as shown at the top right of Figure 6-2, you need to set 'value' on the dataLabels property in renderOptions, as given in Listing 6-3.

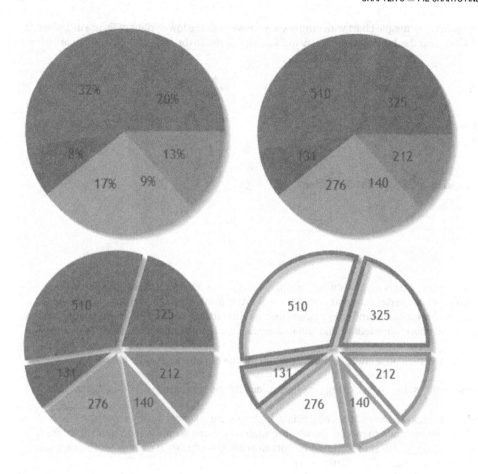

**Figure 6-2.** *Different ways to set a pie chart*

**Listing 6-3.** Ch6_01b.html

```
rendererOptions: {
    showDataLabels: true,
    dataLabels: 'value'
}
```

If you want to add a margin to separate the slices of the pie, as illustrated in the lower-left of Figure 6-2, we need to set the sliceMargin property to 6 (see Listing 6-4).

**Listing 6-4.** Ch6_01c.html

```
rendererOptions: {
    showDataLabels: true,
    dataLabels: 'value',
    sliceMargin: 6
}
```

Furthermore, if you want to show the pie chart with empty slices, as seen in the lower-right of Figure 6-2, you can set the fill property to 'false' and the lineWidth property to 5 in order to shade the slices, with lines that are a little thicker (see Listing 6-5).

***Listing 6-5.*** Ch6_01d.html

```
rendererOptions: {
    showDataLabels: true,
    dataLabels: 'value',
    sliceMargin: 6,
    fill: false,
    // stroke the slices with a little thicker line.
    lineWidth: 5
}
```

# Donut Charts

One of the main problems with pie charts is their inability to display multiple series simultaneously. Hence, you must decide whether to represent each series separately, with a pie chart or, preferably, to use a donut (also spelled "doughnut") chart. This kind of chart requires and uses options that are identical to those of pie charts; therefore, the transition from pie chart to donut chart is immediate.You will look at the simplicity of such a transition with an easy example.

First, as with the pie chart, you need to include a specific plug-in in order to obtain a donut chart:

```
<script type="text/javascript" src="../src/plugins/jqplot.donutRenderer.min.js"> </script>
```

The only change you have to make in the options object is to replace the pieRenderer object with DonutRenderer in the renderer call and then to modify the starting angle of the first sector in the rendererOptions object. By default the chart starts on the left side of the circle, but normally it must start at the top. So, it is necessary to set the startAngle property to –90 degrees (see Listing 6-6).

***Listing 6-6.*** Ch6_02.html

```
var options = {
    seriesDefaults: {
    // Make this a pie chart.
        renderer:$.jqplot.DonutRenderer,
        rendererOptions: {
            showDataLabels: true,
            dataLabels: 'value',
            sliceMargin: 3,
            startAngle: -90
        }
    }
};
jQuery.jqplot ('myChart', [data], options);
```

In this way, you get a donut chart (see Figure 6-3), which is very similar to the pie chart in the lower right of Figure 6-2.

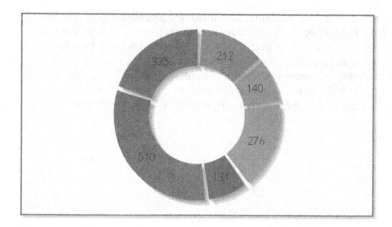

**Figure 6-3.** *A simple donut chart*

But, we choose to use a donut chart instead of a pie chart because it allows us to represent multiple series at the same time and thus to compare the proportions of its components. Therefore, to continue with the example, you can compare the food consumed by two different groups of people. Listing 6-7 illustrates how to add another data array.

**Listing 6-7.** Ch6_02.html

```
var data2 = [
    ['Dairy', 185],['Meat', 166], ['Grains', 243],
    ['Fish', 166],['Vegetables', 499], ['Fruit', 370]
];
```

Adding this second array to data, you modify the listing:

```
$.jqplot ('myChart', [data, data2], options);
```

Figure 6-4 presents the donut chart reporting the two series of values.

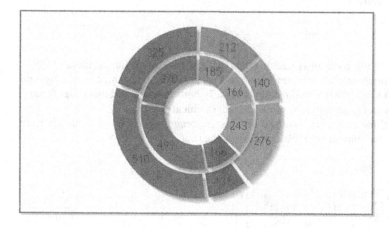

**Figure 6-4.** *A multiseries donut chart*

Looking at Figure 6-4, you can see at once that something fundamental is missing: a legend. A legend is required because the plug-in automatically assigns a color to each sector, and so without a color reference, it is very hard to understand the chart. Hence, after you set the show property of the legend to 'true', you can select the location of the legend. To determine in which position to place the legend, jqPlot uses the location property, to which values corresponding to the cardinal directions are assigned: 'n' (north),'s' (south), 'e' (east), and 'w' (west). But, it is also possible to use a combination, for instance, 'ne', to indicate the northeast position.

Let us say you decide to locate the legend on the right side of the chart, so you assign 'e' to the location property (see Listing 6-8).

*Listing 6-8.* Ch6_02.html

```
legend: {
    show:true,
    location: 'e'
}
```

The legend automatically reports the labels contained in the data arrays, as displayed in Figure 6-5.

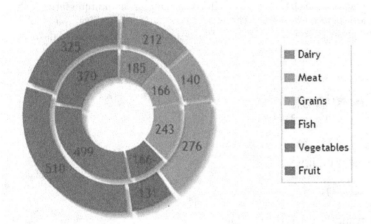

*Figure 6-5.* *A multiseries donut chart with a legend*

# Multilevel Pie Charts

The multilevel pie chart is a modern format that is good for visualizing data that are used for displaying hierarchical relationships. This kind of chart offers a hierarchical structure, starting from a root node in the center of the circle, and you can follow the memberships as they gradually move into the outer circles. To better understand this kind of chart, let us take as an example a series of animals and gradually determine their hierarchical groups.

As input data array, you want to insert three arrays (see Listing 6-9). This will generate three levels of hierarchy. In the first array, you insert the last level, up to the third array, which represents the root.

*Listing 6-9.* Ch6_03.html

```
var data = [ ['Cat', 1],['Dog', 1], ['Mouse', 1],['Snake', 1],
    ['Turtle', 1], ['Jellyfish', 1], ['Cuttlefish', 1] ];
var data2 = [ ['Mammals', 3],['Reptiles', 2], ['Mollusks', 2] ];
var data3 = [ ['Vertebrates', 5],['Invertebrates', 2] ];
```

To generate a multilevel pie chart, you actually need to modify a donut chart, setting the diameter of the inner hole to zero. Instead of displaying a numerical value, in this case you need to show the name of the animal or animal group represented by the label; you must set the dataLabels property to 'label'. The last thing to modify is the set of colors. The default colors provided by jqPlot are not adequate, and it is necessary to define a set of colors for each level of the hierarchy.It is preferable to assign similar colors to animals belonging to the same group and to do likewise for the successive levels of the hierarchy. In Listing 6-10, special attention is paid to the sequence of colors that are assigned to each series (hierarchical level).

*Listing 6-10.* Ch6_03.html

```
var options = {
    seriesDefaults: {
        renderer:$.jqplot.DonutRenderer,
        rendererOptions: {
            showDataLabels: true,
            dataLabels: 'label',
            startAngle: -90,
            innerDiameter: 0,
            ringMargin: 2,
            shadow: false
        }
    },
    series: [
    {
        seriesColors: ['#4bb2c5', '#4baacc', '#4b88aa', '#bbb2c5',
                       '#bbaa99', '#c5dd99', '#dddd77']
    },
    {
        seriesColors:  ['#4bbbbb', '#ccb2c5', '#c5ff99']
    },
    {
        seriesColors:  ['#aa5555', '#a3ffaa']
    }]
};

$.jqplot ('myChart', [data, data2, data3], options);
```

In the end, your efforts are rewarded with the multilevel pie chart in Figure 6-6.

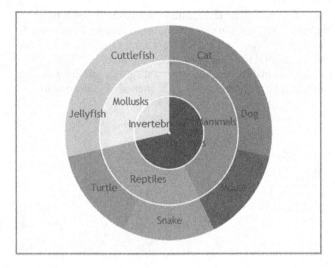

***Figure 6-6.*** *A multilevel pie chart*

## Summary

In this chapter, you have seen how the jqPlot library allows you to represent your data by means of a **pie chart** (with a single series of data) or with a **donut chart** (with multiples series of data) while also obtaining a quick overview of some of the main properties and how to set them in options. In the last part of the chapter, you created a **multilevel pie chart**: a classic example of how you can generate a type of chart that is not among the standard charts proposed by the library by modifying certain properties appropriately.

In the next chapter, you will see how the jqPlot library lets you realize **candlestick charts** and how to handle the particular data format **open-high-low-close (OHLC),** which is the basis of this kind of chart.

■ ■ ■

# CHAPTER 7

# Candlestick Charts with jqPlot

Candlestick charts are widely used in the analysis of a currency over time or of price movements. This chart consists of a series of vertical bars, called **candlesticks**. They show the opening, closing, lowest, and highest price in a given time period (see Figure 7-1). For this reason, this kind of chart is often called an **OHLC chart** (when it reports open-high-low-close values) or an **HLC chart** (when it reports onlyhigh-low-close values).

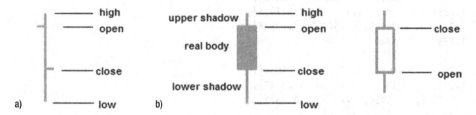

**Figure 7-1.** *Different ways to represent OHLC data: (a) line, (b) real body*

Candlesticks may be depicted as simple lines or as boxes (called real body) with lines at the ends (called wicks or shadows). The height of each candlestick indicates the price range for a given period. In a box representation the real body is the area between the opening and closing price.If, however, the candlestick is represented by a simple vertical line, two small horizontal ticks indicate the opening (tick to the left) and closing (tick to the right) price. In addition, in candlestick charts, data plots are colored differently, according to whether prices rise or fall.

In this chapter, you will see how particular OHLC data can be represented. You will also learn how to format such charts with either lines or real bodies. First, though, you need to include the *OHLCRenderer* plug-in.

## OHLC Charts

To enable jqPlot to draw candlestick charts, you must include a specific plug-in in your web page: *OHLCRenderer*.

You need to include the *DateAxisRenderer* plug-in as well, because in candlestick charts, you usually place date values on the x axis:

```
<script type="text/javascript" src="../src/plugins/jqplot.dateAxisRenderer.min.js">
</script>
<script type="text/javascript" src="../src/plugins/jqplot.ohlcRenderer.min.js">
</script>
```

In regard to the input data array, you have to respect a specific order:
['timestamp', open, max, min, close]

For this example, you are using a set of real data available online. The data are taken from a comma-separated values (CSV) file generated by a free tool, called Dukascopy, which is also available online (www.dukascopy.com). You choose euro–US dollar exchange values from a period of approximately one month in 2012. Let us assign all these values to a variable, as in Listing 7-1.

***Listing 7-1.*** Ch7_01a.html

```
var ohlc = [
['8/08/2012 0:00:01', 1.238485, 1.2327, 1.240245, 1.23721],
['8/09/2012 0:00:01', 1.23721, 1.22671, 1.23873, 1.229295],
['8/10/2012 0:00:01', 1.2293, 1.22417, 1.23168, 1.228975],
['8/12/2012 0:00:01', 1.229075, 1.22747, 1.22921, 1.22747],
['8/13/2012 0:00:01', 1.227505, 1.22608, 1.23737, 1.23262],
['8/14/2012 0:00:01', 1.23262, 1.23167, 1.238555, 1.232385],
['8/15/2012 0:00:01', 1.232385, 1.22641, 1.234355, 1.228865],
['8/16/2012 0:00:01', 1.22887, 1.225625, 1.237305, 1.23573],
['8/17/2012 0:00:01', 1.23574, 1.22891, 1.23824, 1.2333],
['8/19/2012 0:00:01', 1.23522, 1.23291, 1.235275, 1.23323],
['8/20/2012 0:00:01', 1.233215, 1.22954, 1.236885, 1.2351],
['8/21/2012 0:00:01', 1.23513, 1.23465, 1.248785, 1.247655],
['8/22/2012 0:00:01', 1.247655, 1.24315, 1.254415, 1.25338],
['8/23/2012 0:00:01', 1.25339, 1.252465, 1.258965, 1.255995],
['8/24/2012 0:00:01', 1.255995, 1.248175, 1.256665, 1.2512],
['8/26/2012 0:00:01', 1.25133, 1.25042, 1.252415, 1.25054],
['8/27/2012 0:00:01', 1.25058, 1.249025, 1.25356, 1.25012],
['8/28/2012 0:00:01', 1.250115, 1.24656, 1.257695, 1.2571],
['8/29/2012 0:00:01', 1.25709, 1.251895, 1.25736, 1.253065],
['8/30/2012 0:00:01', 1.253075, 1.248785, 1.25639, 1.25097],
['8/31/2012 0:00:01', 1.25096, 1.249375, 1.263785, 1.25795],
['9/02/2012 0:00:01', 1.257195, 1.256845, 1.258705, 1.257355],
['9/03/2012 0:00:01', 1.25734, 1.25604, 1.261095, 1.258635],
['9/04/2012 0:00:01', 1.25865, 1.25264, 1.262795, 1.25339],
['9/05/2012 0:00:01', 1.2534, 1.250195, 1.26245, 1.26005],
['9/06/2012 0:00:01', 1.26006, 1.256165, 1.26513, 1.26309],
['9/07/2012 0:00:01', 1.26309, 1.262655, 1.281765, 1.281625],
['9/09/2012 0:00:01', 1.28096, 1.27915, 1.281295, 1.279565],
['9/10/2012 0:00:01', 1.27957, 1.27552, 1.28036, 1.27617],
['9/11/2012 0:00:01', 1.27617, 1.2759, 1.28712, 1.28515],
['9/12/2012 0:00:01', 1.28516, 1.281625, 1.29368, 1.290235] ];
```

In options you activate the *OHLCRenderer* plug-in by calling it on the series object. Because you need to handle date values on the x axis, you must activate the dateAxisRenderer object in the xaxis object. With this type of chart, it is better to define the period of time you want to represent, regardless of the input data, in order to have more precise control over what is displayed. To this end, you specify the min and max properties in xaxis object. You can also see that with dateAxisRenderer, you can choose the tick interval, using literal expressions ('1 day', 'n days', '1 week', 'n weeks', '1 month', 'n months', where n is any integer greater than 1). Furthermore, note that yaxis has not been defined or rather that y values have been attributed to y2axis. This has been done in order that the y axis be situated on the right edge of the chart rather than the default left edge (see Listing 7-2).

*Listing 7-2.* ch12_01a.html

```
var options = {
    title: 'EUR-USD Exchange',
    seriesDefaults:{ yaxis: 'y2axis'},
    axes: {
        xaxis: {
            renderer: $.jqplot.DateAxisRenderer,
            tickOptions: {formatString: '%b %e'},
            min: "08-07-2012 16:00",
            max: "09-12-2012 16:00",
            tickInterval: "1 weeks"
        },
        y2axis: {
            tickOptions:{ formatString: '$%.2f'}
        }
    },
    series: [{ renderer: $.jqplot.OHLCRenderer}]
};

$.jqplot('myChart', [ohlc], options);
```

You now have the OHLC chart shown in Figure 7-2.

*Figure 7-2.* *An OHLC chart with lines*

Insofar as you had integers, you represented them just as they are entered in the input data array. But, this is not always possible. Often, you must deal with numbers that have many digits after the decimal point and that are not of the same length. It is therefore necessary to standardize these numbers, reporting only the significant digits. You can accomplish this by setting the formatString property. This particular case requires a float value with two decimal points: '%.2f'.

# Using Real Bodies and Shadows

The candlestick chart you have just seen is formatted with bar lines. If you want a box representation, with real bodies and shadows, you need to set an additional property: the candlestick (see Listing 7-3).

*Listing 7-3.* ch12_01b.html

```
series: [{
    renderer: $.jqplot.OHLCRenderer,
    rendererOptions:{ candleStick: true }
}]
```

Now, let us look at the real bodies that replace the horizontal ticks on bar lines. In Figure 7-3 the white boxes indicate when the price rises (the opening price is lower than the closing price), black boxes, when the price falls (the closing price is lower than the opening price).

*Figure 7-3.* *An OHLC chart with boxes*

# Comparing Candlesticks

Ocassionally, you will need to compare candlesticks representing different categories at particular time. In such cases, you do not have dates on the x axis, but the names of the subjects themselves. The input data array will be different; you must separate the OHLC data, using the labels of the categories from which they were taken. For each entity, you insert an array with five values:

[n, open, max, min, close]

Here, instead of the timestamp, n is an integer corresponding to the index of the tick array. Thus, you define these OHLC values in the data1 array, as shown in Listing 7-4. In the ticks array, you use four different labels to indicate each of the four OHLC values.

*Listing 7-4.* Ch7_02.html

```
var data1 = [[1, 75, 80, 40, 55], [2, 30, 60, 15, 50],
            [3, 64, 75, 48, 50], [4, 67, 78, 20, 36]];
var ticks = ['Apple', 'Ubuntu', 'Microsoft', 'Android'];
```

You replace the call to the *DateAxisRenderer* plug-in with one to the *CategoryAxisRenderer* plug-in:

```
<script type="text/javascript" src="../src/plugins/jqplot.categoryAxisRenderer.min.js">
</script>
<script type="text/javascript" src="../src/plugins/jqplot.ohlcRenderer.min.js">
</script>
```

As you can see in Listing 7-5, the settings in options are very simple. First, you have to replace $.jqplot.DateAxisRenderer with $.jqplot.CategoryAxisRenderer in the renderer property. Furthermore, you assign the ticks array to the ticks object in the xaxis.

***Listing 7-5.*** Ch7_02.html

```
var options = {
    axes: {
       xaxis: {
           renderer: $.jqplot.CategoryAxisRenderer,
           ticks: ticks
       },
    },
    series: [{
       renderer: $.jqplot.OHLCRenderer,
       rendererOptions:{ candleStick: true}
    }]
};

$.jqplot ('myChart', [data1], options);
```

This chart gives a perfect picture of a box representation with real bodies; the box is filled when the price falls and empty when the price rises (see Figure 7-4).

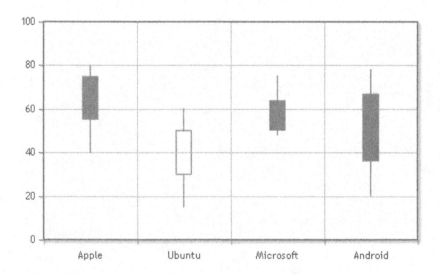

***Figure 7-4.*** *A comparative candlestick chart*

# Summary

In this chapter, you have seen how, by means of a **candlestick chart,** particular **OHLC** data can be represented. You have also learned how to format such charts with either lines or real bodies.

In the next chapter, I will discuss a whole class of charts sharing a common feature: their aim is to represent a **distribution** of data. Through this exploration, you will discover how to realize **scatter charts**, **bubble charts**, and **block plots** with the jqPlot library.

■ ■ ■

# CHAPTER 8

# Scatter Charts and Bubble Charts with jqPlot

In this chapter, I will discuss a category of charts that are particularly useful when representing a data distribution. It is likely you will often find yourself interested in how a set of data is distributed along the space defined by two different parameters, shown along the x axis and y axis. Such data distribution can suggest correlation or clustering.

The scatter chart is the best choice for the display of data distribution, especially when a large set of data needs to be analyzed. Thus, you will first learn how to realize this kind of chart, using a simple example. Subsequently, you will see how, once two different data groups (clusters) are defined, it is possible to highlight correlations between the x and y variables via trend lines.

Finally, you will analyze two other types of charts: bubble charts and block charts. These may be considered variations of the scatter chart—variations in which data points are replaced with bubbles or blocks. Bubble charts are used when you need to represent data with three different parameters (the scatter chart works only with two); the third parameter is represented by the radius of the bubble. The block chart, is a particular kind of scatter chart, in which, instead of data points, you use a box containing a label.

## Scatter Chart (xy Chart)

At first glance, you might think that a scatter chart (also called a scatter plot or xy chart) is a line chart in which the points are not connected, but this would be a mistake. In fact, scatter charts, along with bubble charts and block charts, are a particular type of chart. In a scatter chart, points are represented by the (x, y) pair, but you can get many points with the same x value, making it both difficult and unnecessary to join them with a line. The purpose of a line chart is to follow the progress of a y value in the range of an x value. The purpose of a scatter chart is to display a collection of points that may or may not have some sort of relationship (which can be nonlinear). Furthermore, you may want to analyze these points and their distribution in an (x, y) space, as when, for example, they are distributed in spatially separate groups.

You use the default settings (as in a line chart), disabling the line between the points. Let us take, for instance, two collections of (x, y) data that may present some form of relationship, as shown in Listing 8-1.

***Listing 8-1.*** Ch8_04a.html

```
var data = [[400, 35], [402, 37], [650, 55], [653, 56], [650, 50],
           [700, 55], [600, 37], [601, 43], [450, 38], [473, 37],
           [480, 42], [417, 37], [510, 41], [553, 44], [570, 39],
           [527, 41], [617, 41], [625, 49]];
var data2 = [[100, 40], [600, 80], [200, 50], [300, 55], [400, 60],
            [500, 70], [123, 43], [110, 41], [157, 45], [160, 48],
            [237, 49], [248, 55], [287, 50], [321, 59], [359, 52],
            [387, 62], [466, 68], [533, 74], [344, 60], [323, 51],
            [430, 65]];
```

The points that you have entered do not follow any order, unlike those in a line chart. As previously stated, you use the default settings, disabling the lines between the points by setting the showLine property to 'false' (see Listing 8-2).

***Listing 8-2.*** Ch8_04a.html (Disabling the lines between the points using 'false')

```
var options = {
    title: 'Scatter Chart',
    seriesDefaults: {
        showLine: false,
        showMarkers: true
    }
};
$.jqplot ('myChart', [data, data2], options);
```

You thus obtain the scatter chart in Figure 8-1, in which the two collections of data cover two different areas of the chart. The points are divided into well-defined groups.

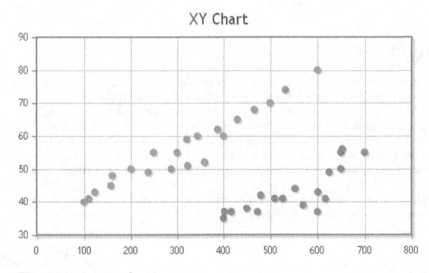

***Figure 8-1.*** *A scatter chart*

Only once the two data collections are represented does it makes sense to determine whether they follow a linear or exponential trend. Here, you can use the trend line functionality of jqPlot. You therefore include the *Trendline* plug-in:

```
<script type="text/javascript" src="../src/plugins/jqplot.trendline.min.js"></script>
```

Or, if you prefer to use a content delivery network (CDN) service, you may do so as follows:

```
<script type="text/javascript" src="http://cdn.jsdelivr.net/jqplot/1.0.8/plugins/jqplot.trendline.
min.js"></script>
```

Then, activate the *Trendline* plug-in for both series, assigning each line a different color (see Listing 8-3).

***Listing 8-3.*** Ch8_04b.html

```
var options = {
    title: 'Scatter Chart',
    seriesDefaults: {
        showLine: false,
        showMarkers: true
    },
    series: [{
        trendline: {
            show: true,
            color: '#0000ff',
            type: 'exponential'
        }
    },{
        trendline: {
            show: true,
            color: '#ff0000'
        }
    }]
};
```

As a result, you get a scatter chart with two different series, each with its own trend line, as illustrated in Figure 8-2.

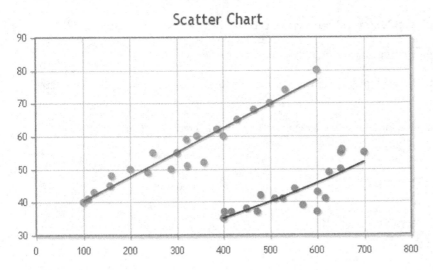

**Figure 8-2.** *A scatter chart with trend lines*

# Bubble Chart

You use a bubble chart when you need to display data in three dimensions. Each entity is therefore represented by a triplet (v1, v2, v3) of independent values. Two of these values are expressed by plotting a disk with an (x, y) point as center. The third value is expressed by the disk radius (r). Hence, the (v1, v2, v3) triplet must be converted to (x, y, r). Which of the three (v1, v2, v3) values is the radius and which is x or y depends on the skill of the chart designer.

Similar to xy charts, bubble charts are often used to identify probable relationships between the data represented or even to see whether they fall into different groups. Such an approach is commonly found in scientific, medical, and economic data analysis.

There is a specific plug-in for bubble charts in jqPlot: *BubbleRenderer*. It is therefore necessary to include this plug-in in your web page:

```
<script type="text/javascript" src="../src/plugins/jqplot.bubbleRenderer.min.js"></script>
```

Or, if you prefer to use a CDN service, you may do so as follows:

```
<script type="text/javascript" src="http://cdn.jsdelivr.net/jqplot/1.0.8/plugins/jqplot.
bubbleRenderer.min.js"></script>
```

The input data array has four values per item:
[x, y, radius, <label or object>]

The first two values represent the (x, y) coordinates, the third value (pay attention!) is proportional to the radius of the bubble, and the last value represents the reference label (you can actually pass an object, too; more on this in a moment). Listing 8-4 defines an array containing characteristic values of seven European nations: as a value for x, you will insert the surface area; for y, the population; and the radius will represent an economic value. The fourth value is a label reporting the name of the state.

***Listing 8-4.*** Ch8_01a.html

```
var data = [[301,60,29392,"Italy"], [675,65,34205,"France"],
            [506,46,30625,"Spain"], [357,81,37896,"Germany"],
            [450,9,37333,"Sweden"], [30,11,37736,"Belgium"],
            [132,11,27624,"Greece"]]];
```

Now, let us analyze how to set the options variable (see Listing 8-5). You need to activate the *BubbleRenderer* plug-in in the seriesDefault object and set the bubbleGradients property to 'true'. This will fill the "bubbles" with a color gradient, giving a sense of depth: the disks are thus made to appear as if they were spheres. As you can see, for this plug-in, you do not need to create an array containing labels for the bubbles and then assign it explicitly to an object in options; the labels are automatically read by the same input data array.The settings to be specified in options are few and simple.

***Listing 8-5.*** Ch8_01a.html (Setting the options variable)

```
var options = {
    title: 'Bubble Chart with Gradient Fills',
    seriesDefaults: {
        renderer: $.jqplot.BubbleRenderer,
        rendererOptions: {
            bubbleGradients: true
        },
        shadow: true
    },
    axes: {
        xaxis: {
            label: "Total area [*1000 km3]"
        },
        yaxis: {
            label: "Population [million]"
        }
    }
};

$.jqplot ('myChart', [data], options);
```

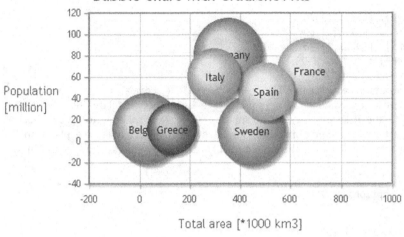

**Figure 8-3.** *A bubble chart*

Finally, with these few rows of code, you get the wonderful bubble chart shown in Figure 8-3.

Earlier, we I mentioned the possibility of passing an object as the fourth value in the input data array. Here, you can see in detail what this involves. You can pass, simultaneously, an object that allows you to define both the label and the color to be attributed to each individual element (bubble). Using the previous example (see Listing 8-5), you attach colors that are different from those of the default sequence. For example, let us say you want to emphasize the value of one country over that of the others. You take Sweden and assign it the color red. You assign the other countries various shades of brown. You then move the Sweden data to a new array, data2; this is to ensure that the "Sweden" bubble is always in the foreground and that it is not overlapped by other bubbles (see Listing 8-6).

**Listing 8-6.** Ch8_02.html

```
var data = [[301, 60, 29392, {label: 'Italy',color:'#b39524'}],
            [675, 65, 34205, {label: 'France', color:'#c39564'}],
            [506, 46, 30625, {label: 'Spain',color:'#a39544'}],
            [357, 81, 37896, {label: 'Germany', color:'#b39524'}],
            [30, 11, 37736, {label: 'Belgium',color:'#c39544'}],
            [132, 11, 27624, {label: 'Greece', color:'#a39564'}]];
var data2 = [[450, 9, 37333, {label: 'Sweden', color:'#ff2524'}]];
```

Using the same options, you need only modify the jqplot() function, as shown in Listing 8-7. You take this smallshortcut, knowing that the rightmost array item is the one that will be drawn last and that it will, consequently, appear in the foreground.

**Listing 8-7.** Ch8_02.html (modifying the jqplot() function)

```
$.jqplot ('myChart',[data, data2], options);
```

Figure 8-4 presents the result.

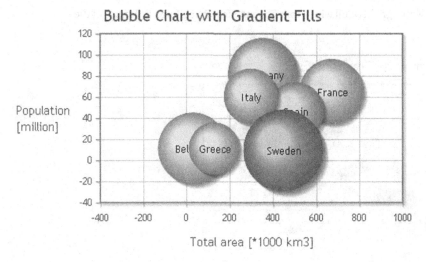

**Figure 8-4.** *A bubble chart with a selected state in the foreground*

The default sequence of colors suits you fine here, but you decide to change the gradient fill to a transparent effect. To accomplish this, you must add the bubbleAlpha property and assign the desired value of transparency to it, as demonstrated in Listing 8-8.

**Listing 8-8.** *Ch8_01b.html*

```
seriesDefaults: {
    renderer: $.jqplot.BubbleRenderer,
    rendererOptions: {
        bubbleGradients: true,
        bubbleAlpha: 0.6
    },
    shadow: true
},
```

Figure 8-5 shows the bubbles with a gradient fill with a transparent effect that affords a glimpse of the underlying bubbles.

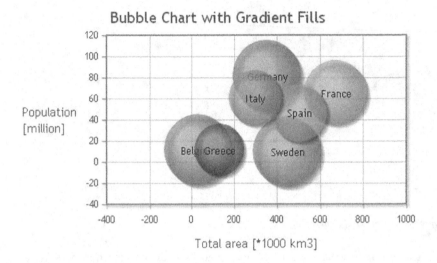

**Figure 8-5.** *A bubble chart with transparency*

# Block Chart

A block chart (also called a block plot) is very similar to the bubble chart, but instead of disks, it uses rectangles. Here, the size of the rectangles has no significance except to provide space for those in which a label is applied to a given (x, y) pair.

As with the bubble chart, it is necessary to include the *BlockRenderer* plug-in in the web page:

```
<script type="text/javascript" src="../src/plugins/jqplot.blockRenderer.min.js"></script>
```

Or, if you prefer to use a CDN service, you may do so as follows:

```
<script type="text/javascript" src="http://cdn.jsdelivr.net/jqplot/1.0.8/plugins/jqplot.
blockRenderer.min.js"></script>
```

In this example you will use three series of data. The input data array should have this format:
[x, y, 'Label'],
Now, you define three different arrays, as shown in Listing 8-9.

**Listing 8-9.** Ch8_03.html

```
var data1 = [[10, 30, 'Copper'], [100, 40, 'Gold'], [50, 50, 'Silver'],
             [12, 78, 'Lead'], [44, 66, 'Brass']];
var data2 = [[68, 15, 'Maple'], [33, 22, 'Oak'], [10, 90, 'Ebony'],
             [94, 30, 'Beech'], [70, 70, 'Ash']];
var data3 = [[22, 16, 'PVC'], [56, 76, 'PE'], [33, 78, 'PET'],
             [27, 60, 'PC'], [70, 44, 'PU']];
```

In options, you need only activate the *BlockRenderer* plug-in in the seriesDefault object (see Listing 8-10).

***Listing 8-10.*** Ch8_03.html (Activating the `BlockRenderer` plug-in)

```
var options = {
    seriesDefaults:{
        renderer: $.jqplot.BlockRenderer
    }
};

$.jqplot ('myChart', [data1, data2, data3], options);
```

Figure 8-6 gives the block chart you have just defined, in which each series is marked by a different color.

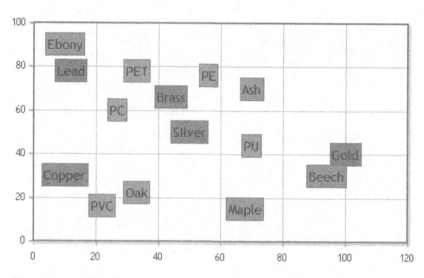

***Figure 8-6.*** *A block chart*

# Summary

In this chapter, you have learned how to represent a **distribution**. You will probably often find yourself interested in examining how data are distributed in space in order to uncover any possible trends or clusters. Depending on what you want to stand out more, you can choose to represent data by means of a **scatter chart**, a **bubble chart**, or a **block chart**. In addition, you have seen how to highlight the trend of a distribution.

In the next chapter, I will gather other types of charts that you have not yet looked at but that are standard types belonging to the jqPlot library. First, you will study **funnel charts** and how to set their properties through `options`. Then, you will discover **Bezier curves**—what they are and how they can be implemented by jqPlot.

# CHAPTER 9

■ ■ ■

# Funnel Charts with jqPlot

Funnel charts are used to show the progressive reduction of data as they go down one level to the next. The chart consists of an inverted pyramid, or funnel, divided into different levels. Each level has its own area, which is proportional to a given percentage value. A funnel chart is similar to a pie chart in that both express a whole divided into its constituent parts. But, the funnel chart specifies levels, which succeed one another in a very precise sequence. This sequence may express a hierarchical order, the steps of a process, and so on. A pie chart cannot do this.

## Creating a Funnel Chart

Even for this specialized chart, jqPlot provides a specific plug-in: *FunnelRenderer*. You therefore need to include it:

```
<script type="text/javascript" src="../src/plugins/jqplot.funnelRenderer.min.js"></script>
```

Or, if you prefer to use a content delivery network (CDN) service, you can do so as follows:

```
<script type="text/javascript" src="http://cdn.jsdelivr.net/jqplot/1.0.8/plugins/jqplot.funnelRenderer.min.js"></script>
```

With jqPlot, you must be aware of a behavior that is specific to this renderer plug-in: *FunnelRenderer* reorders the data, in descending order. The largest value is displayed at the top of the funnel, with the lesser values placed below. The area of each funnel section corresponds to the value of its data point, relative to the sum of all values (percentage). With this renderer, you need to use the following format for the input data array:
['label',value]
Thus, for this example, you define the data array as shown:

```
var data = [['Sony', 1], ['Samsung', 13], ['LG', 14], ['Philips', 5]];
```

For options, you have to activate the *FunnelRenderer* plug-in in the seriesDefaults object, and, optionally, you can add a legend reporting the labels of the series, as presented in Listing 9-1.

***Listing 9-1.*** Ch9_01a.html

```
var options = {
    seriesDefaults: {
        renderer: $.jqplot.FunnelRenderer
    },
    title: {
        text: 'Basic Funnel Chart'
    },
    legend: {
        location: 'e',
        show: true
    }
};

$.jqplot('myChart', [data], options);
```

Figure 9-1 is a basic funnel chart.

## Basic Funnel Chart

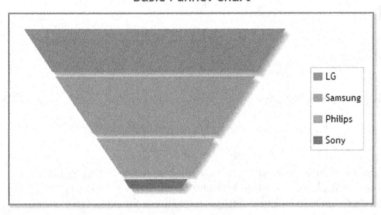

***Figure 9-1.*** *A simple funnel chart*

As you can see, the order of items has been changed, with the element with the highest value at the top, and so on, down to the item with the lowest value. This is the basic chart, but you can enrich it, for example, by adding labels reporting the percentages. To this end, you must add the dataLabel property, setting it to 'percent' and then enabling it with showDataLabel, set to 'true' (see Listing 9-2).

***Listing 9-2.*** Ch9_01b.html

```
seriesDefaults: {
    renderer: $.jqplot.FunnelRenderer,
    rendererOptions: {
        dataLabels: 'percent',
        showDataLabels: true
    }
},
```

As you can see in Figure 9-2, percentage values are now reported in their corresponding sections of the funnel chart.

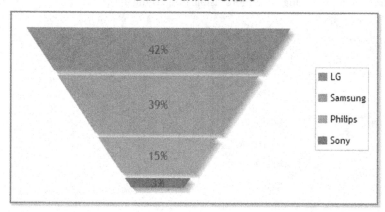

**Figure 9-2.** *A funnel chart with a legend and percentages*

You can make further changes. For example, let us say you want to decrease the spacing between funnel sections, as in Figure 9-3. You can accomplish this through the values passed to the sectionMargin property. By assigning the value 0 to the sectionMargin property, you eliminate the space between the sections completely (see Listing 9-3).

**Listing 9-3.** Ch9_01c.html

```
rendererOptions: {
    dataLabels: 'percent',
    showDataLabels: true,
    sectionMargin: 0
}
```

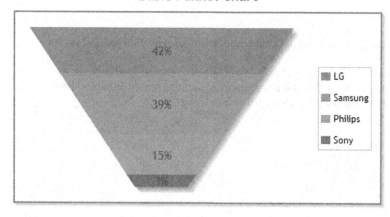

**Figure 9-3.** *A funnel chart without spaces between sections*

Alternatively, you may want to represent the various sectors as unfilled and increase the width of their boundary lines, as in Figure 9-4. To do this, you need to use two properties: fill and lineWidth. First, you set the fill property to 'false' which causes jqPlot to draw the section with an empty area; then, you set the lineWidth property to 4, thereby increasing the thickness of the sections' edges, making them more visible (see Listing 9-4).

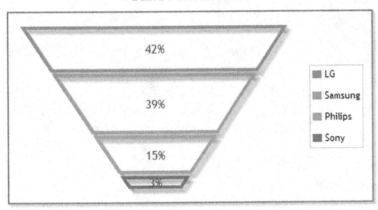

*Figure 9-4.* *A funnel chart with no filled sections*

*Listing 9-4.* Ch9_01d.html

```
rendererOptions: {
    dataLabels: 'percent',
    showDataLabels: true,
    fill: false,
    lineWidth: 4
}
```

# Summary

In this chapter, you learned how to make certain types of **funnel charts** and how to change their properties through options.

In the next chapter, I will cover a topic I have touched on in previous chapters: controls. I will describe the importance of introducing controls in a chart, understanding that a property of options is hidden behind every control. This affords the user the opportunity to select a property's attributes in real time.

# CHAPTER 10

■ ■ ■

# Adding Controls to Charts

Sometimes, it can be useful to change settings directly from the browser at runtime and then replot the chart with these new settings. A typical way of doing this is to add active controls. These controls make the chart interactive, allowing the user to make choices in real time, such as deciding how the chart should be represented. By inserting controls, you give the user the ability to control the values of the chart's attributes, which you would normally have to set in options.

In this chapter, you will look at introducing controls within your web page. You will also consider the factors that lead to the choice of one type of control over another. A series of examples featuring three of the most commonly used controls, will take you deeper into this topic.

## Adding Controls

One way to group controls is according to their functionality. Some controls (e.g., buttons, menus) work as switches (command controls) with which the user can trigger a particular event or launch a command. Other controls (e.g., check boxes, radio buttons, combo boxes, sliders) are bound to a specific value or property. With this type of control, the user makes a choice or enters values through a text field (text area). Still other controls (e.g., scrollbars) have a navigation function and are especially suitable in situations in which it is necessary to move an object, such as a selected item in a list or a large image enclosed in a frame or in the web page.

Here, you will be investigating those controls that are linked to values and that let the user interact with a chart by making choices. These controls should, in some way, graphically represent the values that a particular property can assume (the same values that you would usually assign to the properties within the options object, limited to those that you want to make available to the user). Your choice of control will depend on the property to set and the values that it can assume:

- To enable the user to make a single selection from a set of values (e.g., one of three possible colors), the choice of mutually exclusive **radio buttons** as controls is optimal (see Figure 10-1a).

- To let the user select which series should be visible in a chart, you will need to use **check boxes** (see Figure 10-1b).

- To allow the user to choose within a range of values for a particular attribute (e.g., changing the color of an object through adjustment of the red-green-blue (RGB) values that define the color), a **slider** is generally the best choice (see Figure 10-1c) (in this case, you would use three sliders as controls, corresponding to the colors red, green, and blue).

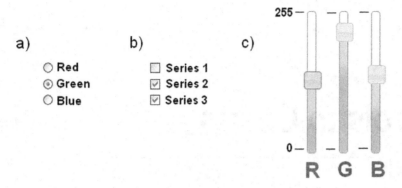

**Figure 10-1.** *Three of the most commonly used controls: (a) radio buttons, (b) check boxes, (c) sliders*

The list of possible controls does not end there. But, an understanding of the mechanisms that underlie these controls enables a chart developer to handle the vast majority of cases, including those that are the most complex.

In the following examples, you will discover how to apply these three controls to your chart.

# Using Radio Buttons

To illustrate the use of controls, let us first look at radio buttons. Radio buttons are a set of small buttons grouped in list form (see Figure 10-1a). They are generally represented as small, empty circles, with text to the side. As previously stated, this type of control is linked to a certain value or property. The particularity of radio buttons is that their values are mutually exclusive; therefore, the user can choose only one of them.

By way of illustration, let us take a simple multiseries line chart, in which, instead of displaying all the series, you want to allow the user to decide which series will be shown. To make a selection, the user will click one of the radio buttons, filling the circle with a dot. The series corresponding to that control will then be drawn on the chart.

## Adding Radio Button Controls

First, you need to write the HTML page, importing all the necessary libraries (see Listing 10-1).

*Listing 10-1.* ch10_01.html

```
<HTML>
<HEAD>
<TITLE>Selection series with controls</TITLE>
<!--[if lt IE 9]>
<script type="text/javascript" src="../src/excanvas.js"></script>
<![endif]-->
<script type="text/javascript" src="../src/jquery.min.js"></script>
<script type="text/javascript" src="../src/jquery.jqplot.min.js"></script>
<link rel="stylesheet" type="text/css" href="../src/jquery.jqplot.min.css"/>
<script>
$(document).ready(function(){

    //add your code here

});
</script>
</HEAD>
```

```
<BODY>
<div id="myChart" style="height: 300px; width: 500px;"></div>
    <!-- add the table with the controls here -->
</BODY>
</HTML>
```

Or, if you prefer to use the content delivery network (CDN) service, you use the following code:

```
<!--[if lt IE 9]>
<script src="http://cdn.jsdelivr.net/excanvas/r3/excanvas.js"></script>
<![endif]-->
<script src="http://code.jquery.com/jquery-1.9.1.min.js"></script>
<script type="text/javascript"
    src="http://cdn.jsdelivr.net/jqplot/1.0.8/jquery.jqplot.min.js"></script>
<link rel="stylesheet" type="text/css"
    href="http://cdn.jsdelivr.net/jqplot/1.0.8/jquery.jqplot.min.css"/>
```

You start with a line chart in which you will be representing four sets of values. Every element in each series will be represented by an (x, y) pair of values; you insert the values of these four series in a data set defined within the jQuery $(document).ready() function, as shown in Listing 10-2.

**Listing 10-2.** ch10_01.html

```
var dataSet = {
    data1: [[1, 1], [2, 2], [3, 3], [4, 2], [5, 3], [6, 4]],
    data2: [[1, 3], [2, 4], [3, 5], [4, 6], [5, 5], [6, 7]],
    data3: [[1, 5], [2, 6], [3, 8], [4, 9], [5, 7], [6, 9]],
    data4: [[1, 7], [2, 8], [3, 9], [4, 11], [5, 10], [6, 11]]
};
```

But, instead of displaying all four series with lines of different colors, as seen previously, you provide the user the opportunity to display only one series at a time. Once the chart is loaded in the browser, the user will be able to select any one of the four series and switch between them, without having to load a new page.

You begin by representing only the first series (data1) (see Listing 10-3).

**Listing 10-3.** ch10_01.html

```
var options = {
    seriesDefaults: {
        showMarker: false
    },
    title: 'Series selection',
    axes: {
        xaxis: {},
        yaxis: {
            min: 0,
            max: 12
        }
    }
};

var plot1 = $.jqplot ('myChart', [dataSet.data1], options);
```

189

> ■ **Note**   In this example, you store the value returned by the $.jqplot() function within the plot1 variable. This allows you to access the contents of jqplot object, change the values, and call its methods, including the replot() function, which lets you draw the chart again, including the new changes.

The user will be selecting an option from a set of possible choices; the radio buttons is the best choice of control for this purpose. Therefore, let us assign one series to each radio button. As you can see in Listing 10-4, all the controls (buttons) are contained in an inner list within a table. Each button is specified by an <input> element in which the four series are also specified as values.

***Listing 10-4.***  ch10_01.html

```
<table>
<tr>
  <td>
    <div>
      <ul>
        <li><input name="dataSeries" value="data1" type="radio" checked />First Series</li>
        <li><input name="dataSeries" value="data2" type="radio" />Second Series</li>
        <li><input name="dataSeries" value="data3" type="radio" />Third Series</li>
        <li><input name="dataSeries" value="data4" type="radio" />Fourth Series</li>
      </ul>
    </div> </td>
</tr>
</table>
```

However, setting the controls definition in an HTML page is not enough; you must also create functions that relate the radio buttons to the jqPlot chart. Depending on which radio button is in the checked state, a different set from the data set will be loaded in the chart.

In selecting a different radio button, the user changes the checked attribute from 'false' to 'true'. The status change of a radio button involves the activation of the change() function, which detects this event. This function assigns a new set from the data set to the plot1 variable (containing all the information about your jqPlot chart) and finally forces the replot of the chart. The new data are thus represented in the chart, without having to reload the page (see Listing 10-5).

***Listing 10-5.***  ch10_01.html

```
$(document).ready(function(){
    ...
    var plot1 = $.jqplot ('myChart', [dataSet.data1], options);
    $("input[type=radio][name=dataSeries]").attr("checked", false);
    $("input[type=radio][name=dataSeries][value=data1]").attr("checked", true);
    $("input[type=radio][name=dataSeries]").change(function(){
        var val = $(this).val();
        plot1.series[0].data = dataSet[val];
        plot1.replot();
    });
});
```

To customize the elements within the table of controls, you can add a little bit of Cascading Style Sheets (CSS) style, as demonstrated in Listing 10-6.

**Listing 10-6.** ch10_01.html

```
<style>
li {
    font-family: "Verdana";
    font-size: 16px;
    font-weight: bold;
    text-shadow: 1px 2px 2px #555555;
    margin: 3px;
    list-style: none;
}
</style>
```

If you load this web page in the browser, you obtain the chart in Figure 10-2.

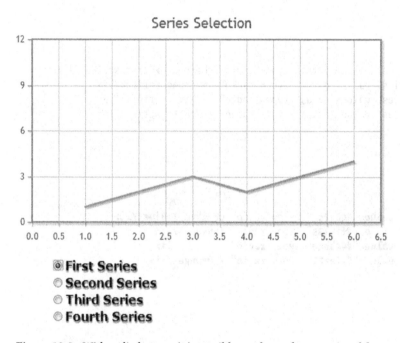

**Figure 10-2.** *With radio buttons it is possible to select only one series of data*

Now, the user can choose which series will be shown in the chart. Having selected the radio button as a control, the chart will display only one set of data at a time.

## Accessing Attributes after the Chart Has Already Been Drawn

So far, you have used the options object to define the property values of your chart (by changing the default values) and then passed it as an argument to the $.jqplot() function. But, this applies only when you want to characterize your chart before it is drawn. What can you do if you need to access the attribute values subsequently?

In fact, by introducing the controls as an argument, you have also introduced the possibility of changing these attributes after the chart has been drawn. Therefore, there must be a way to access these values, edit them, and then run the command to redraw the chart (as when you used the replot() function) (see Listing 10-5).

You have seen that you can receive the entire jqplot object as the value returned by the $.jqplot() function and store it in a variable (in the previous example, the plot1 variable) so that you can access its content later.

A jqplot object contains practically all the objects—their properties and methods—that define the whole jqPlot library, and every particular instance (e.g., plot1) is realized in the representation of a specific chart.

Thus, when you are writing a JavaScript code to define the functions that handle particular events (such as the use of controls by the user), you can access these values and change them after the page has designed the chart and then run the command to redraw it with the desired changes. This adds the interactivity you need in your charts.

Continuing with the previous example (see Listings 10-1 to 10-6), you note that the lines are all drawn in blue. Let us now make some changes so that this time the user can choose the color with which the series will be drawn.

To do this, you add another set of controls to the table: a second column of radio buttons, each representing a color (see Listing 10-7).

*Listing 10-7.* ch10_02.html

```
<table>
<tr>
  <td>
    <div>
      <ul>
        <li><input name="dataSeries" value="data1" type="radio" checked />First series</li>
        <li><input name="dataSeries" value="data2" type="radio" />Second series</li>
        <li><input name="dataSeries" value="data3" type="radio" />Third series</li>
        <li><input name="dataSeries" value="data4" type="radio" />Fourth series</li>
      </ul>
    </div>
  </td>
  <td>
    <div>
      <ul>
        <li><input name="colors" value="#4bb2c5" type="radio" checked />Blue</li>
        <li><input name="colors" value="#ff3333" type="radio" />Red</li>
        <li><input name="colors" value="#44bb44" type="radio" />Green</li>
        <li><input name="colors" value="#ffaa22" type="radio" />Orange</li>
      </ul>
    </div>
  </td>
</tr>
</table>
```

Next, you add the rows highlighted in bold in Listing 10-8 to your JavaScript code.

*Listing 10-8.* ch10_02.html

```
$("input[type=radio][name=dataSeries]").attr("checked", false);
$("input[type=radio][name=dataSeries][value=data1]").attr("checked", true);
$("input[type=radio][name=dataSeries]").change(function(){
    var val = $(this).val();
    plot1.series[0].data = dataSet[val];
    plot1.series[0].renderer.shapeRenderer.strokeStyle = col;
    plot1.replot();
});
```

```
var col = "#4bb2c5";
$("input[type=radio][name=colors]").change(function(){
    col = $(this).val();
});
```

Figure 10-3 illustrates how the user can decide the series to represent, selecting among four different colors. This is an example of how adding controls increases the interactivity between the user and chart.

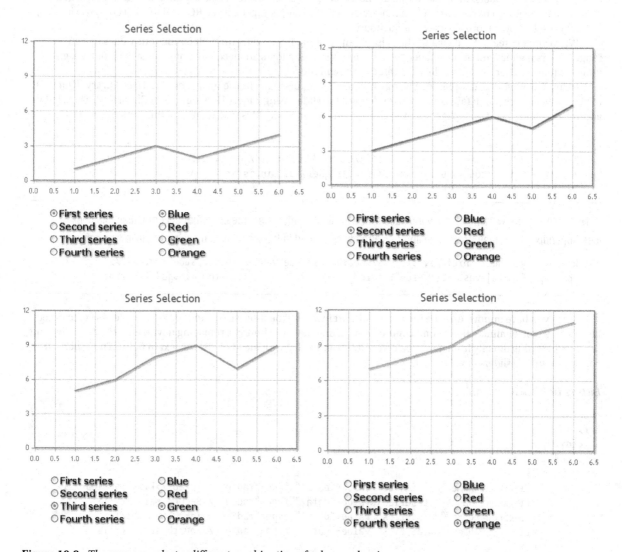

***Figure 10-3.*** *The user can select a different combination of colors and series*

# Using Sliders

In the previous example the user first set the color by checking one of the radio buttons in the second column and then chose the series to be represented with that color by selecting it from the first column. This process, therefore, involved two selections, made at two different times. This time, you will keep unchanged the first column, from which the user selects the series to be displayed (mutual exclusion), but in place of the column of radio buttons, you will insert a set of three sliders. In this scenario, the user selects the series to be displayed, and, once it is drawn on the chart, in a predefined color, he or she can modify this color by adjusting the three RGB values that compose it. Now, you have a selection, followed by a fine adjustment.

When you are required to change the value of an attribute by scrolling through contiguous values in a given range, sliders are the kind of control needed. In this case, three sliders are necessary, one for each color (red, green, blue), so that the user can adjust the RGB values to obtain the desired color.

Using the previous example (see Listings 10-7 and 10-8), first you choose the jQuery Interface library (jQuery UI) to obtain the sliders (for details on how to implement the slider using jQuery UI widgets, see Chapter 2). Thus, before adding the sliders to the web page, you must import all the necessary files that are part of this library:

```
<link rel="stylesheet"
    href="http://code.jquery.com/ui/1.10.3/themes/smoothness/jquery-ui.css"/>
<script src="http://code.jquery.com/ui/1.10.3/jquery-ui.min.js"></script>
```

■ **Note**   If you are working in the workspace made available with the source code that accompanies this book (see Appendix A), you may access the libraries already contained in the workspace by using the following references:

```
<link rel="stylesheet" href="../src/css/smoothness/jquery-ui-1.10.3.custom.min.css"/>
<script type="text/javascript" src="../src/js/jquery-ui-1.10.3.custom.min.js"></script>
```

Once you have imported all the files, you can start inserting the three sliders in the HTML table. As you can see in Listing 10-9, you eliminate the second column, containing the radio buttons, replacing it with a set of <div> elements (if you are starting directly from here, you can copy the entire listing instead of just the text in bold). The jQuery UI will convert them into sliders (see Chapter 2).

***Listing 10-9.*** ch10_04.html

```
<table>
<tr>
   <td>
      <div>
         <ul>
            <li><input name="dataSeries" value="data1" type="radio" checked />First series</li>
            <li><input name="dataSeries" value="data2" type="radio" />Second series</li>
            <li><input name="dataSeries" value="data3" type="radio" />Third series</li>
            <li><input name="dataSeries" value="data4" type="radio" />Fourth series</li>
         </ul>
      </div>
   </td>
   <td>
      <div id="red">
         <div id="slider-text">
            <div id="0">0</div>
            <div id="1">255</div>
```

```
                </div>
            </div>
            <div id="green">
                <div id="slider-text">
                    <div id="0">0</div>
                    <div id="1">255</div>
                </div>
            </div>
            <div id="blue">
                <div id="slider-text">
                    <div id="0">0</div>
                    <div id="1">255</div>
                </div>
            </div>
        </td>
    </tr>
</table>
```

Furthermore, you have also added two numerical values to each slider with the slider-text id. These values are nothing more than labels that are used to display the minimum and maximum for the range of values (0–255) covered by the three sliders. This methodology can be very useful when you have to represent a scale for each slide in the web page.

Let us now add all the CSS style directives to make sure these new controls can be displayed correctly in the context of the existing page (see Listing 10-10).

***Listing 10-10.*** ch10_04.html

```
<style>
...
#red, #green, #blue {
    float: left;
    margin: 15px;
    left: 50px;
}
#red .ui-slider-range {
    background: #ef2929;
}
#red .ui-slider-handle {
    border-color: #ef2929;
}
#green .ui-slider-range {
    background: #8ae234;
}
#green .ui-slider-handle {
    border-color: #8ae234;
}
#blue .ui-slider-range {
    background: #729fcf;
}
#blue .ui-slider-handle {
    border-color: #729fcf;
}
```

```
#slider-text div {
    font-family: "Verdana";
    font-size: 10px;
    position: relative;
    left: 17px;
}
</style>
```

With regard to the section of code in JavaScript, you keep only the part that manages the radio buttons for the selection of the desired series, integrating it with a new section of code that handles the RGB values, adjusted through the three sliders, as shown in Listing 10-11. The three RGB values are then converted to hexadecimal numbers through an appropriate function and combined to form the HTML color code, expressed by a pound sign (#), followed by six hexadecimal characters ('rrggbb'), where each pair represents a value from 0 to 255, translated into hexadecimal format.

*Listing 10-11.* ch10_04.html

```
$(document).ready(function(){

...

    $("input[type=radio][name=dataSeries]").attr("checked", false);
    $("input[type=radio][name=dataSeries][value=data1]").attr("checked", true);
    $("input[type=radio][name=dataSeries]").change(function(){
        var val = $(this).val();
        plot1.series[0].data = dataSets[val];
        plot1.series[0].renderer.shapeRenderer.strokeStyle = "#" + col;
        plot1.replot();
    });

    var col = "4bb2c5";

    function hexFromRGB(r, g, b) {
        var hex = [
            r.toString( 16 ),
            g.toString( 16 ),
            b.toString( 16 )
        ];
        $.each( hex, function( nr, val ) {
            if ( val.length === 1 ) {
                hex[ nr ] = "0" + val;
            }
        });
        return hex.join( "" ).toUpperCase();
    };

    $( "#red, #green, #blue" ).slider({
        orientation: "vertical",
        range: "min",
        max: 255,
        change: refreshPlot
    });
```

```
// set col to default "#4bb2c5";
    $( "#red" ).slider( "value", 255 );
    $( "#green" ).slider( "value", 140 );
    $( "#blue" ).slider( "value", 60 );

    function refreshPlot() {
        var r = $( "#red" ).slider( "value" );
        var g = $( "#green" ).slider( "value" );
        var b = $( "#blue" ).slider( "value" );
        var col = hexFromRGB(r, g, b);
        plot1.series[0].renderer.shapeRenderer.strokeStyle = "#" + col;
        plot1.replot();
    }

    $("[id=0]").css('top','90px');
    $("[id=1]").css('top','-20px');

});
```

The last two lines of code in Listing 10-11 use the jQuery css() function to assign a CSS style to a specific selection of HTML elements (see Chapter 2). The selection is made on all elements with id = 0 and id = 1, that is, the <div> elements containing the labels for the sliders' scale.You set the CSS top attribute to place each scale label next to the corresponding slider, at a specific height.

In Figure 10-4 the user can decide the series to display and change its by modifying the RBG values through three sliders.

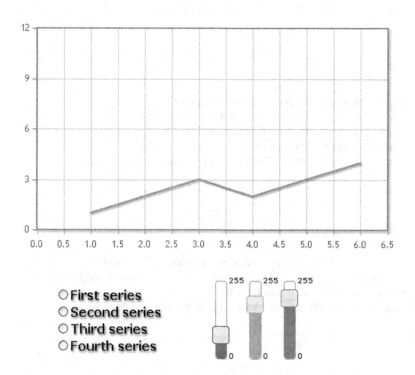

***Figure 10-4.*** *A chart with three slider widgets added to adjust the RGB levels*

# Using Check Boxes

In the previous examples, the user could choose only one among the number of series that could be displayed. However, typically the user will want to be able to decide which series should be displayed and which should not, choosing, for instance, to display two or more sets at the same time. This entails dealing with multiple choices within the same group. To enable the user make this kind of choice, you have to opt for check boxes.

Generally, check boxes are grouped in a list, represented by empty boxes (see Figure 10-1). Unlike radio buttons, these controls are not mutually exclusive, but rather multiple choice. Thus, you can select all, some, or none of the values that they represent (whereas with radio buttons an item has to be selected).

Similar to radio buttons, there is a check box for each series, and if a check box is checked, the corresponding series is shown in the chart. Yet, unlike radio buttons, check boxes are independent of each other: their state (checked or unchecked) does not affect the status of the others.

Often, when you have a list of check boxes, it can be very useful to add two buttons with the "CheckAll/UncheckAll" functionality, thereby allowing the choice of selecting/deselecting all the check boxes with one click.

Using the previous example (see Listing 10-9 to 10-11), the data set and options settings are the same; the only thing you need to change is the data passed in the $.jqplot() function. In this case, the whole data set will be passed as an argument.

```
var plot1 = $.jqplot ('myChart', [dataSet.data1, dataSet.data2, dataSet.data3, dataSet.data4], options);
```

Let us delete the table containing the previous controls (radio buttons, sliders) and substitute it with a new one containing check boxes, as shown in Listing 10-12 (if you are starting directly from here, you can copy the entire listing without considering the previous controls). Moreover, in addition to the four controls for as many series, you can add a button at the end to manage the feature "CheckAll/UncheckAll".

***Listing 10-12.*** ch10_03.html

```
<table>
<tr>
   <td>
      <div>
         <ul>
            <li><input name="data1" type="checkbox" checked />First series</li>
            <li><input name="data2" type="checkbox" checked />Second series</li>
            <li><input name="data3" type="checkbox" checked />Third series</li>
            <li><input name="data4" type="checkbox" checked />Fourth series</li>
            <li><input type="button" name="checkall" value="Uncheck All"></li>
         </ul>
      </div>
   </td>
</tr>
</table>
```

As with radio buttons, you have to add jQuery methods to bind the events that have occurred with these controls. First, you define the status of each check box. Normally, they should all be checked. Then, you define five jQuery methods, enabling or disabling the series to be represented, and then force the replot.

From the code, you must delete all the rows that handled the previous controls and in their place, write the methods in Listing 10-13.

***Listing 10-13.*** ch10_03.html

```javascript
$("input[type=checkbox][name=data1]").change(function(){
    if(this.checked){
        plot1.series[0].data = dataSet.data1;
        plot1.replot();
    } else {
        plot1.series[0].data = [];
        plot1.replot();
    }
});

$("input[type=checkbox][name=data2]").change(function(){
    if(this.checked){
        plot1.series[1].data = dataSet.data2;
        plot1.replot();
    } else {
        plot1.series[1].data = [];
        plot1.replot();
    }
});

$("input[type=checkbox][name=data3]").change(function(){
    if(this.checked){
        plot1.series[2].data = dataSet.data3;
        plot1.replot();
    } else {
        plot1.series[2].data = [];
        plot1.replot();
    }
});

$("input[type=checkbox][name=data4]").change(function(){
    if(this.checked){
        plot1.series[3].data = dataSet.data4;
        plot1.replot();
    } else {
        plot1.series[3].data = [];
        plot1.replot();
    }
});

$("input[type=button][name=checkall]").click(function(){
    if(this.value == "Check All"){
        plot1.series[0].data = dataSet.data1;
        plot1.series[1].data = dataSet.data2;
        plot1.series[2].data = dataSet.data3;
        plot1.series[3].data = dataSet.data4;
        $("input[type=checkbox][name=data1]").prop("checked", true);
        $("input[type=checkbox][name=data2]").prop("checked", true);
        $("input[type=checkbox][name=data3]").prop("checked", true);
        $("input[type=checkbox][name=data4]").prop("checked", true);
```

```
      this.value = "Uncheck All";
      plot1.replot();
   } else {
      plot1.series[0].data = [];
      plot1.series[1].data = [];
      plot1.series[2].data = [];
      plot1.series[3].data = [];
      $("input[type=checkbox][name=data1]").prop("checked", false);
      $("input[type=checkbox][name=data2]").prop("checked", false);
      $("input[type=checkbox][name=data3]").prop("checked", false);
      $("input[type=checkbox][name=data4]").prop("checked", false);
      this.value = "Check All";
      plot1.replot();
   }
});
```

As shown in Figure 10-5, the user can now select the series he or she wants to see displayed in the chart.

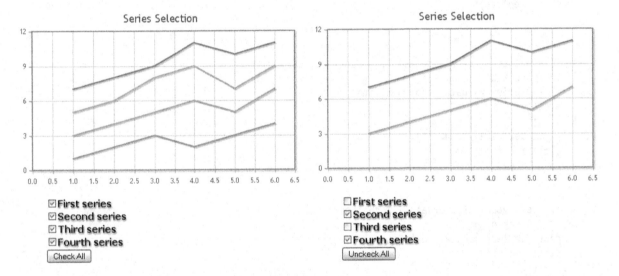

**Figure 10-5.** *A custom legend with check boxes and a button*

If you click the button labeled "Uncheck all", all the check boxes will be unchecked, and the corresponding series will be hidden in the plot. Subsequently, the button will show the label "Check All." When clicking it this time, all the check boxes will be checked, and the corresponding series will be shown in the chart.

The features covered in this last example are very similar to the legend provided by the *EnhancedLegendRenderer* plug-in (see the section "Handling Legends" in Chapter 5). In that case, by clicking the colored square corresponding to a series, you can decide whether that series should be represented in the chart. But, here you have also added the possibility of checking and unchecking all the series with just one click, and this functionality is not at present implemented in the plug-in (although someone is proposing it). This is another small example of how to expand the functionality that a library provides through the use of controls.

# Summary

In this chapter, you have seen how to use various controls, such as **radio buttons**, **sliders**, and **check boxes**, to increase the interactivity of a chart. With the introduction of controls, we, as programmers, are no longer the only ones to have direct control of the values of the properties of the chart; through such controls the user is also able to make the appropriate choices.

In addition, you learned how to integrate **jQuery UI widgets** with the jqPlot library, using these widgets **as controls**. In the next chapter, you will complete this integration by using jQuery UI widgets **as containers** for your charts. This combination greatly expands the possibilities for development and representation of charts using the jqPlot library.

▪▪▪

# CHAPTER 11

# Embedding jqPlot Charts in jQuery Widgets

In Chapter 2, you saw several examples of jQuery UI widgets used as containers. In this chapter, you'll exploit such capability to represent the charts within these containers. This enables you to exploit the great potential of the jQuery UI widgets to further improve the way in which your charts are represented.

The advantages of combining jQuery UI and jqPlot libraries are various: you can display more charts occupying the same space in the web page, and at the same time keep the context of the page clean and tidy. Another advantage is that jQuery UI widgets can be resized, and even users can resize a jqPlot chart.

In this chapter, you'll explore three simple cases where the benefits just mentioned will be made evident. You'll also become more confident in working with jQuery UI widgets, even more so than you did in Chapter 2.

## jqPlot Charts on Tabs

The first widget you're going to use as a container is the *tab* (see the section "Tab" in Chapter 2). Inserting charts inside tabs allows you to display different charts on the same page within a limited area. In this example, you'll place three different jqPlot charts within three tabs, called Tab 1, Tab 2, and Tab 3. In the first tab you'll place a bar chart, in the second tab you'll place a multiseries line chart, and in the last tab a pie chart. You won't be analyzing these charts in detail, because they are exactly the same kind of charts used in previous chapters. Each type of chart requires its specific plug-ins, and Listing 11-1 shows a list of the plug-ins that are needed.

*Listing 11-1.* ch11_01.html

```html
<!--[if lt IE 9]>
<script src="http://cdn.jsdelivr.net/excanvas/r3/excanvas.js"></script>
<![endif]-->
<script src="http://code.jquery.com/jquery-1.9.1.min.js"></script>
<script src="http://cdn.jsdelivr.net/jqplot/1.0.8/jquery.jqplot.min.js">
</script>
<link rel="stylesheet" type="text/css"
    href="http://cdn.jsdelivr.net/jqplot/1.0.8/jquery.jqplot.min.css" />
<script src="http://cdn.jsdelivr.net/jqplot/1.0.8/plugins/jqplot.pieRenderer.min.js">
</script>
<script type="text/javascript" src="http://cdn.jsdelivr.net/jqplot/1.0.8/plugins↩
    /jqplot.dateAxisRenderer.min.js"></script>
<script type="text/javascript" src="http://cdn.jsdelivr.net/jqplot/1.0.8/plugins↩
    /jqplot.canvasTextRenderer.min.js"></script>
```

```
<script type="text/javascript" src="http://cdn.jsdelivr.net/jqplot/1.0.8/plugins↵
    /jqplot.canvasAxisTickRenderer.min.js"></script>
<script type="text/javascript" src="http://cdn.jsdelivr.net/jqplot/1.0.8/plugins↵
    /jqplot.categoryAxisRenderer.min.js"></script>
<script type="text/javascript" src="http://cdn.jsdelivr.net/jqplot/1.0.8/plugins↵
    /jqplot.barRenderer.min.js"></script>
```

In addition, you are going to use jQuery widgets as containers, and these also require some files to be included:

```
<link rel="stylesheet" href="http://code.jquery.com/ui/1.10.3/themes/smoothness/jquery-ui.css" />
<script src="http://code.jquery.com/ui/1.10.3/jquery-ui.min.js"></script>
```

---

■ **Note** For those of you working on the workspace made available with the book's source code, you can use the libraries already contained in the workspace. Use the following references:

```
<script src="../src/js/jquery-1.9.1.js"></script>
<script src="../src/jquery.jqplot.min.js"></script>
<link rel="stylesheet" type="text/css" href="../src/jquery.jqplot.min.css" />

<link rel="stylesheet" href="../src/css/smoothness/jquery-ui-1.10.3.custom.min.css" />
<script src="../src/js/jquery-ui-1.10.3.custom.min.js"></script>
<script src="../src/plugins/jqplot.pieRenderer.min.js"></script>
<script src="../src/plugins/jqplot.dateAxisRenderer.min.js"></script>
<script src="../src/plugins/jqplot.canvasTextRenderer.min.js"></script>
<script src="../src/plugins/jqplot.canvasAxisTickRenderer.min.js"></script>
<script src="../src/plugins/jqplot.categoryAxisRenderer.min.js"></script>
<script src="../src/plugins/jqplot.barRenderer.min.js"></script>
```

---

With the introduction of so many graphic elements on the web page, the use of Cascading Style Sheets (CSS) styles becomes increasingly important. You need to define some settings in order to modify the tabs' appearance so that they will fit to your needs. Add the style settings in Listing 11-2.

*Listing 11-2.* ch11_01.html

```
<style>
.ui-tabs {
    width: 690px;
    margin: 2em auto;
}
.ui-tabs-nav {
    font-size: 12px;
}
.ui-tabs-panel {
    font-size: 14px;
}
.jqplot-target {
    font-size: 18px;
}
```

```css
ol.description {
    list-style-position: inside;
    font-size: 15px;
    margin: 1.5em auto;
    padding: 0 15px;
    width: 600px;
}
</style>
```

You are going to use three different charts, which have already been used in previous chapters (see Chapter 4 for the line chart, Chapter 5 for the bar chart, and Chapter 6 for the pie chart). This chapter, therefore, doesn't cover the details of their settings. Add them to our web page, replacing the usual target name myChart with chart1, chart2, and chart3. As you can see in Listing 11-3, in these charts you have defined the options objects directly within the three jqplot() functions. Their return values are stored in three different variables: plot1, plot2, and plot3. These variables will be used to handle the respective charts within the JavaScript code.

***Listing 11-3.*** Ch11_01.html

```javascript
var bar1 = [['Germany', 12], ['Italy', 8], ['Spain', 6],
            ['France', 10], ['UK', 7]];
var data1 = [1, 2, 3, 2, 3, 4];
var data2 = [3, 4, 5, 6, 5, 7];
var data3 = [5, 6, 8, 9, 7, 9];
var data4 = [7, 8, 9, 11, 10, 11];
var pie1 = [
    ['Dairy', 212], ['Meat', 140], ['Grains', 276],
    ['Fish', 131], ['Vegetables', 510], ['Fruit', 325]
];

var plot1 = $.jqplot ('chart1', [bar1], {
    title: 'Foreigner customers',
    series:[{renderer:$.jqplot.BarRenderer}],
    axesDefaults: {
       tickRenderer: $.jqplot.CanvasAxisTickRenderer ,
       tickOptions: {
          angle: -30,
          fontSize: '10pt'
       }
    },
    axes: {
       xaxis: {
          renderer: $.jqplot.CategoryAxisRenderer
       }
    }
});

var plot2 = $.jqplot ('chart2', [data1, data2, data3, data4],{});
```

```
var plot3 = $.jqplot ('chart3', [pie1], {
    seriesDefaults: {
        renderer: jQuery.jqplot.PieRenderer,
        rendererOptions: {
            showDataLabels: true,
            dataLabels: 'value',
            fill: false,
            sliceMargin: 6,
            lineWidth: 5
        }
    }
});
```

Now it is time to add the jQueryUI tabs() function at the end of the $(document).ready() function, as shown in Listing 11-4.

***Listing 11-4.*** ch11_01.html

```
$(document).ready(function(){
...
    $("#tabs").tabs();
});
```

This call creates the tabs container, and consequently you need to bind the tabs to your plots (see Listing 11-5).

***Listing 11-5.*** ch11_01.html

```
$('#tabs').bind('tabsshow', function(event, ui) {
    if (ui.index === 0 && plot1._drawCount === 0) {
        plot1.replot();
    }
    else if (ui.index === 1 && plot2._drawCount === 0) {
        plot2.replot();
    }
    else if (ui.index === 2 && plot3._drawCount === 0) {
        plot3.replot();
    }
});
```

Selecting a tab will replot the content of the chart within it. Now, in the `<body>` part of the web page, you need to add the `<div>` elements that the jQuery UI library will convert into tabs. The way to do that is to specify a `<div>` element with `tabs` as id. Inside it, you define a list of three items, each representing a tab. After the list, you must define another three subdivisions of tabs: three additional `<div>` elements called `tabs-1`, `tabs-2`, and `tabs-3`. You are going to put these into your charts: `chart1`, `chart2`, and `chart3` (see Listing 11-6).

***Listing 11-6.*** ch11_01.html

```
<div id="tabs">
    <ul>
        <li><a href="#tabs-1">Tab 1</a></li>
        <li><a href="#tabs-2">Tab 2</a></li>
        <li><a href="#tabs-3">Tab 3</a></li>
    </ul>
    <div id="tabs-1">
        <p>This is the bar chart</p>
        <div id="chart1" style="height:300px; width:650px;"></div>
    </div>
    <div id="tabs-2">
        <p>This is the line chart</p1>
        <div id="chart2" style="height:300px; width:650px;"></div>
    </div>
    <div id="tabs-3">
        <p>This is the pie chart</p>
        <div id="chart3" style="height:300px; width:650px;"></div>
    </div>
</div>
```

Figure 11-1 shows the final result.

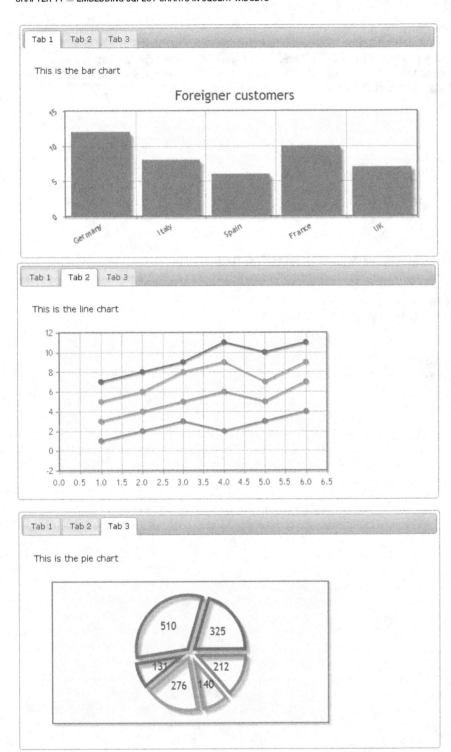

***Figure 11-1.*** *A page with three tabs containing different charts*

# jqPlot Charts on Accordions

Another commonly used type of jQuery container is the *accordion*. This time you'll put the previous three charts into accordions. The list of plug-ins to include with the web page remains the same as in the previous example. You need to make some changes in the CSS styles; there are specific CSS classes for accordions, and their attributes need to be specified. They are shown in Listing 11-7.

*Listing 11-7.* ch11_02.html

```css
<style type="text/css">
.ui-accordion {
    width: 690px;
    margin: 2em auto;
}
.ui-accordion-header {
    font-size: 12px;
}
.ui-accordion-content {
    font-size: 14px;
}
.jqplot-target {
    font-size: 18px;
}
ol.description {
    list-style-position: inside;
    font-size: 15px;
    margin: 1.5em auto;
    padding: 0 15px;
    width: 600px;
}
.section {
    width: 400px;
    height: 200px;
    margin-top: 20px;
    margin-left: 20px;
}
</style>
```

As you did in the previous example, you must create the jQueryUi widget. You can do this by calling the accordion() function:

```
$("#accordion").accordion();
```

You also need to bind this accordion to your charts, as shown in Listing 11-8. When you select an accordion tab, the event makes sure that the respective chart is redrawn inside it, calling the replot() function.

***Listing 11-8.*** ch11_02.html

```
$('#accordion').bind('accordionchange', function(event, ui) {
    var index = $(this).find("h3").index ( ui.newHeader[0] );
    if (index === 0) {
        plot1.replot();
    }
    else if (index === 1) {
        plot2.replot();
    }
    else if (index === 2) {
        plot3.replot();
    }
});
```

As you can see, the way in which you define the accordions is very similar to the way you define the tabs. In the same way, you now define the <div> elements that will be converted into accordion tabs in the HTML code (see Listing 11-9).

***Listing 11-9.*** ch11_02.html

```
<div id="accordion" style="margin-top:50px">
  <h3><a href="#">Section 1</a></h3>
  <div>
    <p>This is the bar chart</p>
    <div class="section" id="chart1" data-height="200" data-width="400"></div>
  </div>

  <h3><a href="#">Section 2</a></h3>
  <div>
    <p>This is the multiseries line chart</p>
    <div class="section" id="chart2" data-height="200" data-width="400"></div>
  </div>

  <h3><a href="#">Section 3</a></h3>
  <div>
    <p>This is the pie chart</p>
    <div class="section" id="chart3" data-height="200" data-width="400"></div> </div>
</div>
```

As you can see in Figure 11-2, the result is similar to the previous one, but this time the different charts are replaced by sliding the accordion tab vertically.

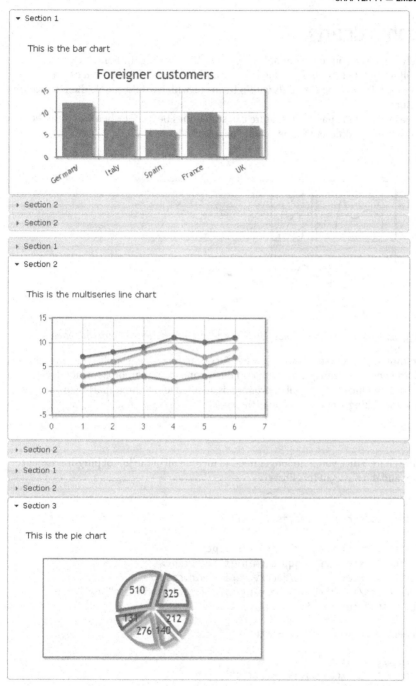

*Figure 11-2.* *An accordion widget containing three charts*

# Resizable and Draggable Charts

Two other features that you can widely exploit in your charts enable users to resize and drag the container area.
A resizable frame within a web page allows you to arbitrarily change its size and the size of the objects it contains.
This feature could be combined with the ability to drag elements within the page, which would enable them to occupy
different positions relative to the original.

In addition to giving fluidity to the layout of the page, this feature can sometimes be useful when you want the
user to interactively manage spaces occupied by different frames on the page (see Figure 11-3).

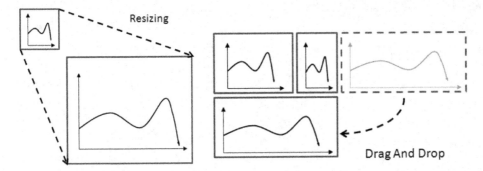

**Figure 11-3.** *Enclosing the charts in jQueryUI containers enables you to resize and move them around the page*

In this section, you'll see two examples. In the first example, you will focus on the resizing applied to a line chart.
You'll see how easy it is to resize a chart contained within a container. In the second example, you'll further develop
the example by adding two more line charts. Once the draggable property is enabled for all three charts, you will see
how you can change their positions to your liking, or even exchange them.

## A Resizable Line Chart

In this example you'll use a simple line chart. Thus, you'll no longer need to include all of the jqPlot plug-ins, except
those needed for the jQuery container and the basic jqPlots library:

```
<!--[if lt IE 9]>
<script type="text/javascript" src="../src/excanvas.js"></script>
<![endif]-->
<script type="text/javascript" src="../src/jquery.min.js"></script>
<script type="text/javascript" src="../src/jquery.jqplot.min.js"></script>
<link rel="stylesheet" type="text/css" href="../src/jquery.jqplot.min.css" />
<link rel="stylesheet" href="../src/css/smoothness/jquery-ui-1.10.3.custom.min.css" />
<script src="../src/js/jquery-ui-1.10.3.custom.min.js"></script>
```

Or if you prefer to use a content delivery network (CDN) service:

```
<!--[if lt IE 9]><script type="text/javascript"
src="http://cdn.jsdelivr.net/excanvas/r3/excanvas.js"></script><![endif]-->
<script src="http://code.jquery.com/jquery-1.9.1.min.js"></script>
<script type="text/javascript"
src="http://cdn.jsdelivr.net/jqplot/1.0.8/jquery.jqplot.min.js"></script>
<link rel="stylesheet" type="text/css" href="
http://cdn.jsdelivr.net/jqplot/1.0.8/jquery.jqplot.min.css" />
<link rel="stylesheet" href="http://code.jquery.com/ui/1.10.3/themes/smoothness/jquery-ui.css" />
<script src="http://code.jquery.com/ui/1.10.3/jquery-ui.min.js"></script>
```

Even here it is necessary to specify some CSS styles, as shown in Listing 11-10.

**Listing 11-10.** ch11_03.html

```
<style type="text/css">
.chart-container {
    border: 1px solid darkblue;
    padding: 30px 0px 30px 30px;
    width: 900px;
    height: 400px;
}
#chart1 {
    width: 96%;
    height: 96%;
}
</style>
```

To the <body> part of the web page, you now add the <div> element, which will be the container enclosing the line chart called chart1 (see Listing 11-11).

**Listing 11-11.** ch11_03.html

```
<div class="chart-container">
    <div id="chart1"></div>
</div>
```

Now, after you have defined the chart-container as container, you can handle it with two jQuery methods—the resizable() function adds the resizable functionality and the bind() function binds the event of resizing to the replotting of the chart (see Listing 11-12).

**Listing 11-12.** ch11_03.html

```
$(document).ready(function(){
    var plot1 = $.jqplot ('chart1', [[100, 110, 140, 130, 80, 75, 120, 130, 100]]);

    $('div.chart-container').resizable({delay: 20});
    $('div.chart-container').bind('resize', function(event, ui) {
        plot1.replot();
    });
});
```

The result is a resizable chart, shown in Figure 16-4, with a small grey triangle in the bottom-right corner. By clicking on it, the user can resize the container and consequently the jqPlot chart.

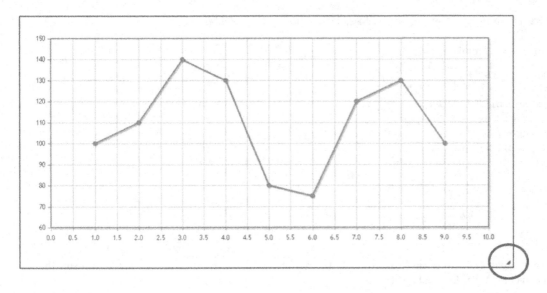

**Figure 11-4.** *A resizable line chart*

## Three Draggable Line Charts

Starting from the previous example, you will add two more line charts by placing them in two independent containers. The goal here—in addition to making all three containers resizable—is to make the containers draggable. The final result is a web page with three line charts, the position of which can be changed by dragging them, even exchanging their positions.

Start by making some small additions to the previous example. In Listing 11-13, you add the other two containers (chart-container2 and chart-container3) with the new line charts inside, naming them chart2 and chart3, respectively.

*Listing 11-13.* ch11_03b.html

```
<BODY>
<div class="chart-container">
    <div id="chart1"></div>
</div>
<div class="chart-container2">
    <div id="chart2"></div>
</div>
<div class="chart-container3">
    <div id="chart3"></div>
</div>
</BODY>
```

Now that you have created the container for the new line chart, it is necessary to define them through three distinct $.jqplot() functions (see Listing 11-14). The values returned by these three functions will be passed to the three variables: plot1, plot2, and plot3. This is because you need to redraw each of the three charts whenever a change is made to the container, by using the replot() function on these three variables.

*Listing 11-14.* ch11_03b.html

```
$(document).ready(function(){
    var plot1 = $.jqplot ('chart1', [[100, 110, 140, 130, 80, 75, 120, 130, 100]],
        {seriesColors: [ "#bb0000" ]});
    var plot2 = $.jqplot ('chart2', [[120, 90, 150, 120, 110, 75, 90, 120, 110]],
        {seriesColors: [ "#00bb00" ]});
    var plot3 = $.jqplot ('chart3', [[ 130, 110, 140, 100, 80, 135, 120, 90, 110]],
        {seriesColors: [ "#0000bb" ]});

    $('div.chart-container').resizable({delay:20});
    ...
});
```

Now you'll activate the draggable feature for the three containers. Doing this is really quite simple; you need to add the function to the three jQuery selections applied to each container, as shown in Listing 11-15. Moreover, you'll add the resizing feature for the two new containers the same way as was done for the first container.

*Listing 11-15.* ch11_03b.html

```
$(document).ready(function(){
    ...
    var plot3 = $.jqplot ('chart3', [[130, 110, 140, 100, 80, 135, 120, 90, 110]],
        {seriesColors: ["#0000bb"]});

    $('div.chart-container').draggable({cursor: 'move'});
    $('div.chart-container2').draggable({cursor: 'move'});
    $('div.chart-container3').draggable({cursor: 'move'});

    $('div.chart-container').resizable({delay: 20});
    $('div.chart-container').bind('resize', function(event, ui) {
        plot1.replot();
    });
    $('div.chart-container2').resizable({delay: 20});
    $('div.chart-container2').bind('resize', function(event, ui) {
        plot2.replot();
    });
    $('div.chart-container3').resizable({delay: 20});
    $('div.chart-container3').bind('resize', function(event, ui) {
        plot3.replot();
    });
});
```

Nothing remains but to add CSS styles, thus defining the initial position and size of each container, as shown in Listing 11-16.

*Listing 11-16.* ch11_03b.html

```
<style type="text/css">
.chart-container {
    border: 1px solid darkblue;
    padding: 30px 0px 30px 30px;
    width: 300px;
    height: 200px;
    position: relative;
    float: left;
}
.chart-container2 {
    border: 1px solid darkblue;
    padding: 30px 0px 30px 30px;
    width: 200px;
    height: 200px;
    position: relative;
    float: left;
    margin-left: 20px;
}
.chart-container3 {
    border: 1px solid darkblue;
    padding: 30px 0px 30px 30px;
    width: 500px;
    height: 200px;
    position: relative;
    float: left;
    margin-left: 20px;
}
#chart1 {
    width: 96%;
    height: 96%;
}
#chart2 {
    width: 96%;
    height: 96%;
}
#chart3 {
    width: 96%;
    height: 96%;
}
</style>
```

In Figure 11-5, you can see the page layout when the page is initially loaded. Figure 11-6 shows a situation in which the user has changed the position and the size of the third chart to align it below the other two.

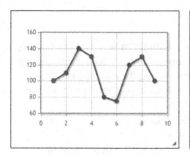
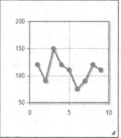
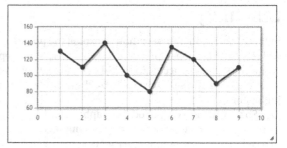

*Figure 11-5. The web page shows the three line charts enclosed in three different containers*

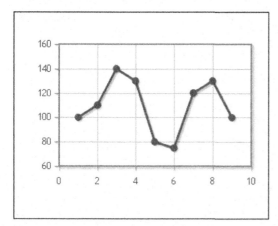
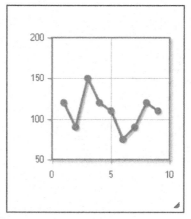
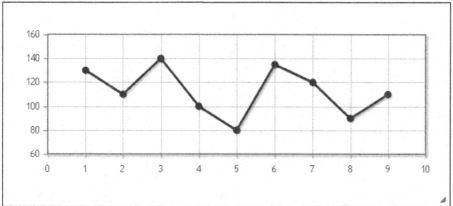

*Figure 11-6. By dragging and resizing the containers, the original layout can be changed*

# Summary

In this chapter you have seen how to exploit the potential of widgets that the jQuery UI library makes available to you, widgets that help you improve the way your charts are represented. You have seen how to enclose more charts inside **containers, such as accordions and tabs**, so that you can view them one by one, even when they occupy the same area. You have also seen how to **resize** these **containers,** extending such capability to the charts developed with the jqPlot library.

So far you have deepened the graphical and representational aspects of your chart. In the next chapter, you'll learn about the core of your charts: **data management**. So far the variety of data defined in the page has been limited, in order to make the examples easier to comprehend. In reality, it is very unlikely that data will be defined on the same web page that contains the code management chart. More likely, the data are provided by external files or by databases through SQL queries.

# CHAPTER 12

■ ■ ■

# Handling Input Data

Once you have dealt with all the graphical aspects of a chart, it is time to analyze input data in more detail. In the previous chapters, you assigned the values of input data to arrays. These arrays were defined in the same HTML page within which the jqPlot code resides. You have frequently used these two ways:

```
var plot1 = $.jqplot ('chart1', [[100, 110, 140, 130, 80, 75, 120, 130, 100]]);
```

and

```
var data = [[100, 110, 140, 130, 80, 75, 120, 130, 100]];
```

In actuality, it is often necessary to interface with other technologies in order to obtain such data, and to do so you need to find a way that is well suited to any source of data. The need to use a common text format that can be easily handled by different scripting languages (especially JavaScript) and that remains comprehensible to humans, led to the use of the JavaScript Object Notation (JSON) format. You have briefly read about this kind of format in Chapter 1, but now you'll see how to use it concretely to handle input data from external sources.

This chapter studies in detail the JSON format, first illustrating the structure of the data in this format and then showing you how to use them with the jqPlot library. To this purpose, you'll see two different ways to handle JSON data—the first makes use of a jqPlot plug-in and the second uses a jQuery function that specializes in parsing JSON data.

Regardless of how the data coming from an external source are structured, if you want to have a complete overview of the management and handling of real data, you also need to take into account how this data are generated and the consequent acquisition mode. Therefore, in the last part of the chapter, you'll develop a real-time chart exclusively using the jqPlot library.

In fact, regardless of the format of the input data, many times the data source is not only external, but it is also continuous—the input data consists of a train of data in which the values are produced one at a time, serially and uninterrupted. Hence, the chart that will display this type of data will not only have to manage a format of data coming from an external source but needs also to be able to update itself continuously, thereby ensuring that the data representation (in this case, the real-time chart) is always updated.

## Using the JSON Format

This section covers the JSON format, including various options for using it with the library jqPlot. First of all, you will learn how there can be structured data in the JSON format, by analyzing some syntax diagrams. Then you will move on to practical examples.

# The JSON Format

JSON is a data exchange format. Thanks to its tree structure, in which each element is referred as a name-value pair, it is easy for humans to read and write it and for machines to parse and generate it. This is the main reason for its increasingly prevalent use.

The JSON structure is built on the combination of two different structures: arrays and objects (see Figure 12-1). Within them you can define all of the classic primitive values commonly used, even in other languages: numbers, Booleans, strings, and null value. This allows values contained in it to be exchanged between various programming languages. (At www.json.org, you can find a list of all languages that handle the JSON format, along with a list of all the related technologies, such as libraries, modules, plug-ins, and so on.)

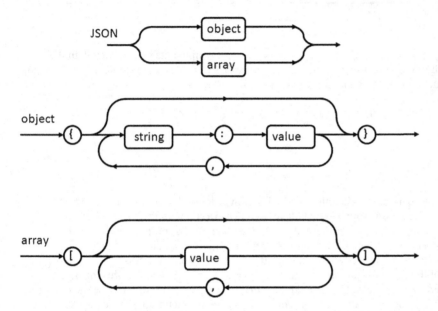

**Figure 12-1.** *Syntax diagrams for JSON*

Just to understand the syntax diagrams in Figure 12-1 better, you can analyze how a JSON format is structured. You must take into account two things. The first is that both the objects and the arrays contain a series of values identified by the value labels in the diagrams. value refers to any type of value, such as a string, a number, or a Boolean, and it can even be an object or an array.

In addition to this, you can easily guess that the JSON structure is a tree structure with different levels. The tree will have as nodes either arrays or objects; the leaves are the values contained in them.

Consider some examples. If you have a JSON structure with only one level, you will have only two possibilities:

- An array of values

- An object with values

If you extend the structure to two levels, the possibilities are four (assuming for simplicity that the tree is symmetrical):

- An array of arrays

- An array of objects

- An object with arrays

- An object with objects

And so on; the cases gradually become more complex.

The classic JSON structure is precisely the structure of the jqPlot library options object that you have already used frequently in this book. In fact, you have seen that, thanks to the objects that have a string associated with each value, these tree structures can describe any type of element. Even very complex elements, such as charts, can be easily understood and manipulated.

## A Practical Case: The jqPlot Data Renderer

Referring to JSON as an exchange format, this section considers the simple case in which the external data source is a text file. In this example, you will use data rendered directly by the jqPlot library: the json2 plug-in. This plug-in allows you to read the data in JSON format contained in a file in order to use them as input data. For your part, the only thing you are required to do is assign the external source to the dataRenderer property.

Start by implementing a blank HTML page, as shown in Listing 12-1.

***Listing 12-1.*** ch12_01a.html

```
<HTML>
<HEAD>
    <TITLE>Chapter 12</TITLE>
<!--[if lt IE 9]>
<script type="text/javascript" src="../src/excanvas.js"></script>
<![endif]-->
<script type="text/javascript" src="../src/jquery.min.js"></script>
<script type="text/javascript" src="../src/jquery.jqplot.min.js"></script>
<link rel="stylesheet" type="text/css" href="../src/jquery.jqplot.min.css" />
<script>
$(document).ready(function(){
    //Add the JavaScript code here
});
</script>
</HEAD>
<BODY>
<div id="myChart" style="height:300px; width:500px;"></div>
</BODY>
</HTML>
```

In order to have the data renderer interpret the data, the external source must return a valid jqPlot data array. To extend the chart with this functionality, you need to include the jqplot.json2 plug-in:

```
<script type="text/javascript" src="../src/plugins/jqplot.json2.min.js"></script>
```

Or use the content delivery network (CDN) service:

```
<script type="text/javascript"
    src="http://cdn.jsdelivr.net/jqplot/1.0.8/plugins/jqplot.json2.min.js"></script>
```

As an external source, you can choose a TXT file containing the data. For this example, you'll create a new TXT file with Notepad or any other text editor. After you have edited the data as reported in Listing 12-2, save the file as jsondata.txt.

*Listing 12-2.* jsondata.txt

```
[[30, 12, 24, 54, 22, 11, 64, 33, 22]]
```

On the web page where you want to manage the data in an external file, you need to add the code in Listing 12-3.

*Listing 12-3.* ch12_01a.html

```
$(document).ready(function(){
    var ajaxDataRenderer = function(url, plot, options) {
        var ret = null;
        $.ajax({
            async: false,
            url: url,
            dataType: "json",
            success: function(data) {
                ret = data;
            }
        });
        return ret;
    };
    var jsonurl = "./jsondata.txt";
    var options = {
        title: "AJAX JSON Data Renderer",
        dataRenderer: ajaxDataRenderer,
        dataRendererOptions: {
            unusedOptionalUrl: jsonurl
        }
    };
    $.jqplot ('myChart', jsonurl, options);
});
```

You'll get the chart shown in Figure 12-2, which derives its data directly from the TXT file.

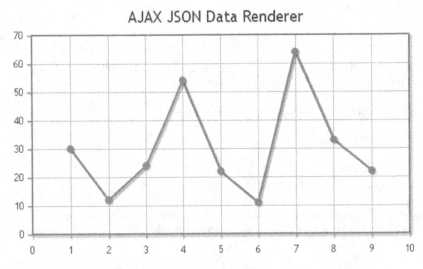

*Figure 12-2. A line chart representing data from the* jsondata.txt *file*

If you want to insert more than one series, the format of data within the TXT file remains the same as the format used for the input data arrays (see Listing 12-4). After you have copied this data in a file with an editor, save this file as jsondata2.txt.

**Listing 12-4.** jsondata2.txt

```
[[1,3,2,4,3,4,1,2],
[6,7,9,6,8,9,10,9],
[15,12,11,9,11,12,13,14]]
```

Figure 12-3 shows a chart with the three series read from the TXT file.

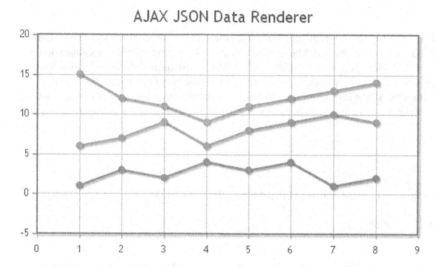

**Figure 12-3.** *A multiseries line chart representing data from a TXT file*

## JSON and $.getJSON()

There is another way to use external JSON data in your jqPlot charts. Instead of using the json2 jqPlot plug-in as a data renderer, jQuery provides a method that performs the same functions; it's called $.getJSON().

This method reads a JSON file and parses it. It also can load JSON-encoded data directly from a server by making an HTTP GET request. It is widely used in many applications on the Web, not only for jqPlot. This method has three arguments:

```
$.getJSON(url, data, success(data, textStatus, jqXHR));
```

Only url is mandatory; the other two arguments are optional. url is a string containing the URL of the JSON file or the URL of the server for the request. data is a string to be sent to the server with the request, and success() is a callback function that will be executed if the request succeeds.

The data contained in the file must follow the rules for JSON encoding. Because you are using them in order to be encoded by jqPlot, they should have this format:

```
{ "series_name1": [ value1, value2, value3, ...],
  "series_name2": [ value1, value2, value3, ...], ... }
```

Create a new TXT file and save it as jsondata3.txt. This file contains data from four distinct series, as shown in Listing 12-5.

**Listing 12-5.** jsondata3.txt

```
{"data1": [1,2,3,2,3,4],
 "data2": [3,4,5,6,5,7],
 "data3": [5,6,8,9,7,9],
 "data4": [7,8,9,11,10,11]}
```

The next step consists of the call to the getJSON() method:

```
$.getJSON('./jsondata3.txt', '', myPlot);
```

You must pay attention to write the right URL. In this example, the TXT file is in the same directory of the HTML file, so you need to add ./ as a prefix to the name of the file. The second argument is an empty string, because you do not need to send any data to the URL (it is a file, not a server application). myPlot is the returned value of the function, which checks if the loading of $.jqplot() is good. As you can see in Listing 12-6, you only need to add your own function, within which you have defined the $.jqplot() function. In this case, the data to pass—such as data1, data2, and so on—belongs to the data object and must be therefore passed as data.data1, data.data2, and so on.

**Listing 12-6.** ch12_02.html

```
$(document).ready(function(){
    var myPlot = function (data, textStatus, jqXHR) {
        $.jqplot ('myChart', [data.data1, data.data2, data.data3, data.data4]);
    };
    $.getJSON('./jsondata3.txt', '', myPlot);
});
```

You thus obtain a multiseries line chart (see Figure 12-4) as if you had written the data directly on the web page, but the chance to work with servers and other applications extends your capabilities enormously.

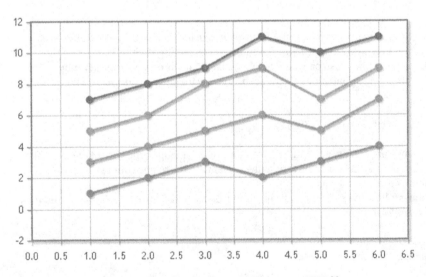

**Figure 12-4.** A multiseries line chart representing data on a TXT file

# Real-Time Charts

Real-time charts automatically update themselves, thus allowing you to represent streams of data from a source that produces data continuously. This source can be a server, an application, a device connected to a PC, and so on. It is in such cases that a chart assumes the role of a true indicator, that is, a device which provides a visual indication of how a certain property varies over time.

You are now going to develop a simple real-time line chart using only the jqPlot library. Consider, for instance, that you want to implement an indicator of a magnitude that varies from 0 to 100%. This quantity could be, for example, the consumption of a resource (such as CPU), but can be applied to many other things such as temperature, the number of participants or connections, and so on. In this case, you'll start with the value of 50% and generate random variations in real time, simply for the sake of simulating a data source. It is possible to adapt this example to any other case, just by replacing the random function with a function that acquires data externally.

You'll implement a web page in which a line chart is represented, a chart in which there is only a small stretch set to the value of 50% (see Figure 12-5). This will be the starting point for the values of the streaming data.

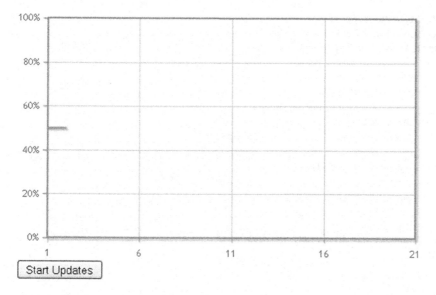

***Figure 12-5.*** *The real-time chart before acquiring data shows only a small stretch as its starting point*

Listing 12-7 shows all that is needed to obtain the chart shown in Figure 12-5. In options, you define the limits of the range of the axes so that there are no variations during the chart update. To give the animation a more fluid effect, you eliminate the markers on the line and enable the smooth mode. Under the chart, you'll insert a button to start the update in real time.

*Listing 12-7.* ch12_03.html

```
<HTML>
<HEAD>
<TITLE>Real-time chart</TITLE>
<!--[if lt IE 9]>
<script type="text/javascript" src="../src/excanvas.js"></script>
<![endif]-->
<script type="text/javascript" src="../src/jquery.min.js"></script>
<script type="text/javascript" src="../src/jquery.jqplot.min.js"></script>
<link rel="stylesheet" type="text/css" href="../src/jquery.jqplot.min.css"/>
<script class="code" type="text/javascript">
$(document).ready(function(){
    data = [50, 50];
    var options = {
        axes: {
            xaxis: {min: 1, max: 21, numberTicks: 5},
            yaxis: {min: 0, max: 100, numberTicks: 6,
                tickOptions:{formatString: '%d%'}
            }
        },
        seriesDefaults: {
            showMarker: false,
            rendererOptions: {smooth: true}
        }
    };
var plot1 = $.jqplot ('myChart', [data], options);
});
</script>
</HEAD>
<BODY>
<div id="myChart" style="height: 300px; width: 500px;"></div>
<button>Start Updates</button>
</BODY>
</HTML>
```

Inserting Listing 12-8, you now capture the click event of the button and link it to the execution of the doUpdate() function. Once the button is pressed, you can delete it from the web page.

*Listing 12-8.* ch12_03.html

```
$(document).ready(function(){
    ...
    var plot1 = $.jqplot ('myChart', [data], options);
    $('button').click( function(){
        doUpdate();
        $(this).hide();
    });
});
```

Hence, in Listing 12-9, you implement the function that generates random variations.

***Listing 12-9.*** ch12_03.html

```
$(document).ready(function(){
    ...
    $('button').click( function(){
        doUpdate();
        $(this).hide();
    });
    function getRandomInt (min, max){
        return Math.floor(Math.random() * (max - min + 1)) + min;
    }
});
```

This function generates integer values between min and max values (which can be negative). These values are passed as arguments to the function. You set a possible variation between -3 and 3, which will be applied to the last values acquired. The real-time values are stored in an array called data, which operates as a sort of buffer. This array contains only 20 values, so that the first (the eldest) will be deleted and a new acquired value will be inserted in the last position of the array. As you can see in Figure 12-4, at the beginning you'll see an oscillating line that extends the length of the chart. Then the right end of the line will move, following the trend of the magnitude observed.

To obtain an animation you need to refresh the chart, so for each update you need to destroy the current chart (plot1), replace the data array with the new one, and then replot the whole plot1 chart. At the end, you need to call the setTimeout() function, which will in turn call the doUpdate() function again. Thus, the cycle is repeated endlessly. You can update the chart every second (1,000 milliseconds), but these values, in other cases, will be chosen depending on the source data.

Go ahead and add Listing 12-10 to your code.

***Listing 12-10.*** ch12_03.html

```
$(document).ready(function(){
    ...
    function getRandomInt (min, max) {
        return Math.floor(Math.random() * (max - min + 1)) + min;
    }
    function doUpdate() {
        var last = data[data.length-1];
        if(data.length > 19){
            data.shift();
        }
        var newlast = last + getRandomInt(-3, 3);
        if(newlast < 0)
            newlast = 0;
        data.push(newlast);
        if (plot1) {
            plot1.destroy();
        }
        plot1.series[0].data = data;
        plot1.replot( {resetAxes: true} );
        plot1 = $.jqplot ('myChart', [data], options);
        setTimeout(doUpdate, 1000)
    }
});
```

Figure 12-6 demonstrates how the real-time chart shows the stream of data varying around the value of 50%.

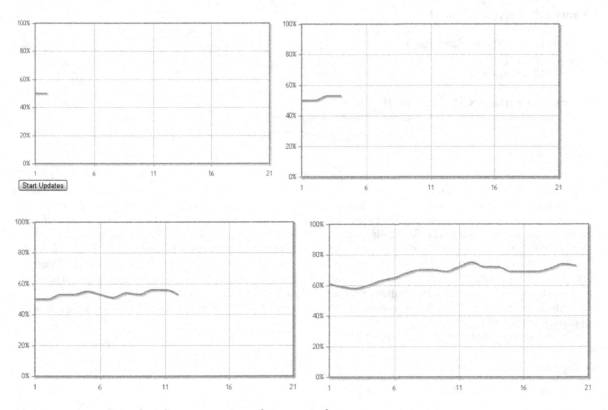

***Figure 12-6.*** *A real-time line chart representing values moment by moment*

# Summary

In this chapter you have seen how input data often come from external sources and how it is possible to handle them. In a particular way, you have seen how external data in **JSON format** can be used as input data arrays for the charts developed with the jqPlot library. In regard to the management of the data generated in real time, you have seen a simple but effective example in which you implemented a **real-time line chart** that is updated as the acquired data vary.

■ ■ ■

# Guidelines for the Examples in the Book

This appendix provides guidelines on how to use XAMPP and Aptana Studios together to create a development environment on your PC that will allow you to develop, run, and fix the examples given in the book.

## Installing a Web Server

Nowadays, on the Internet, you can easily find free software packages containing everything you need to set up a test environment for all your examples and for everything related to the web world in general.

These packages minimize the number of programs that need to be installed.More important, they may be acquired with a single installation. The packages generally consist of an Apache HTTP server; a MySQL database; and interpreters for the programming languages PHP, Perl, and Python. The most complete package is XAMPP (available for download at the Apache Friends web site [`www.apachefriends.org/en/index.html`]). XAMPP is totally free, and its key feature is that it is a cross-platform package (Windows, Linux, Solaris, MacOS). Furthermore, XAMPP also includes a Tomcat application server (for the programming language Java) and a FileZilla FTP server (for file transfer). Other solutions are platform specific, as suggested by the initial letter of their name:

- **WAMP** (Windows)
- **MAMP** (MacOS)
- **LAMP** (Linux)
- **SAMP** (Solaris)
- **FAMP** (FreeBSD)

In fact, XAMPP is an acronym; its letters stand for the following terms:

- **X**, for the operating system
- **A**, for Apache, the web server
- **M**, for MySQL, the database management system
- **P**, for PHP, Perl, or Python, the programming languages

Thus, choose the web server solution that best fits your platform, and install it on your PC.

# Installing Aptana Studio IDE

Once the Web server has been installed, it is necessary to install an integrated development environment (IDE), which you need to develop your JavaScript code. In this appendix, you will install Aptana Studio as your development environment.

Visit the Aptana site (www.aptana.com), and click the Products tab for the Aptana Studio 3 software (at the time of writing, the most recent version is 3.6.0). Download the stand-alone edition (with the Eclipse IDE already integrated): Aptana_Studio_3_Setup_3.6.0.exe.

After the download is complete, launch the executable file to install the Aptana Studio IDE. At the end of the installation, in launching the application, you should see the workbench opening, as shown in Figure A-1.

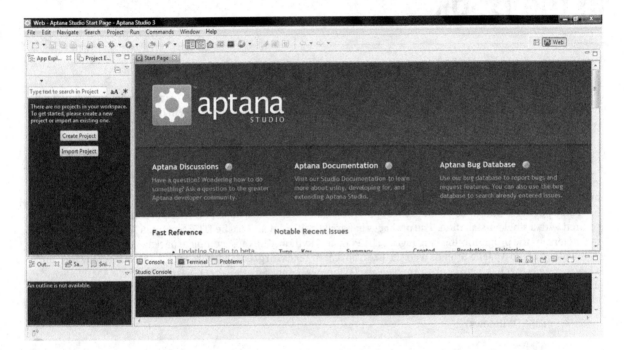

***Figure A-1.*** *The Aptana Studio IDE workbench*

During the installation of Aptana Studio, the software detects the various browsers and the web server installed and configures itself accordingly.

# Setting the Aptana Studio Workspace

Before starting to develop the examples in the book, you must create a workspace. First, you should set the workspace on Aptana Studio, where the Web server document root is.

These are typical paths with XAMPP:

- Windows: C:\xampp\htdocs

- Linux: /opt/lamp/htdocs

- MacOS: /Applications/XAMPP/xamppfiles/htdocs

Whereas with WAMP, this is the path:

- C:\WAMP\www

Thus, select File ➤ Switch Workspace ➤ Other . . . from the menu. Then, insert the path of the web server document root in the field, as demonstrated in Figure A-2.

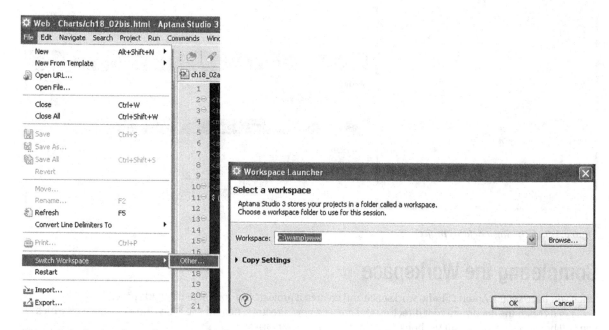

***Figure A-2.*** *Setting the workspace on the document root*

# Creating a Project

The next step in creating your workspace consists of creating a project in Aptana Studio:

1.  Select New ➤ Web Project from the menu.

2.  A window such as that shown in Figure A-3 appears. Select Default Project, and click Next.

3.  Insert "charts" as the name of the project. This will be the directory in the workspace in which you will write all the example files described in the book, using Aptana Studio.

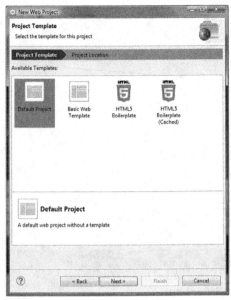

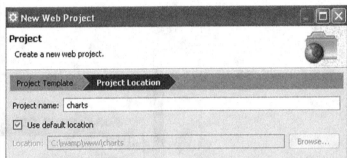

**Figure A-3.** *Creating a default project*

# Completing the Workspace

Once you have set the Aptana Studio workspace and created a project, you complete the workspace.

Let us open the document root directory and create a new directory, named src. Now, the workspace on which you will be working throughout the book is composed of two directories:

- src

- charts

The src directory should contain all the files related to libraries.

The charts directory should contain all HTML, images and Cascading Style Sheets (CSS) files related to the examples in the book (which is in fact a project). Each example file should be created in this directory (if you prefer to do things differently, that's fine, but it is important to take note of the different path reference in HTML pages in order to include the library files and images).

---

■ **Note**   The source code that accompanies this book (available from the Source Code/Download area of the Apress web site [www.apress.com]) is practically already packaged in a workspace. With it, you will find two versions of the charts project: content delivery network (CDN) and local. The charts_CDN directory contains all the examples referring to libraries remotely distributed from CDN services. The charts_local directory offers all the examples referring to libraries found within the src directory.

---

# Filling the src Directory with the jqPlot Library

If you have chosen to develop HTML pages by referring to libraries locally, it is necessary to download all their files. These files will be collected in the src directory. This is a good approach, as you can develop several projects that will make use of the same libraries without having to copy them for each project.

The versions listed in this appendix are those used to implement the examples in the book. If you install other versions, there may be issues of incompatibility, or you may observe behavior different from that described.

**jqPlot library version 1.0.8 (includes jQuery library version 1.9.1)**

1. Visit the jqPlot web site (https://bitbucket.org/cleonello/jqplot/downloads/), and download the compressed file (.zip, .tar.gz or tar.bz2) for the library: jquery.jqplot.1.0.8r1250.

2. Extract all content. You should get a directory named dist, containing the following subdirectories and files:

   - doc

   - examples

   - plugins

   - A series of files (jquery.min.js, jquery.jqplot.min.js, and so on)

3. Copy the set of files and the plugins directory, and place in src.

**jquery UI library version 1.10.3, with the smoothness theme**

1. Visit the JQuery user interface library (jQuery UI) site (http://jqueryui.com/themeroller/), and download the library from ThemeRoller, with the smoothness theme: jquery-ui-1.10.3.custom.zip.

2. Extract all content. You should get a directory named jquery-ui-1.10.3.custom, with the following directories inside:

   - css

   - js

   - development-bundle

3. Copy the css and js directories, and place in src.

You have thus obtained the src directory, which should contain the subdirectories and files shown in Figure A-4.

| | |
|---|---|
| css | jquery.jqplot.min.js |
| js | jquery.js |
| plugins | jquery.min.js |
| changes.txt | MIT-LICENSE.txt |
| copyright.txt | optionsTutorial.txt |
| excanvas.js | README.txt |
| excanvas.min.js | usage.txt |
| gpl-2.0.txt | LICENSE |
| jqPlotCssStyling.txt | d3.v3.js |
| jqPlotOptions.txt | d3.v3.min.js |
| jquery.jqplot.css | |
| jquery.jqplot.js | |
| jquery.jqplot.min.css | |

***Figure A-4.*** *The files and subdirectories contained in the* `src` *directory*

---

■ **Note**   By convention you are developing the examples in the `charts` directory. If you want to do otherwise, you need to consider the new path when you will include the other files in a web page.

If you are developing the HTML page inside the `charts` directory, you need to use the following code:

```
<script type="text/javascript" src="../src/jquery.min.js"></script>
```

In contrast, if you prefer to develop it directly, in the document root, you use this:

```
<script type="text/javascript" src="src/jquery.min.js"></script>
```

In short, it is important to take the path of the file you are including into account, with respect to the page you are implementing.

---

# Running the Examples

Once you have created or copied an HTML file in the workspace, to run it in Aptana Studio IDE, select Run ➤ Run from the menu, or click the Run button on the toolbar (see Figure A-5).

***Figure A-5.*** *The Run button from the toolbar*

Immediately, your default browser will open, with the selected HTML page loaded.

Look at Run Configurations (see Figure A-6), selecting Run Configurations . . . from the context menu of the Run icon. Let us set, for example, `http://localhost/` as your base URL; to do so, you select the Append project name option, as shown. Then, you click the Apply button to confirm your settings.

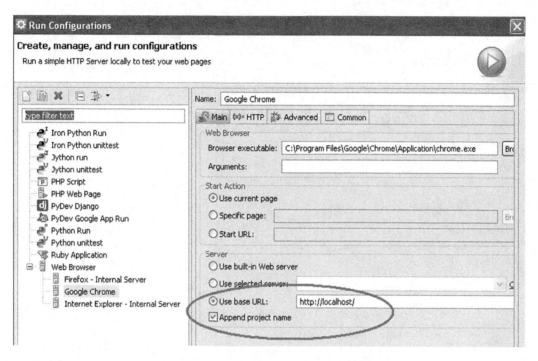

**Figure A-6.** *The run configuration for each browser must be set correctly*

Now, you have everything required to work easily on all the examples in the book.

Once you reach a certain familiarity with the Aptana IDE, you will find that it is an excellent environment for developing many other projects, both in JavaScript and in other programming languages (e.g., PHP).

And, now, have fun!

# Summary

This appendix provides guidelines on how to use XAMPP and Aptana Studios together to create a development environment on your PC. The choice of using these applications is not mandatory, and many other solutions are possible; there are many applications available on the Internet for performing similar operations. But, if you wish to implement and quickly test the examples described in the book, this environment will prove a good choice.

# APPENDIX B

■ ■ ■

# jqPlot Plug-ins

This appendix shows the complete list of available plug-ins in the jqPlot distibution (see Table B-1). Not all these plug-ins have been treated in this book; for more information, please visit the jqPlot web site (www.jqplot.com).

*Table B-1.* *Available Plug-ins in the jqPlot Distribution (version 1.0.8)*

| Name | Type | Description |
| --- | --- | --- |
| **$.jqplot.BarRenderer** | Renderer | Draw a bar chart. |
| **$.jqplot.BezierCurveRenderer** | Renderer | Draw lines as stacked Bezier curves. |
| **$.jqplot.BlockRenderer** | Renderer | Draw an xy block chart. A block chart has data points displayed as colored squares, with a text label inside. |
| **$.jqplot.BubbleRenderer** | Renderer | Draw a bubble chart. A bubble chart has data points displayed as colored circles, with an optional text label inside. |
| **$.jqplot.CanvasAxisLabelRenderer** | Renderer | Draw axis labels, with a canvas element to support advanced features, such as rotated text. This renderer uses a separate rendering engine to draw the text on the canvas. |
| **$.jqplot.CanvasAxisTickRenderer** | Renderer | Draw axis ticks, with a canvas element to support advanced features, such as rotated text. This renderer uses a separate rendering engine to draw the text on the canvas. |
| **$.jqplot.CanvasOverlay** | Plug-in | Draw lines overlaying the chart. |
| **$.jqplot.CanvasTextRenderer** | Renderer | Modified version of the canvastext.js plug-in, written by Jim Studt (http://jim.studt.net/canvastext/). |
| **$.jqplot.CategoryAxisRenderer** | Renderer | Render a category style axis, with equal pixel spacing between y data values of a series. |
| **$.jqplot.ciParser** | Plug-in | A function to convert a custom JavaScript Object Notation (JSON) data object into jqPlot data format. |
| **$.jqplot.Cursor** | Plug-in | A class representing the cursor, as displayed on the plot. |
| **$.jqplot.DateAxisRenderer** | Renderer | Render an axis as a series of date values. |

*(continued)*

**Table B-1.** (*continued*)

| Name | Type | Description |
| --- | --- | --- |
| **$.jqplot.DonutRenderer** | Renderer | Draw a donut chart; x values, if present, are used as slice labels, and y values give slice size. |
| **$.jqplot.Dragable** | Plug-in | Make plotted points that the user can drag. |
| **$.jqplot.EnhancedLegendRenderer** | Renderer | Draw **a legend** with advanced features**.** |
| **$.jqplot.FunnelRenderer** | Renderer | Draw a funnel chart; x values, if present, are used as labels, and y values give area size. Funnel charts draw a single series only. |
| **$.jqplot.Highlighter** | Plug-in | Highlight data points when they are moused over. |
| **$.jqplot.Json2** | Plug-in | Create a JSON object containing two methods: `stringify()` and `parse()`. |
| **$.jqplot.LogAxisRenderer** | Renderer | Render a logarithmic axis. |
| **$.jqplot.MekkoAxisRenderer** | Renderer | Used along with the *MekkoRenderer* plug-in; displays the y axis as a range from 0 to 1 (0 to 100 percent) and the x axis with a tick for each series, scaled to the sum of all the y values. |
| **$.jqplot.MekkoRenderer** | Renderer | Draw a Mekko-style chart that shows three-dimensional data on a two-dimensional graph. |
| **$.jqplot.MeterGaugeRenderer** | Renderer | Draw a meter gauge chart. |
| **$.jqplot.Mobile** | Plug-in | jQuery mobile virtual event support. |
| **$.jqplot. OHLCRenderer** | Renderer | Draw open-high-low-close, candlestick, and high-low-close charts. |
| **$.jqplot.PieRenderer** | Renderer | Draw a pie chart; x values, if present, are used as slice labels, and y values give slice size. |
| **$.jqplot.PointLabels** | Plug-in | Place labels at the data points. |
| **$.jqplot.PyramidAxisRenderer** | Renderer | Used along with the *PyramidRenderer* plug-in; displays the two x axes at the bottom and the y axis at the center. |
| **$.jqplot.PyramidGridRenderer** | Renderer | Used along with the *PyramidRenderer* plug-in; creates a grid on a `canvas` element. |
| **$.jqplot.PyramidRenderer** | Renderer | Draw a pyramid chart. |
| **$.jqplot.Trendline** | Plug-in | Automatically compute and draw trend lines for plotted data. |

# Index

# ■ L

# Get the eBook for only $10!

Now you can take the weightless companion with you anywhere, anytime. Your purchase of this book entitles you to 3 electronic versions for only $10.

This Apress title will prove so indispensible that you'll want to carry it with you everywhere, which is why we are offering the eBook in 3 formats for only $10 if you have already purchased the print book.

Convenient and fully searchable, the PDF version enables you to easily find and copy code—or perform examples by quickly toggling between instructions and applications. The MOBI format is ideal for your Kindle, while the ePUB can be utilized on a variety of mobile devices.

Go to www.apress.com/promo/tendollars to purchase your companion eBook.